HORATIO'S BOYS

HORATIO'S BOYS

The Life and Works
of
Horatio Alger, Jr.

EDWIN P. HOYT

CHILTON BOOK COMPANY

Radnor, Pennsylvania

Published in Radnor, Pa., by Chilton Book Company
and simultaneously in Ontario, Canada
by Thomas Nelson & Sons, Ltd.
Designed by Donald E. Cooke

Manufactured in the United States of America

Library of Congress Cataloging in Publication Data

Hoyt, Edwin Palmer.
  Horatio's boys.

  Includes bibliographical references.
  1. Alger, Horatio, 1832-1899. I. Title.
PS1029.A3Z68   813'.4 [B]   74-10672
ISBN 0-8019-5966-7

Contents

Chapter One • Crossroads... 1

Chapter Two • Budding Writer... 7

Chapter Three • Fair Harvard... 17

Chapter Four • The Reverend Horatio Alger, Jr.... 29

Chapter Five • The First Boys' Book... 36

Chapter Six • Paul Prescott's Charge... 49

Chapter Seven • The Brewster Affair... 60

Chapter Eight • The Arrival of Ragged Dick... 64

Chapter Nine • Lion Among the Juveniles... 76

Chapter Ten • Rough and Ready... 85

Chapter Eleven • The Established Writer... 99

Chapter Twelve • The Saga of Tattered Tom... 109

Chapter Thirteen • The New Crusade... 115

Chapter Fourteen • Experimentation... 129

Chapter Fifteen • Way Out West... 140

Chapter Sixteen • Painting America... 153

Chapter Seventeen • Shifting With the Wind... 169

Chapter Eighteen • Horatio Out West... 184

Chapter Nineteen • The Unchangeable Alger... 189

Chapter Twenty • More of the Same... 199

Chapter Twenty-one • In the Mold... 211

Chapter Twenty-two • End of an Era... 227

Chapter Twenty-three • Horatio Alger in History... 236

Chapter Twenty-four • The Published Alger... 243

Notes and Acknowledgments... 250

Index... 260

HORATIO'S BOYS

Chapter One

Crossroads

It was a blustery, cold Tuesday afternoon in the sprawling little white frame village of Brewster on the upper shank of Cape Cod, one of those chill March days when the wind sweeps across the cape, bringing mist and a coldness that paints the faces of the young and seeps into the very bones of old Cape Codders. And yet, so bemused was the little band of villagers who assembled for the monthly meeting of the First Unitarian Parish of Brewster that no man among them could have given you the temperature or even gauged the wind. The room was hushed, as S. H. Gould, the Moderator of the Parish Committee, rose to mention what was on every man's mind. He was reluctant—God knew they were all reluctant—to face the matter that was to come before them.

Now, he said, they came to the question of reengaging the minister, Mr. Alger, for the coming year. Was there any discussion?

Mr. Alger, the Reverend Horatio Alger, Jr., had been serving as Unitarian minister to the Brewster parish since the end of November, 1864. Earlier, Alger had been engaged as supply

1

minister for several months, with high recommendation that he could meet the community's emotional and religious needs. The relationship had started as auspiciously as could be hoped. The minister had come down from the Boston area by train, and the parishioners had met him at the station.

He saw a group of sturdy, mostly lanky, small-town New Englanders whose common interest centered on the old white clapboard church on the post road high above the beach. These Brewster Unitarians were ardent in the fall of 1864; the old church had been boarded up for years, but that summer enough people with get-up-and-go had decided to reinstitute regular services.

They saw a pleasant-faced grey-eyed young man of thirty-two, five feet two in his patent leather boots, weighing about a hundred and thirty pounds, thinning a little on top, but sporting a dandy little moustache that lent him the dignity his size tried to deny. He was soft-spoken and in polite conversation he stammered a little, but when he moved into the pulpit all that vanished. Here he was an accomplished orator and elocutionist. He had acquired these in years of debate and forensics at Harvard College and Harvard Divinity School. Alger's credentials were impeccable. His father, the Reverend Horatio Alger, Sr., was minister of the old and eminently respectable Unitarian Church at South Natick, a day's journey via Boston to the west, and the Algers came from a New England stock that numbered Mayflower passengers among its forebears.

Each weekend during the early fall of 1864 Horatio Alger, Jr. came down to Brewster from Boston. On Sunday mornings he led the services and preached the sermons. He visited around the parish on Sunday afternoons and was "to dinner" at the house of a Parish committeeman. During social calls he discoursed on his recent trip to Europe and on Unitarian affairs. The Parish committee in 1864 found young Alger likable and soft-spoken, and without any visible jarring qualities. Toward the end of the autumn, the committee met one Sunday afternoon and voted to ask Mr. Alger to "settle over that Society" if the terms could be made satisfactory. When the young minister reached home from his weekly stint, he found a letter, and he replied. Since he was a bachelor the committee did not offer him a house and upkeep, but a straight salary of $800 a year. This was neither stingy nor overly generous; it was a fair sum for a young man who had never before held a pulpit. There was every indication that if he joined the community and married and settled down that this amount could be increased and his future needs met without any trouble. It was settled then, at the end of November, 1864, that the young Reverend Mr. Alger would come to Brewster, and if for some reason he did not like this parish, or if the parishioners found they did not like him, minister or parish could dissolve their ties by giving three month's notice to the other.

Thus the young man had packed up his carpetbag and come to Brewster. The marriage of parish and pastor could not have been happier. On December 8, the Reverend Horatio Alger, Sr. came down from South Natick with several other ministers of note. The junior Mr. Alger was installed as the pastor of the Brewster Church by the Reverend W. P. Tilden of New South Church in Boston and the Reverend Edward E. Hale of the South Congregational Church. The senior Alger beamed, and the parishioners smiled. "Altogether," said the Yarmouth *Register* the next week, "there was an auspicious commencement of Mr. Alger's ministry, and we doubt if either the townspeople or guests will soon forget the pleasant and profitable event."

Well, this gray March afternoon fifteen months later, several parishioners sitting near the stove were wishing they could forget the event—that it had never happened—that they had been lucky enough to avoid any mention of the name Horatio Alger, Jr.

Yes, said Elisha Bangs and Thomas Crocker, there was an important matter for discussion in relation to the pastor.

As they all knew Alger had come to the village proud of his recent success as an author of books for boys. He had charmed the ladies with his talks on Europe, and more so because the committee charged admission and the proceeds were given to the Ladies Library of Brewster. He did all that ministers are supposed to do; he visited the sick, he comforted the aged, he ran the first May festival with the éclat of a circus ringmaster. He doted on the boys. His second boys' book, *Paul Prescott's Charge,* was published in the summer of 1865, and publication made of the diminutive minister a virtual social lion. The Yarmouth *Register* noted the fact, and that was important, for in the fourth year of the Civil War the *Register* had little room for local news. Parishioners were pleased with the book, it was all that a book for boys ought to be. It told how a boy volunteered to run the family farm so his father could become a soldier, and how by a combination of Character and Steam and Zest, the boy managed to outwit the Wicked Squire who held the mortgage on the farm, make a fool of the squire's Wicked Son without doing a single Dishonorable Act, and make a Grand Success of all he undertook. It was the kind of story to show what a boy could do if he put his mind and heart to it.

For it was boys, boys, boys that interested the Reverend Mr. Alger. He organized the Cadets for Temperance, which drew boys from his Sunday School Classes. Unlike other adults he was never too busy for a walk in the woods or a game of ball or a songfest. He organized games and entertainments and events that would appeal to boys in a quiet rural community where so little was available for amusement. His love for boys and the boys' attraction to him were well known. Now, the rueful committee members wished they had been warned by this inordinate fondness for boys, for recently the most dreadful rumors regarding Horatio Alger, Jr. and boys of the parish had been making their way around the community.

Moderator Gould approached the subject gingerly. No one wanted to come out into the open, but Horatio Alger's affection for boys in general had changed from something admirable to something suspect. Several mothers of the parish were very much upset. They felt their boys were up to something. It was not natural that their boys should have such a fondness for a man outside the family, even if he *was* the minister.

It was nothing definite, just a vague, uneasy suspicion. Why wasn't the young Reverend Mr. Alger married? Why didn't he show any particular interest in the young unmarried girls of the parish? Why was it always boys?

The Parish committee, pondering the situation of Mr. Alger and the responsibility to deal with his pastorate, decided that it would not engage this minister again for the following year. Then someone suggested that this decision was hardly fair; should a man be condemned by old wives' tales? The committee voted again, decided to reconsider the whole matter, then adjourned for a week.

At two o'clock on the next Tuesday, March 13, the parish elders met again, and this time, so agitated were some parishioners, they decided they would have to appoint a committee to investigate the rumors regarding Mr. Alger. Elisha Bangs, Moderator Gould and Thomas Crocker were chosen as the investigators. Once again, the parish committee adjourned.

A week later Thomas Crocker, Elisha Bangs and Moderator Gould came in with a dreadful report. Crocker had started at home with his own son, Thomas S. Crocker, and from him had learned that the Reverend Mr. Alger had been buggering him. Not only him, but John Clark too, and perhaps there were others. The shocked senior Crocker wished to go no further. "We learn from John Clark and Thomas S. Crocker that Horatio Alger, Jr. has been practicing on them at different times deeds that are too revolting to relate," Crocker, Bangs and Gould reported to the parishioners. Further, they had called Horatio Alger to appear before them and repeated the accusations of their boys, half hoping that the boys were up to some devilment and that the whole dreadful matter was a mistake.

But no. Braced by the committee, Horatio Alger, Jr. did not deny the charges. He had been "imprudent," he said.

Imprudent! Pederasty was imprudent, was it?

And further, Reverend Alger said with equanimity, under the circumstances he considered his connection with the Unitarian Society of Brewster to be dissolved. He left town that night.

The Unitarian Church meeting left the whole community of Brewster shocked and upset. Luckily for Horatio Alger, Jr., he had slipped out of town on the train immediately after the exposure of his homosexuality and before the shocked reaction of the Parish committee; luckily, because the villagers were up in arms.

"Had he remained longer an arrest or something worse might have occurred," said the committeemen in a letter to the Reverend Charles Lowe, secretary of the American Unitarian Association in Boston.

The committee, composed of good, normal, Christian gentlemen, could not bring itself to disclose the precise acts, nor even how many more boys than the two were involved, although as they said "they have good reason to think there are others."

The Parish felt impelled to tell Mr. Lowe, and through him, the American Unitarian Association,

That Horatio Alger, Jr. who has officiated as our minister for about fifteen months past has recently been charged with gross immorality and a most heinous crime, a crime of no less magnitude than the abominable and revolting crime of unnatural familiarity with *boys,* which is too revolting to think of in the most brutal of our race—the commission of which under any circumstances, is to a refined or Christian mind too utterly incomprehensible—

The object of this fulmination, other than to ease consciences and clear the air in Brewster, was to be sure that "this pretended Christian teacher" did not have a chance to bugger any little boys in other communities. The committeemen trusted that the Reverend Mr. Lowe would put out the word about Alger.

But there was no need. Horatio Alger, Jr. knew what he had done; he had burned every bridge to his past. He could never again seek a pulpit, that much was sure, for no matter how discreetly, Mr. Lowe would have to inform any new parish committee that Mr. Alger had left Brewster under embarrassing circumstances involving boys—and no more need be said.

Horatio knew full well; but it did not make any difference. He had never wanted to be a minister anyhow, but a writer. Already, while acceding to his father's wishes and joining the church, he had made enough success to call himself a writer. Now he had no choice. He would sink or swim in the ink of his pen. There was no turning back.

Chapter Two

Budding Writer

WHEN THE Brewster committee finished with Horatio Alger, he stuffed his meagre belongings into his carpetbag and fled Cape Cod forever before the word got out and he was lynched. Horatio's erstwhile friends and admirers supposed that Horatio had gone to Boston, which had for many years been the center of the Alger world. But no such thing. Horatio headed like a homing pigeon for the Great Anonymity, New York City, where even a minister who buggered little boys could live in peace and not be asked too many embarrassing questions as long as he paid his weekly bill at the boardinghouse.

The new life he was undertaking was vastly different from anything this sheltered young man had ever known before.

The Algers came from Pilgrim stock. The direct progenitor, Thomas Alger, had settled in Taunton, Massachusetts, before 1700, and the Algers had never strayed far from that base. Alger men served honorably with the revolutionaries in the war against England, one became a brigadier general and another, Edmund Lazell, whose mother was an Alger, was a member of the Constitutional Convention.

7

As with nearly all Americans, the early Algers were farmers. As the country grew and the towns sprang up, some drifted into professions, some became skilled artisans and some became churchmen.

The great, great grandfather of the writer was Israel Alger, Jr., a farmer of Bridgewater, whose son was James, and whose grandson was also called James. The farm, located on Milstone Plain, passed down from one boy to the next. Horatio Alger (the elder) was born in 1806 in the house on Milstone Plain. As a younger son, this Horatio had no hope of getting the farm, and his frail physique and short stature led the family to decide Horatio Alger, Sr. would be a scholar. He showed skill far beyond his age in reading and writing and when he was fifteen years old was able to substitute for a sick teacher in the district school.

James Alger and his brother were successful in the iron business, and it was not much strain for James to send his son to Harvard College in Cambridge. Even so, young Horatio worked part of his way there, tutoring others and teaching at country schools during vacation. He graduated high in his class of 1825—a celebrated class that included such lights as Oliver Wendell Holmes, the poet—and then Horatio Alger decided that he would enter the Divinity School and become a man of the cloth. He inclined toward the Unitarian profession and decided to accept that following.

The Unitarians of Massachusetts were an independent and even quarrelsome lot. It was not at all unusual for a pastor to discover after a few years that he was involved in argument over matters of doctrine. This happened in Chelsea, northeast of Cambridge, to the Reverend Joseph Tuckerman after more than twenty years in the pulpit of the town's Unitarian Church. Two other preachers followed him, but they were unable to heal the rifts in the congregation and lasted but a few months each. The dissidents finally split away from the main body in 1829, leaving a much smaller, poorer, and yet still quarrelsome congregation that could not seem to agree on any established minister. All this came to a head just at the time that Horatio Alger, Sr. was finishing up his studies at the Harvard Divinity School. Before the end of the summer he was offered the permanent post as minister of the Unitarian Church and he accepted. He was to have $400 a year, and he was to find his own lodgings.

One of the deacons of the Unitarian Church in Chelsea was John Fenno, a Chelsea farmer and businessman, who had an unmarried daughter named Olive Augusta. She was a painful girl, drab and frightened as a rabbit, and a good three inches taller than the minister. But she was single, and her parents encouraged the Reverend Mr. Alger to come and call, and to spend Christmas with them. One thing led to another; by the following Christmas the young people were engaged, and on March 31, 1831, they were married.

Deacon Fenno was a wealthy man. He built a house for his son-in-law, a saltbox of the kind so common in that day, a seven-room house that would give the couple room to build a family.

Almost immediately they obliged. By fall Olive Fenno Alger was very noticeably pregnant, and on January 13, 1832 their first son was born. They christened him Horatio Alger, Jr., after his father.

The parson Alger was a strict and dedicated little man who believed his calling to be the most important in the world, and he decided even when the boy was a baby, that little Horatio would follow in his footsteps. The father was a born manager. He managed the church and pushed the parishioners into improving it, buying a bell for the tower and keeping the paint up. He badgered the townspeople, the state legislature, even Congress, until he secured a post office for Chelsea. He was made the first postmaster, which in those days meant he also delivered the mail when it came in from Boston and took care of getting it out three times a week. Soon the young preacher was the town's leading citizen, never failing to take up a good cause of civic improvement. In recognition of his service and leadership, he was elected by his fellow townsmen to the Massachusetts legislature.

Baby Horatio did not do well. A sister, Olive Augusta, came along twenty-two months later, but she grew larger and faster than Horatio, Jr. and was able to talk before he could and to walk and do all the things that children do to please their parents, while the boy fell behind. Little Horatio was spindly and asthmatic, and his family worried over his survival. Another baby was born, a brother James, but still Horatio languished. At six he could make sounds, but not very intelligible ones. It was another year before he began to communicate satisfactorily.

Even then he stuttered so much that contact with the outside world was painful.

So little Horatio Alger, Jr. grew up a bookworm. He learned to read, and forged ahead as his father had done before him. When he was eight years old his father gave him a Bible. A few months later the minister started the boy on the study of Greek, Latin and the classics, and soon little Horatio was spouting memorized portions, chapter and verse.

All the way, the Reverend Horatio Alger worked to bring his son up as a God-fearing boy who would join the church. When Horatio, Jr. was nine, he was accompanying his father on house calls; after his chores he played with his brother and sister, but very seldom with the other, rougher children of Chelsea.

The town was small. Not even a thousand souls lived there yet, and it was difficult to keep a school in the winter months when children should be learning. For a time the Reverend Alger taught school in addition to all else, but only because the schoolmaster who had been engaged ran away and left the townspeople flat. In 1839 the town came to grips with the problem and built a new schoolhouse, and the Alger children were among the first to attend in the new building.

Young Horatio had his problems, some of them his own and many of them forced upon him by his father. Other boys wore rough homespun during the week, and in the summers went barefoot. Not Horatio. He wore his Sunday suit and tight shoes all week long, to school and as he accompanied his father on the ministerial rounds. It was only proper, said the Reverend Alger, for a boy who was going into the church to be trained carefully from his earliest youth. In school they called him Holy Horatio, and he was the butt of the jokes of the ruder, bigger boys, so much so that he complained tearfully to his mother; she stood up (or rather, down) to the feisty minister, and Horatio was permitted to dress more in the fashion of his fellows.

But the principle remained the same—young Horatio was committed to the church, and he was never allowed for a day to forget it.

Small, timid and shy, the young Horatio was the one selected by his fellows to bear the abuse of the moment. Ralph D. Gardner, Alger collector and one of his biographers, interviewed a number of people who had secondhand information about the Algers and they told many tales of his boyhood, which, while probably apocryphal, indicated the spirit of the day. When the boys played bandit and posse, little Horatio was chosen to be the bandit. There was, one day, a very good probability that his companions were going to make an experiment in hanging, with him on the end of the rope, until a farmer shooed the whole gang off his property and the noose was taken from around Horatio's neck. The village also had its bully, and Horatio was his natural prey, suffering untold indignities at the hands of this large, strong fellow. The lessons learned were burned deep in his soul, as the future would show.

The young Alger's participation in boyhood play was never more than sporadic, for his father made serious demands on the boy's time. There were extra studies, languages, for one destined for the ministry. There was the matter of house calls—to get the feel for the calling. There was the matter of dignity; like most small men the Reverend Mr. Alger was intensely conscious of his personal dignity, and he wanted Horatio Jr. to be the same. That the boy won prizes for his academic prowess pleased the father. He was ill much of every winter, and the father accepted this frailty as a cross to be borne.

The father dominated the household and became the most important figure in the boy's life.

Like nearly all ministerial families in New England, the Algers lived in genteel poverty, but that did not keep them from having five children: Horatio, Olive Augusta who was called Gusti by her brother, James, Ann and Francis, the last born in the summer of 1842. The large family brought more problems, and the hard times (for these were hard times in New England) meant that the Algers took much of their pay in kind. But even the apples and potatoes and cast-off clothing that came to the minister's family were not enough, and when he was refused an increase in annual salary in 1844, the Reverend Alger began looking around for a new pastorate. He found one in Marlborough, where the Unitarian Church had been looking for a man. It meant a salary of $750 a year plus a supply of wood to heat the house and warm the cookstove. The Reverend Mr. Alger felt the call, heeded it and moved to this newer community west of Boston.

Rev. Horatio Alger, Sr.

Horatio's mother, Olive Augusta Fenno Alge

Horatio's brother, Francis

Alger house (where Horatio was born), Revere, Massachusetts

Sister,
Olive Augusta Alger Cheney

Horatio's brother,
James

Alger house,
Marlborough, Massachusetts

For young Horatio, the slow starter, it meant leaving associations that had just begun to become pleasant for him, in his thirteenth year. He had attended the Chelsea Grammar School for only eighteen months, and that period had increased his association with other boys. The memories were keen.

> I remember the schoolhouse [he wrote later] a square brick building, whose walls the storms of more than a century had beaten without producing any decided effect. Through panes encrusted with the accumulated dirt of many years, the light streamed in....

Young Horatio had distinguished himself as a scholar, particularly of English, and this, too, made it hard to leave, but in December, the family moved.

At first they rented a house, but when the Chelsea house was sold and the money collected, the Reverend Mr. Alger purchased a nine-room clapboard house just off the post road that connected Boston with New York and Philadelphia. The house was within walking distance of the church and also of Gates Academy, the school operated by Obadiah Wheelock Albee. As schools went, Gates was already tried and successful, for Mr. Albee had kept it here since his graduation from Brown College in 1832.

That winter of 1844, Horatio took the entrance examinations for the school, was accepted and began a course of study that was designed to prepare him for college.

Later, an adult Horatio Alger, Jr. recalled his impressions of Marlborough, "a pleasant town, little more than 25 miles distant from Boston...notable for the numerous hills which on all sides surround the main village and its abundance of fruit trees."

Of Gates, he recalled chiefly that he was impressed by the huge elm trees in front of the schoolhouse, and as spring came and brought with it blue skies and the hum of bees, the young Horatio and his fellows sat out under the trees and studied their Greek, Latin and mathematics, the rigorous courses that would qualify them for college entrance.

Alger had already read far more widely than most of his companions, "whatever came my way, from Josephus' *History of the Jews* and works of theology to the *Arabian Nights' Entertainments* and the wonderful adventures of *Jack the Giant Killer.*" Now he concentrated on the classics, and in three years he received the best of what Schoolmaster Albee had to offer.

The Reverend Mr. Alger prospered in bustling Marlborough and as always plunged himself deeply into community affairs. He bought shares in the Gates Academy and served on the committee of the district or public school, whose purpose was to make good citizens of those who had no intention of going into the world of letters. He was sought to lead committees and lend a genteel air to many proceedings; his dignity was tremendous and his probity unquestioned. In time he became an officer of the Marlborough Savings Bank. He was in every way a pillar of the community.

Young Horatio was still very much the minister's son. His father took the boy along when he drove out to visit parishioners or to attend public functions, and there was never any question about the reason for the trips: Horatio, Jr. was learning the ways of the ministry for he would go into it himself. He accepted this calling and never rebelled. He was, in any case, hardly fitted for the rowdy world of business, for in his teens he still stuttered and was uncomfortable in any public role. Under the guidance of Schoolmaster Albee, he did learn public speaking and debating, since it was essential that a preacher be able to preach and that he conquer his nervousness and the stutter before he finished divinity school.

In the summer of 1847 the young Alger had exhausted the resources of Gates Academy, but he was still not ready for college in the practiced eye of his father, who knew the requirements of Harvard College. He spent the next year reading, working on modern languages and testing himself for the college entrance examinations. He did family chores, he got odd jobs to build up a bank account; even though the minister's salary had been increased by half here in Marlborough, it would be a strain to find the money to send Horatio to Harvard—the cost was almost exactly the amount of the increase. But from his own experience, the Reverend Mr. Alger knew that there were prizes and scholarships to be won by the deserving. He had assisted his own education thus, and he expected his son to do the same. It would be hard, but that was to be expected. Horatio would go to college, he must to pursue the calling, and so in the winter of his sixteenth year young Alger applied to Harvard College for admission and in due time received a letter informing him that he was to present himself at the college on August 17 for examination. The world was beckoning.

Chapter Three

Fair Harvard

In the summer of 1847, young Horatio Alger, Jr. presented himself as directed at Harvard College and took the two days of entrance examinations in the classics and mathematics which were then required. He did not do as well as had been expected, but he was accepted conditionally as a probationary student. He would have to make up a great deal of work if he was to remain at Harvard.

But young Horatio was willing to work. He welcomed the academic effort, and he survived. Through the efforts of his father and some Harvard friends, Horatio secured an appointment as the President's freshman, which meant he ran errands during his spare time for President Edward Everett. In exchange he received his room and forty dollars a year. Alger lived in the Yard, as did all the students except the commuters, and went to classes all day long from early morning chapel until the lights were snuffed out at night.

In a few months the probation was removed. The young Alger had more than proved himself capable of mastering the work. He was appointed monitor for lectures, which meant he took attendance and assisted the professor with discipline and management of the classroom. But within him, too, there was a surge of rebellion against the straight and narrow pathway his father had led the boy along all his life. Outside the yard, Harvard Square and Brattle Street called, and down the Charles was the busy, wicked city of Boston. It was not long before the Reverend Mr. Alger back in Marlborough received some distressing news of his son: the boy had been privately admonished by President Everett for unexcused absences from prayers. Of all the offenses young Horatio could have committed, this one hurt his father the most. What could be expected of a budding minister who did not have any interest in the affairs of the Lord? It was the first sign that Horatio's yearnings were not for the church but for a more worldly life. Yet in the Reverend Mr. Alger's mind there was no question; he had dedicated his son to the ministry when he was born, and Horatio *would* become a preacher. Even young Alger knew it.

Writing was the studious endeavor that interested the young Alger most, and Harvard gave him plenty of practice. He wrote papers in Greek, papers in Latin and papers in English, for thus young men then learned to write. His style was lucid and educated, as befitted a Harvard student, and although as flowery as was proper in that day, it was a strong style and he was soon winning prizes for his writing. He did well in winning awards, money was found from various funds to help him continue his college education. In the spring of 1849 he achieved another success, the *Pictorial National Library,* a monthly magazine published in Boston, published a short article he had written on the subject of chivalry and paid him for it. In June the same magazine published Alger's poem *Voices of the Past.* In the fall, when young Alger returned from the long vacation, the same magazine bought another article on Miguel Cervantes. At the age of seventeen he was a *writer.*

Preoccupation with the wider world had a decided impact on the young man's studies. Alger found himself conditioned again in 1849, and he had to labor mightily to work off the extra burden, but he did. In total Alger's sophomore year was far more successful. He began flowering a little.

The young Horatio,
Harvard days

That year the young Horatio was venturesome enough to sign with others a petition to President Jared Sparks (Everett had resigned) asking for better care of the rooms of students at Stoughton Hall. He was also taken into the Institute of 1770, a literary and debating society.

When one of the medical college's professors, John W. Webster, was tried for the murder of a society leader, Dr. George Parkman, New York newspapermen descended on sleepy Cambridge in droves. Young Horatio got a job helping the reporters dig up their stories and thus made the acquaintance of Charles A. Dana, who would later become editor of the New York *Sun.*

The facts of Horatio's college life are sparse. Indeed, of the few men who were as important in their time as Horatio Alger, Jr. was in his, perhaps none have left behind as little mark as human beings. One reason for this paucity of information was the family habit of destroying papers. Toward the end of her life, Alger's sister Olive Augusta destroyed all of Horatio's letters that she could find and all his manuscripts. In many ways, Horatio's personality was doomed to be as dimly limned as that of one of his heroes, Alexander Turney Stewart, the great New York merchant of Scotch-Irish descent. Stewart spent the last years of his life living in a marble mansion on Fifth Avenue, eradicating all evidence of his existence—going so far as to burn paintings of himself. But there was a difference. Horatio, particularly in his later years, had no such urge for anonymity. His shyness helped keep him from the public eye, but he would give any reporter a newspaper interview. It was not his fault that the interviewers found the truth so prosaic that they indulged instead in flights of fancy.

Thus developed the great error regarding Horatio Alger, Jr.'s life which seeped into every respectable publication that mentioned his name until the second half of the twentieth century. The basis of this error was a literary hoax perpetrated by author Herbert Mayes in 1928 and published by Macy-Masius Publishers of New York. The era of the 1920s was a period of debunking biographies, when heroes were not just presented with their warts, the warts were all that could be seen of the heroes. Publisher George Macy thought he would cash in on the surge of the "exposé" tide. Mayes, then a budding writer, fabricated a biography of Alger: *A Biography Without a Hero,* which attributed to Horatio a penchant for high-living, a schizoid personality and any number of love affairs. The first affair was supposed to have occurred in the Harvard days. The girl was a gentle young creature named Patience Stires. Herbert Mayes made the romance out of whole cloth. He later admitted that nearly all his biography of Alger was fiction, but such careful writers as the late Stewart H. Holbrook were taken in by it and the spurious facts found their way into the dignified *Dictionary of American Biography.* Even in 1963, social historian and teacher John Tebbel based a biographical study of Alger *(From Rags to Riches: Horatio Alger and the American Dream)* entirely on the Mayes book. Tebbel was hardly to blame. The whole literary community believed the Mayes biography was "authoritative," and all the more so because Mayes had then risen to become editor of *Good Housekeeping,* a director of the honest and upright *Saturday Review* and finally President of the *McCall* Corporation. It was hard to believe the king could do such wrong, even if he had done it in the days before he was a crown prince. The Mayes reputation stood for years behind the spurious biography. Among critics of the first half of the twentieth century only Malcolm Cowley found it odd that all

Mayes facts were so "exclusive" that they could not be documented at all.

Although the "facts" were not facts, yet in some ways Herbert Mayes succeeded in capturing Alger in life. There *was* a deep, dark streak in Horatio. It was not a lust for girls, as Mayes suggested, but quite the opposite. Mayes had Horatio pining for Patience, while stern father Alger moved mountains to break up the relationship and finally succeeded.

The fact is that even in his college days, Horatio was tutoring young boys, and whatever his relationships with them in that period, there is no hint anywhere in what is known of his life that he ever looked at a girl, except his sister, and that in a most brotherly way. Not for nothing had Horatio grown up with the nickname bestowed on him by his schoolmates—Holy Horatio. His father's constant insistence that he prepare for a minister's life turned him inward. From the early days his rejection by roughneck boys hurt him. By the time he was in college he had all the makings of a homosexual: a domineering father, a weak and patient mother, a strong and not very attractive sister and a grave feeling of inferiority in the world of men.

College was a release, but it was not far enough away from these influences.

Home for the summer of 1850, Horatio was caught up in his father's enthusiasm for the cause of Abolition. It was the year of Henry Clay's great compromise, which, north and south agreed, solved no problem at all. Such prominent antislavery men as William Lloyd Garrison moved around the Boston area speaking with heat against the infamous "Institution." The Reverend Mr. Alger, in spite of criticism from within his parish, insisted on joining hands with the Abolitionists and invited Garrison to speak at his church. It was the time for men to take sides, the senior Alger said, and so the issue of slavery permeated both the pulpit and the family home. Horatio became an abolitionist and at the same time a temperance man, for the two professions went hand in hand.

Back at college, many of the sessions of the Institute of 1770 were devoted to intellectual discussions of slavery. Harvard College drew from north and south impartially and there were slave-holders in Horatio's classes. Sometimes the debates were as heated as Mr. Garrison's speeches.

This junior year, Horatio distinguished himself in Greek and in English. He had a certain gentle humor: one of his papers was a study of *The Immortality of Boot Soles*. Such tomfoolery helped alleviate the grim nature of the times and the plain hard work at the college.

The next year, 1851, Horatio won several honors. He took first prize for his Bowdoin Dissertation, *Athens in the Time of Socrates*. He won an English prize for a study, *The Poetry of the Troubadors*. He won other prizes. His writing was clear (although his Greek had errors). Nearly all of Horatio's writing was for his classes, but he was writing constantly.

He stood eight of ninety in his class and took a lively interest in college affairs. For a time he drilled with a group of students who felt they should learn something about arms (his father would have shuddered at the thought). He and several other young men formed a chapter of the national fraternity Psi Upsilon. He joined the college's Natural History Society, which Horatio claimed existed to provide a home for the owls of the society president. Finally, he was elected to Phi Beta Kappa, the scholarship honorary society. When commencement came, Horatio was chosen to compose the Class Ode, and he made the English oration, a dramatic rendering of *Cicero's Return from Banishment*. These were considerable accomplishments for a shy, tongue-tied minister's son who had always been regarded as something of a sissy.

It was the custom of Harvard's departing seniors to write a page of reminiscences in their own hand in the class book. In neat penmanship, Horatio wrote a little about his early life. He recalled the old brick schoolhouse, but now with the flourish of a Harvard man:

> The light streamed in upon a scene which might well have furnished employment for the pencil of Hogarth....
>
> The room displayed long rows of desk and bench; the former stained and streaked with blots and trickles of dried ink, lumbered with maps and slates, and well-thumbed books, and carved with rough initials.

Long shall I cherish the memory of this ancient edifice which has long since fallen a victim to the spirit of modern improvement....

Harvard Commencement was a happy time for Horatio. He was going forth into the world, and he knew now that whatever else he did, he wished to write. That was the promise and the vision.

But there was a sadness, and he felt it deeply.

No period of my life has been one of such unmixed happiness as the four years which have been spent within college walls [he wrote in the class book]. Whatever may be the course of my life hereafter, I shall never cease to regard it with mingled feelings of pleasure and regret—pleasure which the recollection of past happiness never fails to excite—regret that it is gone forever.

The course of that life was still to be decided, and Horatio was not at all eager at this moment to take the drastic step his father urged on him, a commitment to the Harvard Divinity School. He really wanted to be an author or a journalist.

On Alger's return to Marlborough that summer, he taught school and wrote stories and poems to amuse himself and his students, but always with an eye to publication. He was not very successful; the initial success with *The Pictorial National Library* was not repeated. He began to accumulate rejection slips. But in the fall, while the senior Alger was pressing him to go to Divinity School, Horatio was offered a commission to write a history of Massachusetts' Middlesex County. He had been loath to bring up the matter of Divinity School with his father. Now he temporized, telling his father he wanted to delay the educational process for a time, while he finished the book.

The Reverend Mr. Alger was not pleased, but he was no fool. He suggested that Horatio give his idea a year's trial—knowing full well that the chance of Horatio being able to support himself as a writer after one year's effort was infinitesimal. So Horatio had his chance, and he turned to it with every bit of himself.

All fall and winter, Horatio labored on the history of Middlesex County. Betweentimes he wrote poems. These writings were pastoral or moral, nothing a budding minister need be in the least ashamed to have written; *The Death of Little Alice, A*

Chant of Life, A Welcome to May, The Cottage by the Sea, A Child's Prayer; all poems published by newspapers and magazines. Mostly he received no pay at all; it was the custom of newspapers in particular to regard verse as a contribution to be published, with pride of authorship as the only reward. But by inquiring, Horatio did secure from the editor of *Gleason's Pictorial Drawing Room Companion,* a promise that he would be paid at least two dollars for future contributions. Thus as he estimated he would have to sell 250 poems or stories a year, to conceivably make a living as a writer.

This gloomy prospect loomed just as Horatio lost his sinecure; the authorities who had commissioned the county history announced that times being hard, they were retrenching, and there would be no more funds for the history. So Horatio was flat out of a job, and his record of the past year in terms of sales of writing was such that the Reverend Mr. Alger need have no fears about the outcome. In the spring of 1853, Horatio succumbed to the inevitable and announced that he was going back to Cambridge to enter Divinity School and become a Unitarian minister like his father.

In August Horatio was back in Cambridge, accepting his lot without a whimper. But when September had passed and then October, he found himself growing more and more restless. Boston called him often, and he haunted the offices of various publications. One day a member of the Hale family, which owned and operated the Boston *Daily Advertiser,* offered Horatio a job as an assistant editor. Here was a chance to prove that he could, indeed, make his living in the world of words, so abruptly he withdrew from Divinity School and went to work in Boston at a desk.

What Horatio did not know in his twenty-first year was that although editor and writer could not exist, one without the other, there is a huge gap between performance of the two arts. Horatio was a writer, not an editor, and he so detested the newspaper editing job that no further mention of it is to be found in his scanty papers or even in recollections. He went, he saw, and he decided it was not for him. By May, 1854, he had decided to give it up, and when a friend told him of a job as teacher at the Potowome Boarding School for boys in East Greenwich, Rhode Island, he was glad to give up newspapering forever and go to teaching. The teaching would provide his living, so sadly lacking in the year he had tried on his own, and would still leave him time for writing. Nor would he be burdened by the changing of gears that had precluded him from much effective work in the past six months. True, *Gleason's* had begun publishing stories, many of them imaginative flights, such as "Three Games at Chess" and "Legend of Venice." Another publication, *The Flag of Our Union,* was also publishing his work this year, and many of these were imaginative pieces about far-off lands as well. There was, however a note of morality struck here and there, as in "Margaret's Test" or "Charity Is Its Own Reward," which *Gleason's Pictorial* published just after Horatio took the newspaper job. He was feeling his way, moving more toward the sketch and short story than the poem.

This year, 1854, marked a really productive period as a selling writer: the two magazines published seventeen of Horatio's prose pieces. He discovered that he could write quite well, and the manner he was adopting was straightforward and pleasant to read; he was losing the flowery overly opulent style of the classics student of the day.

It is at this point in Alger's life, that Mayes created a diary for him, and sent the fictional Alger off on a toot that lasted several years. The fictional Alger sailed to Europe with two accomplished roués, Ramsbotham and Emry. Immediately on arriving in London Ramsbotham repaired to the nearest public house and his view of England was that seen through the bottom of a beer mug. They went to Paris, and there Horatio was tempted by wine and women [he was already adept at song, and that was a *fact.*] New passions arose in that timid soul, said biographer Mayes, and they were fanned to flame by Elise Monselet, a short plump blue-eyed singer in a second-rate cafe who taught him to drink and *made a man of him.* Here is the way Mayes's Alger reacted:

Feb. 4th. I was a fool to have waited so long. It is not vile as I thought. Without question I will be better off physically, anyhow I have sometimes thought so. She is more passionate than me...."

Feb. 6th. I ought to know more. Elise makes fun of me. She says she knows I wanted to...I am learning things from her.

Feb. 7th. Should I go on and is it right? What makes it wrong? She doesn't think it is wrong and nobody else does, only I.

Feb. 10th. I won't do it again. If nothing else, from now on I will be clean. I SHALL. They may laugh but I will leave if anything they say to me. I want to be alone and I don't want to see Elise. She must leave me alone. I want to get away somewhere anyhow. My head aches.

Whatever else the diary represented, it was mighty racy reading, much more exciting than the real, live Alger. Horatio then suffered the tortures of the damned, but he did not for a moment—Mayes's fictional Horatio—cease his explorations of Elise's body. He struggled endlessly with his baser nature, and nature always won. This romance continued until he met Charlotte Evans, an English art student, who took Horatio over and completed his sexual education. Mayes hinted at a strange almost bisexual relationship with Charlotte Evans dominating the skinny little Alger completely, until finally he simply ran away from her on the dock at New York in order to escape her dominance. Then, said Mayes, Horatio went home to repent.

One tip-off on the Mayes book should have been the paucity of dates. For it would not have taken very much research for any writer to discover that while Horatio was supposed to be cavorting with questionable ladies in Paris, he was actually either in Divinity School or teaching at such respectable institutions as Potowome Academy. But the sad truth is that after Horatio Alger's death virtually no one in the world was interested in the man. And that is why the Mayes fiction masqueraded as fact for so very long.

Potowome School's fall term had just fairly begun when the damp of Rhode Island in November caused Horatio to come down with an attack of his old enemy—asthma. His doctor sent him home to Marlborough where he would be taken care of and could take bedrest until after the Thanksgiving holiday. So he did come home, fearful lest his father's wrath descend upon him. But the Reverend Mr. Alger was prepared to bide his time, and instead of chastising his wayward son, he reasoned with him. The Reverend Mr. Alger expressed confidence that the boy would turn out all right, and would eventually complete his religious education and accept the call.

At home, Horatio was swept up in the family routine, which in these testy days included constant doses of Abolition politics. He went to fiery prayer meetings where the sins of the South were raked over; his father divided his time these days between consigning drunkards to perdition and upbraiding slaveholders, and in that latter activity, Horatio came to know a good many prominent churchmen. But among the inveighers against strong drink one of the most popular and certainly the most amusing was William Taylor Adams, a school teacher from Boston who was also a writer. Adams was making a fine success of writing stories for boys, under the pen name Oliver Optic. Adams was on the brink now of decision, not quite knowing whether his future lay on the podium or with the pen. He came to Marlborough to speak on the evils of drink, and he and Horatio spent many hours discussing the problems of literature. Horatio was persuaded to show Adams some of his writing. Adams suggested that he might help find a publisher who would bring the stories out in a book.

Adams was as good as his word. He took the stories to Brown, Bazin and Company, Boston publishers, and after a suitable number of readings and adequate mulling, the publishers decided they could make a profit with the material and agreed to publish it. Horatio took a trip to Boston to visit Washington Street, which was then Boston's publishers' row and to talk over with his new friend the conditions under which the book would come out. It was to be called, after one of the tales, *Bertha's Christmas Vision* and was to bear the subtitle, *An Autumn Sheaf,* which would tell the reader he was getting a collection of brief writings.

Horatio went back to Potowome with the publishers' promise to bring out the book and a small advance against royalties. He was now an author.

The year 1855 brought a few more magazine publications. Most of that year was spent in putting together and revising the pieces for the book and teaching at Potowome. *Ballou's Dollar Monthly* published two of Horatio's stories that year. One of them, "Miss Henderson's Thanksgiving Day" was to be a part of the book, *The Saracen Dwarf;* the other, was a little too heady for the purpose. Nearly all the pieces, in one form or another, had already appeared in various newspapers and magazines.

The book was published in the spring of 1856, and it helped persuade Horatio to leave Potowome. Further, he had an offer to take charge of the summer session of Deerfield Academy, which was much nearer home. And so he returned to Massachusetts, and the urgings of his father that he give serious consideration to the ministry once again. Mayes had Horatio still in Paris. How much better a story it would have been if only it were true.

Chapter Four

The Reverend
Horatio Alger, Jr.

WHATEVER the impression Horatio Alger, Jr. made on the boys and the authorities of Deerfield, he was not asked to remain after the summer session of 1856, and so his career was again the big question mark of his life. *Bertha's Christmas Vision* had sold badly, which meant Brown, Bazin and Company was not interested in repeating the experiment. His successes with the magazines careened to a halt. Taking stock at home, Horatio decided that perhaps his father was correct after all and that his calling did lie in the ministry. In the fall the young Alger was at home, worrying. Still, he was not yet ready to give up writing for religion. Many people in the literary world supported themselves by journalism; Horatio already knew this from his experience in Boston on the *Advertiser,* and this year he had an opportunity to try again. The publishers of *True Flag* magazine in that city hired him on the basis of his magazine work and his book to write editorials for the publication. It was a part-time job, but he supplemented his income by tutoring students and by writing for newspapers, notably the Boston *Transcript* and the New York *Sun.* It was a hand-to-mouth existence, and he was not sure which way he should turn. He could devote his full efforts to journalism, but this would mean stopping or slowing his writing pace. Although the two seem to mix, in fact the best journalists generally find that their work demands so much of them that they can manage only an occasional book on the outside. He could continue as he was, living largely on hope. Or, and this was the final and apparently inevitable decision, he could do as his father wished.

The year 1857 opened badly for Wall Street, and thus for the nation and the magazine business. Horatio kept his job until spring, but he was then given notice that his services could not be retained. He thought about going to New York, but just then the gods bestowed on him one of those favors occasioned by the whimsicalities of the public and publishing. That spring William Allen Butler, an intellectual light of some note, had written a long satirical poem taking pokes at the Fifth Avenue society poseurs who symbolized, especially in hard times, conspicuous waste. The Butler poem, *Nothing To Wear,* satirized the gaudy opulence of the rich and caught on immediately with an edgy public. Rudd and Carleton, New York publishers, saw a way to both meet a demand and make some money and reprinted the poem as a little book. It was an instant success, the rage of the publishing world.

Publishers in New York, Boston and Philadelphia pricked up their ears and began looking around for authors who could ape the work and help them cash in on the proceeds. With his poems in New England newspapers and magazines and his prose-poesy book *Bertha's Christmas Vision* behind him, Horatio Alger, Jr. came to the attention of James French and Company of Boston. He was invited for a conference with Editor Knyvet Lowell who outlined the project. When Alger said he thought he could produce, Lowell gave him the assignment.

Horatio was then living in a furnished room in Boston. He repaired there and went to work. In a few days, he had produced a poem in the epic style, and he hastened to the publishing house to present it. Editor Lowell took it, and read:

> Augustus Fitz-Herbert, as all are aware,
> Having crossed the Atlantic, and got a moustache on.
> Likewise being son of a known millionaire,

Stands, of course, on the very top round of fashion.
Being taught to consider himself, from his birth,
As one of the privileged ones of the earth,
He cherishes deep and befitting disdain
For those who don't live on Fifth Avenue,
As entirely unworthy the notice or thought
Of the heir of two millions and nothing to do.
He calls them *canaille,* which I'm credibly told
Is the only French word which he caught when away;
And though, in my case, if I might be so bold,
I should say it scarce paid one for half a year's stay.
The heir of two millions and nothing to do,
Who lives in a palace on Fifth Avenue,
As a matter of course, is no fitting comparison
For the heir of an inkstand and something to do,
Who lodges upstairs, in the house of Miss Harrison

On it went, in that vein, detailing the history of Augustus
Fitz-Herbert, who stemmed from a father who had been a pawnbroker, but who later invented a fake pedigree that went back to
the days of the Black Prince. Horatio told in verse of the stunning
Augustus' European trip from Russia to Spain:

He has stood, it may be, on the very same spot
Where Homer recited his deathless heroics,
Or paused at the portico, knowing it not,
Where Zeno addressed his disciples, the Stoics.
Perchance when he gazed from the brow of the hill
On the once-famous harbor,—the Attic Piraeus,—
Proud trophy of valor reverse could not chill!—
His foot pressed the turf on the breast of Musaeus

Thus were the values of a classical education brought into
full play. The satire of the foolish, ill-educated, uncultured millionaires continued:

From his journal I venture below to record
A single impression received while abroad:
"June 7th, we reached Athens—a sizeable place,
Some three or four miles from the Gulf of Aegina;
It contains a cathedral not equal to Grace

Church in New York, which I think is much finer.
Went up to the top of the famous Acropolis,
Which is visited daily by hundreds of people,
But can't say I think that the view from the top o' this
Is equal to that from our Trinity steeple.
The houses are mostly unsightly and small;
In Minerva and Hermes street noticed a few
Which will do very well, but are nothing at all
Compared to our mansion on Fifth Avenue.
The piles of old ruins one sees here and there
I consider a perfect disgrace to the town;
If they had an efficient and competent mayor,
Like our Mayor Wood, he would soon have them down

The Harvard influence also showed in this spoof. Horatio
had studied natural history under the famous Louis Agassiz:

He inclines, as I think, in regard to the masses,
In a modified form to the view of Agassiz:
As that Adam the first has another for weedin',
And other such jobs in the garden of Eden;
. . .
While from Adam the first are descended the few
Who are blest with long purses and nothing to do
. . .
Conclusively showing that much finer clay
Is required for the rich than the general masses

Horatio ended with a flourish that even his father, no re-
specter of levity, would not find distasteful. Having called on the
reader to consider this case of Augustus Fitz-Herbert, the wastrel,
he ended on a suitable moral note that could be either taken as a
spoof on the moralists or seriously:

And, if, as Faith, Reason, and Scripture all show,
God rewards us in heaven for the good done below,
I pray you take heed, idle worldling, lest you
With that better world should have nothing to do!

Editor Lowell was pleased with what he read and accepted
the epic for publication. Horatio was given a small payment, and

the manuscript was put into production. A few weeks later it appeared, well-bound, illustrated by a picture of a young fop (at the frontispiece) and dedicated by the author to Butler. But the author's name was not mentioned and was never mentioned in connection with the publicity attendant to the book. *Nothing To Do,* succeeded far more modestly than Butler's work, which sold many thousands of copies and was published in England and other foreign climes. There is no indication that author Alger received anything more than the flat fee he was paid for writing it and such admiration as he might gain from family and friends. Horatio's father thought well enough of the work to present a copy of it to the Harvard College library. His friends laughed at it when they met that summer at the fifth anniversary reunion of the class of 1852.

Literature seemed to have reached a dead end for Horatio, and again he went home to Marlborough for the summer. He had discussions with his father and family, and in the end he agreed that whatever he did with his writing, he would return to Harvard to complete the divinity course and become a minister. So in August he was back in Cambridge.

Many of Horatio's old literary markets had vanished or dried up as far as he was concerned. The national economy was not so very healthy in those years on the edge of war. *Ballou's,* for which he had had such hope, had stopped buying, but he turned elsewhere and by the winter of 1857–58 was receiving a certain amount of encouragement from *Gleason's,* which had expanded and now published a magazine called *Gleason's Weekly Line-of-Battle Ship.* In January *Graham's Illustrated Magazine* published the story "Five Hundred Dollars" (which would later be the basis for a book). Combining newspaper work, his divinity studies and writing was pleasant, and the occasional check helped. But the financing of Horatio's divine education came from money granted by Harvard from various charitable funds established to aid poor students. He was also tutoring young boys, but there was not a breath of scandal about him. He was very discreet in his relationships.

In the winter recess of 1858 Horatio went home to Marlborough where his father was now superintendent of schools as well as Unitarian minister. Horatio, Sr.'s influence brought Horatio,

Jr. a temporary job teaching in a district school for which he was paid nearly as much as the $75 he had received at Deerfield as summer sessions headmaster two years before. Then it was back to the grind at Cambridge.

The year 1858 brought a renewed literary success with the Gleason house, *The Weekly Line-of-Battle Ship* published a story, "Matthew Pendleton's Wager," on November 13 and two weeks later published another Alger tale, "Kitty Ray's Perplexity." Then came "Jacob Blount's Will" on December 11, and Horatio was ensconced as a contributor on a regular basis. For the rest of the year he averaged two stories a month in *Gleason's,* which not only brought in income, but gave him a cachet as a solid writer of stories for young people. He was still picking subjects from his student days and romantic tales of his youth: "A Duke in Disguise," "The King and the Abbot" and "The Miser of Nottingham." But there were signs of the style and subject that would one day make him famous: "The Newsboy's Temptation," "Tim, the Blacksmith" and "John Grover's Lesson."

It seemed apparent, now, that Horatio could combine a career as minister of the gospel and writer to both financial advantage and personal satisfaction, and he went to his books of divinity with a good will.

At home the feisty Horatio Alger, Sr. was in trouble. Having cast his lot squarely with the Abolitionists and the Temperance movement he had made his share of enemies among the conservatives and tavern owners. His outspoken nature had brought him a great deal of criticism inside and outside his parish. Further, because of the great energy he put into civic affairs, he was elected to the lower house of the Massachusetts legislature. There in 1859 he became involved in a railway power struggle between two of the little lines that were fighting over rights and privileges in the central part of the state. Many of his parishioners were stockholders in the North Branch Railway which was fighting the South Branch Railway for the right to carry goods from Marlborough and other towns to Boston. The legislature, in spite of the senior Alger's heroic speeches and lobbying, decided in favor of the South Branch line. Alger's constituents thought he had let them down. Since many of those constituents were also parishioners at the Unitarian Church, the atmosphere grew very cool.

When the Reverend Mr. Alger suggested he might resign his pulpit, the resignation was immediately accepted.

Alger agreed to stay on until the parishioners could find a new minister and meanwhile found himself a new sinecure at the First Unitarian Church of South Natick, whose minister would retire in 1860. He never stopped his public works, then, and was one of the leading figures in Marlborough's Bicentennial Celebration planned for the summer of 1860.

The senior Alger was now a man of some substance. He had money in the bank and only half a family to support. Horatio's younger brother James had succumbed to the lure of gold and headed for California, where he wrote seldom and vaguely, but indicated no desire to leave the west. Youngest brother Francis headed for Boston where his grandparents, the Fennos helped him get a job in a clothing store. Sister Olive Augusta remained at home doing parish works and waiting for a husband. Sister Ann languished with what must have been tuberculosis (they called it lung fever) and provided the one pain of sadness in the hearts of the minister and his wife.

All, however, were brightened by the Bicentennial and its hoopla. Horatio, Jr. came home, wrote the Ode, which was sung by a choir during the celebration. He was in good company: William Cullen Bryant had written a hymn especially for this auspicious occasion. Bands played and people marched and orators spoke for hours. In spite of the Reverend Mr. Alger's stiffest complaints (he was chairman of arrangements for the whole festivity but was overruled) a gang of ruffian-minded citizens of the Antiques and Horribles, a merrymaking, cider-drinking, hell-raising association, insisted on parading as part of the celebration. The Alger supporters at least confined the disgraceful spectacle to late afternoon. They ignored the whole matter, and all else that went on in the saloons and taverns after dark.

In all it was grand, and a kind of a send-off for the Algers, who were about to leave the community, even though it meant the Reverend Mr. Alger would have to resign his seat in the legislature. A month later they took the trek to South Natick, some twenty miles away. Horatio went back to Divinity School and graduated at the end of July. Now he was ready to accept the calling.

Chapter Five

The First Boys' Book

Before settling down to the life of a Unitarian minister, Horatio Alger, Jr. decided to see the world. It was still the day of the Grand Tour, which privileged Americans made through the historic lands of Europe, and although Horatio was not privileged in the manner of Augustus Fitz-Herbert and his Fifth Avenue friends, he had managed to turn a pretty penny recently with the inkpot. His contributions to *Gleason's* continued steadily through the spring, now appearing in *Gleason's Literary Companion.* More and more they were tending toward the moral tales for boys that he would write so successfully in a few years. The stories bore titles signifying their uplifting content: "Henry Trafton's Independence," "John Beckwith's Reverses." But it would be a mistake to believe that Horatio Alger, Jr. had only one string to his bow, that the style of the Alger books was arrived at by some effortless sleight of hand or that he was, as some later librarians were to indicate, a careless and ill-conceiving author. An example of one aspect of his style, the travel story, appeared in the *Marlborough Mirror* that spring of 1860, following a brief trip made by Horatio and three friends to Quebec. Horatio defrayed a bit of his expense by writing this article for the hometown paper. The Alger account was low-key and not at all given to flourishes.

> Few who visit Quebec fail to see the Falls of Montmorenci. They are, in fact, one of the chief lions of the neighborhood, and, although not so grand or sublime as Niagara, exceed it in altitude. One fine morning in August, 1859, a party of four, including myself, sallied from Russell's Hotel, and looked about for a carriage in which to make the excursion. Quite a number were drawn up in front of the hotel, and the respective drivers at once assailed us with urgent invitations to avail ourselves of their carriage. The competition was all the more favorable to us, so we stood by quietly, and allowed them to underbid each other. The first price demanded was five dollars for the party, but we at length effected an arrangement with the driver of the best carriage—a good looking barouche—to carry us for three dollars and a half.

Following this are some twelve hundred words of description of the trip to the falls, encounters with Quebecoise along the route and the journey back to the hotel. It is not an astounding story and not in any way earthshaking, but a simple report of a pleasant excursion, and it so rang throughout. The Marlborough newspaper was happy enough with it, however, to accede to Horatio's suggestion that they pay him for reports from Europe on his coming journey. He also made arrangements with the New York *Sun* and the Boston *Transcript* to send them travel articles for pay.

Then, for a few weeks in July and August, the new graduate of Harvard Divinity School helped his father in the South Natick parish and occasionally preached elsewhere as a supply minister. But early in September, he joined his cousin George Fenno and Charles Vinal, a Harvard classmate, to sail from Boston aboard the Cunard liner *Arabia* for Liverpool.

It was a rough voyage, and though the young men were seasick they arrived safe and well. They then set out on a trip, half walking, to see as much as they could in a few months, before returning to Boston and the workaday world. George Fenno would step into the family mercantile business; Charles Vinal had already been given a parish at North Andover; only Horatio was unsettled as to his future, and he hoped that writing would have a large part in it. But for the moment they were bent on enjoyment and exploration, with Horatio chronicling their adventures as they went.

The young men headed off into Wales at first, walking a good deal of the way and visiting castles and churches and quaint villages. Horatio sat up late at night, often by candle, and wrote his travel articles for the newspapers. He told how they took the night boat to Ireland and then stopped at Price's Hotel, just opposite the famous Nelson pillar. Walking, riding donkey carts, they traversed the cobbled streets and rough roads of that green Irish land to Killarney, where they took the train to Belfast, and then took a ship to Glasgow.

In November the three were in a chill, drizzling London that did not excite them; they would rather have left immediately but were honor-bound by the code of the Grand Tourer to go home able to talk about the Tower of London and the Parliament and the other sights. So they stayed and walked through the rain and felt the chill of the unheated hotel rooms in their bones for three weeks. Then they took the boat to France and found the climate just as bad, if not advertised so severely. Horatio fell ill. His weak lungs bothered him, and he stayed in their rooms with a small fire while his companions went roaming the streets. It was almost a week before he was well; then he "did" Paris—Montmartre, the Champs Elysées, Notre Dame and the Louvre. He wrote it all for the newspapers, and Americans were still so unversed in travel that the stories were greeted with very respectable acclaim by readers.

In January they were in Italy, where Horatio practiced the language (he had studied it at home and at Harvard). They went south to see the ruins of Pompeii and got lost on a donkey trip. That was the tenor of their adventures. It was nothing at all like the fictional Alger trip to Europe invented by Herbert Mayes. The only similarity, in fact, was that both real and fictional Horatios had taken a trip. He met no cafe singers, nor any exciting art students. He was a dull, young, just-graduated divinity student out acquiring culture along with two companions. In February the three travelers were back in Paris where they saw the funeral procession of Augustin Eugene Scribe, and Horatio later wrote about it for his papers. He also sent a report of a speech by

Emperor Napoleon III (in French) to the Marlborough paper, along with a report in English. They stayed in Paris until the end of March, encountering classmates and other acquaintances, and they returned to England. From Liverpool they sailed home arriving on April 19, 1861, just a week after the guns had begun to roar at Fort Sumter.

Horatio Alger, Jr. went home to South Natick and immediately volunteered for the Massachusetts regiment being formed. But this skinny, undersized minister with chronic chest trouble was not regarded as good cannon fodder and was rejected by the doctors. He stayed at home then, helping his father and waiting. Friends, particularly his cousins the Fennos, suggested that he might come to Boston and join the militia. He did go to Boston, but he was rejected again for physical reasons, and now he gave up. He spent the rest of 1861 and 1862 tutoring students, without scandal, and working in the faith—and writing. Most of the time he lived in Cambridge, where the demand for his services was greatest, the majority of young men of his age group and intellectual capacity were going off to war. In the spring of that year he was offered a post as Unitarian minister in far-off Alton, Illinois, but Horatio had no desire to move so far from his literary markets, and he declined.

Life went on almost as though there was no war, unless one read the newspapers. But in the summer of 1862 the dreadful nature of the struggle was brought home to Horatio when he attended the tenth anniversary celebration of the Harvard class of 1852. It was held at the Union Club—which in essence emphasized the barrier, now absolute, between members of the class. Horatio learned of the activities of classmates, those fighting for the Union and those for the Confederacy, and those who like himself were not fighting at all.

Horatio put his hand now to far more serious writing than before. He wrote an article on Scribe based on his notes of the funeral and his gleanings while in Paris. It was accepted by the highly respected and very literary *North American Review* and published in the autumn of 1863. He wrote a story ("Job Warner's Christmas") which was taken by the equally influential *Harper's Monthly.*

Alger, then, was tending toward a career as the serious writer of prose he wished to be. He wrote patriotic sketches and poetry for the newspapers. He wrote his first novel, which he called *Marie Bertrand: The Felon's Daughter.* The scene was French, obviously drawn from his experiences there, but only in terms of geographic description and people. Always, Alger was to display a marvelous sense of place that made all his books exciting to those who relished a sense of relation to foreign climes and to those whose imagination was stimulated by good description. *Marie Bertrand* was the story of a French convict who had been sent to the galleys and his daughter; except that the daughter, a poor Parisian seamstress, was not his daughter at all, but the kidnaped heiress to a French fortune. In the end Marie Bertrand was reunited with her mother, a countess, and married to a very eligible young man. Ostensibly, she lived happily ever after.

Marie Bertrand was the kind of romance very common in American literature in the 1860s, and when the editors of the New York *Sun,* to whom it was offered, refused it, Alger sent it to Street & Smith, who published the New York *Weekly.* The *Weekly* accepted the tale and serialized it in 1864. Horatio visited New York, and there began to acquire information for more stories. His technique was to carry a notebook around with him on strolls through the city (as he had done on his travels) and jot down impressions that he would later use in his writing.

But now, as the war continued, the young writer felt a patriotic duty to do something to further the effort through the use of his pen, and he turned to a tale of a young boy who also wanted to help the Union war effort. It would be called *Frank's Campaign.*

Street & Smith did not want a juvenile story that dealt with the war. Horatio took it to his friend Will Adams, or Oliver Optic, who had now become editor of the juvenile magazine *Student and Schoolmate* as well as the magazine's leading writer. Adams was cordial; he was already publishing one Alger, Horatio's sister Olive Augusta, who wrote under a pen name. *Student and Schoolmate* also published a number of prominent New England authors, including Louisa May Alcott and Oliver Wendell Holmes. But Adams did not want *Frank's Compaign* either; what he wanted from Horatio were short stories and poems.

Adams did send Horatio to see A. K. Loring, on Boston's Washington Street. Loring was a well-known bookseller who had recently embarked on a publishing career, and he was looking for a writer who could turn out exciting and uplifting juvenile novels aimed specifically at boys. Early in 1864 Loring took the manuscript and this is what met his eyes.

The Town Hall in Rossville stands on a moderate elevation overlooking the principal street. It is generally open only when a meeting has been called by the Selectmen to transact town business, or occasionally on the evening when a lecture on Temperance or a political address is to be delivered.

One Wednesday afternoon, toward the close of September, 1862, a group of men and boys might have been seen standing on the steps and in the entry of the Town House. Why they had met will best appear from a large placard, which had been posted on barns and fences.

It ran as follows:—

WAR MEETING!

The citizens of Rossville are invited to meet at the Town Hall, on Wednesday, September 24, at 3 P.M. to decide what measures shall be taken toward raising the town's quota of 25 men, under the recent call of the President of the United States. All patriotic citizens, who are in favor of sustaining the free institutions transmitted to us by our fathers, are urgently invited to be present....

Almost pure autobiography, that's what it is. Horatio was here recalling the evening he had returned to South Natick from his trip abroad. That first day home he had attended just such a Call To Arms rally at which his father, the Reverend Mr. Alger, gave an impassioned patriotic speech. The description of the meeting place and the people was very much true to New England life.

But there the similarity ended. Horatio began spinning a tale with the same verve and skill he had already demonstrated in his short stories and the novel *Marie Bertrand*. In the first chapter Alger establishes the basic conflict: Mr. Frost, the hero's father, a quiet, well-spoken man, came into conflict with Squire Haynes, "a short, stout, red-faced man, wearing gold spectacles."

Squire Haynes was to be repeated a hundred times in the next thirty-five years. So was Mr. Frost. So were all the basic characters of this first Alger boys' book.

Frost wanted to give bounty money to volunteers to help their families while they fought for country. Haynes, the wealthiest man in town, objected on the basis that "the consequences of it would be to plunge us into debt and increase our taxes to a formidable amount."

Horatio used one technique that immediately turned his reader. Frost spoke openly and his words were sensible and soft. Physically, Frost was not described—it was not necessary—for one had the feeling of a strong, upright, honest character, to wit:

> "Squire Haynes objects that my proposition, if adopted, will make our taxes heavier. I grant it; but how can we expect to carry on this gigantic war without personal sacrifices. If they only come in the form of money, we may count ourselves fortunate. I take it for granted that there is not a man here present who does not approve the present war,—who does not feel that we are waging it for good and sufficient reasons. Such being the case, we cannot but feel that the burden ought to fall upon the entire community and not wholly upon any particular portion.... The least that those who are privileged to stay at home can do is tax their purses for this end...."

Then, having spoken, Virtue was taunted by Vice:

> "Mr. Chairman," said Squire Haynes sarcastically, "I infer that the last speaker is intending to enlist."
>
> Mr. Frost's face flushed at the insinuation. "Squire Haynes chooses to impute to me interested motives. I need enter no defense before an audience to whom I am well known. I will only inquire whether interested motives have nothing to do with his opposition to voting bounties to our soldiers?"
>
> This forthright statement was such a palpable hit and so turned the audience that Squire Haynes winced under it, and his face turned redder.
>
> "Impudent puppy!" he muttered to himself, "he seems to forget that I have a mortgage of eight hundred dollars on his farm. When the time comes to foreclose it, I will show him no mercy....

And so in what was to become the Alger tradition, the battle was joined within the first fifteen pages. The antagonists had been established in this space, the plot set in motion and the conflict created. Then, enter the youth.

Attending Rossville Academy (which was very obviously the Gates Academy of Horatio's youth) under the charge of James Rathbun, A. M., "a thorough scholar and a skillful teacher," were Frank Frost, sixteen, "medium size, campactly made; has dark chestnut hair, with a slight wave, and is altogether a fine looking boy" (and a typical Alger hero).

Frank's natural enemy, Squire Haynes' son John, was two years older, "and about as opposite to him in personal appearance as can be imagined. He has a thin face, very black hair, is tall for his age, and already beginning to feel himself a young man."

In two paragraphs, Horatio Alger, Jr. established the basis for more conflict. Frank Frost is manly, thoroughly admirable; his enemy is rat-faced, skinny, probably pimply (if the reader has a good imagination) greasy-haired (ditto) and full of himself.

A foil is introduced: Henry Tufts, "mild in his manners, and a respectable student, but possesses no positive character." Frank Frost, of course, was the best scholar in school but there was doubt if he would be able to go on to college because of his father's poverty. Well, not exactly poverty.

> His father is in moderate circumstances, deriving a comfortable subsistence from a small farm, but is able to lay by a very small surplus every year, and this he feels is necessary to hold in reserve for the liquidation of the mortgage held by Squire Haynes.

Here again the dastardly nature of Squire Haynes was emphasized.

The story moves fast: Frank Frost won a prize for his essay *The Duties of Boys in the Present National Crisis,* and all but one of the thirty-nine other students applauded.

> John Haynes turned pale, and then red with anger and vexation. He scowled darkly while the rest of the boys were applauding, and persuaded himself that he was the victim of a great piece of injustice.

The plot thickens. John Haynes told his father that Frank Frost was teacher's pet. The squire spoke darkly of those who insulted people with the power to annoy them (the mortgage). He gave John thirty dollars because he had been defrauded of the prize (a book.)

So the wicked Hayneses were established as being beyond no scurvy trick to gain their ends.

Chapter Three of *Frank's Campaign* opens on the Frosts. Mr. Frost, was an artist who had turned to farming to earn a living for his wife and sons, Frank and Charlie, and daughters, Alice and Maggie. Their house very much resembled Horatio's own childhood home. The family's one extravagance like the Algers was literary: subscriptions to *Harper's* and other magazines, a daily newspaper and a children's magazine. At one point Horatio introduced a dialogue between Mr. Frost and a neighbor about the rewards of reading. The neighbor questioned such wasteful expenditure. Not so, said Mr. Frost. He sold his apples at $2 a barrel instead of the $1.75 the neighbor got, because Mr. Frost had read in his farm paper that apples were going up and had held on until they did.

Not only that, said Mr. Frost: "Education often enables a man to make money."

Mr. Frost dropped a seed for his son when he wished Frank were older so he could look after the farm and family while Mr. Frost enlisted in the army.

This remark caused Frank to look thoughtfully into the fire. Then he got up and lighted a candle and went to bed. "But he did not go to sleep for some time."

Next morning Frank convinced his father that he could take care of the farm, so that Mr. Frost could join the army. Mother, Mary Frost, was informed casually of this decision, while Mr. Frost was helping her to a sausage. No cries, no complaints from Mrs. Frost. She munched her sausage and considered:

> "It will be a great undertaking," she said at last, "but if you think you can trust Frank, I will do all I can to help him. I can't bear to think of having you go, yet I am conscious that this is a feeling which I have no right to indulge at the expense of my country."

So Father Frost went to war, and Frank Frost quit school to run the farm. Squire Haynes rubbed his hands, pulled the mortgage out of his strong box and made ready to foreclose in July and give the farm to son John. Obviously the Frost boy would be unable to manage the farm properly.

Father Frost marched off, leaving $400 in the bank and $50 in cash for expenses. Frank's woes began forthwith. On the road home from taking his father to the depot, Frank and his mother encountered a fugitive slave, Chloe, who had settled in Rossville. Chloe spoke black dialect: "O missus I'se almost dead,... "spect I shan't live til mornin." Her son Pomp, "was as black as the ace of spades, and possessing to the full the mercurial temperament of the Southern negro." But they were good sorts, if down on their luck. The Frosts, mother and son, helped them with provisions and then forgot all about their generosity.

Frank's Campaign is a war book written in the heat of the Civil War, and Horatio took pains to bring to it descriptions of camp life as lived by Soldier Frost, all taken from accounts in the daily newspapers. This concatenation of factual matter with fantasy gave the book a strange, two-sided character.

Into the lives of the Frosts came a stranger, Henry Morton, who was taken by Frank Frost's manly ways and honesty. Morton came to board with the Frosts. There he also encountered Chloe, who had known him in the South. Such characters would be forever popping into Alger books: rich college men, rich merchants or just plain rich. Like Henry Morton they come always from some strange, fantastic milieu, stay long enough to pull the young hero out of the hole into which Horatio had dug him, then disappear.

The battle of Fredericksburg (fact again) intervened in the adventures on the farm: Frank's father was wounded there and Horatio devoted a long passage to description of the battle, again written from the newspapers.

Back on the farm, Frank Frost decided to organize a boy's marching and drilling society. After some close order drill based on Horatio's marching days at Harvard, Frank was elected captain of the troop, which caused John Haynes to resign from it. More villainy.

The factual world again intruded via war tales from Frank's father at the front. First there was the sad news that he had been captured by the Rebels because of the treachery of a woman he had helped (O, perfidy thy name is woman); then there was the happier news that he had escaped, a few paragraphs later, and finally there was the satisfying news that the rebel lady had been arrested.

Meanwhile, back home John Haynes nearly drowned because like an idiot he went sailing in the river without knowing how to sail. Mr. Morton rescued him.

The depth of the squire's wickedness was revealed when Frank came to see him to ask for an extension on the mortgage. Of course, said the squire, unless he had sudden need for the money. But on June 30, the day before the mortgage was due, the squire appeared to speak to Frank and his mother. She spoke:

> "May I inquire what course you propose to take?"
>
> "It will be my painful duty to foreclose the mortgage."
>
> "Squire Haynes," said Frank boldly, "haven't you intended to foreclose the mortgage all along? Hadn't you decided about it when I called upon you ten days ago?"
>
> "What do you mean by your impertinence, sir?" demanded the squire.
>
> "Just what I say. I believe you bear a grudge against my father, and only put me off the other day in order to prevent my being able to meet your demands tomorrow. What do you suppose we can do in less than twenty-four hours?"
>
> "Madam," said the Squire, purple with rage. "Do you permit your son to insult me in this impudent manner?"
>
> "I leave it to your own conscience, Squire Haynes, whether his charges are not deserved. I do not like to think ill of any man, but your course is very suspicious."
>
> "I'll have no mercy on you. I'll sell you out root and branch," said Squire Haynes, trembling with passion, and smiting the floor with his cane. . . .

But that night, in the nick of time, Mr. Morton, who had gone to the city, reappeared. All would be well, said the handsome, debonair, imperturbable Mr. Morton.

Next morning he opened his pocketbook and produced four new crisp hundred dollar notes, which, with the Frost savings, made up the mortgage payment. He refused to take any security. Frank's word was good enough for him.

Squire Haynes stumped up to the farm and demanded his money, then announced he was foreclosing. Mrs. Frost produced the money. Frank counted it out, and Mr. Morton came into the room to witness payment. Then Mr. Morton unveiled. He was really Richard Waring, and the squire had best make restitution of the money he stole from the Waring estate.

The squire blustered.

"Pooh, pooh, your threats won't avail you," said the squire contemptuously.

"You doubt my identity?"

"You may very probably be the person you claim to be, but that won't save you."

"Very well, you have conceded one important point."

He walked quietly to the door of the adjoining room, opened it, and in a distant voice called "James Travers."

At the sound of this name, Squire Haynes sank into a chair, ashy pale.

A man, not over forty, but with seamed face, hair nearly white, and a form evidently broken with ill health, slowly entered.

Squire Haynes beheld him with dismay.

"You see before you, Squire Haynes, a man whose silence has been your safeguard for the last twelve years. His lips are now unsealed. James Travers, tell us what you know of the trust reposed in this man, by my father."

"No, no," said the Squire hurriedly. "It—it is enough. I will make restitution."

And so the squire left the house "with the air of one who had been crushed by a sudden blow," and in the next paragraph but one, Frank Frost's father was promoted to second lieutenant. In a sentence, Squire Haynes was stripped of more than half his property, and Henry Morton bought the Squire's house when he moved out of town (the squire went to Philadelphia for reasons not specified). Mr. Morton, now Richard Waring, guaranteed Frank's college education and Frank's father was promoted to captain. Since the war was not over (in later editions the ending was changed to bring Captain Frost home in one paragraph), Captain Frost remained at the front doing his duty, just as fearless Frank Frost stayed home doing his.

A. K. Loring read what Horatio had wrought of the doings of the Frosts and decided it would fit the times and the publishing tempo of 1864. He agreed to take the book. Thus was Horatio Alger, Jr. launched as a writer of stirring books for boys.

Chapter Six

Paul Prescott's Charge

Perhaps it was the paucity of material and writers—the finest young men of the nation were away at war killing one another—but in the winter of 1864 Horatio Alger, Jr. achieved more success with his writing than he had ever enjoyed before. *Harper's Monthly* took a second story "Ralph Farnham's Romance." *Frank Leslie's Illustrated Newspaper* bought another, and a tale he had written for the magazines, "The Young Hero," was included in an anthology called the *Railway Anecdote Book.*

These were among the better stories of their type and quite in fashion. But even as he was writing for the adult magazines, Alger was turning more to publication for the young. One reason for this was his friendship with Editor Adams of *Student and Schoolmate*. He began with poetry, creating "The Song of the Croaker" and a pathetic poem about the War, "Where is My Boy Tonight."

> When the Clouds in the western sky
> Flush red with the setting sun,
> When the veil of twilight falls,
> And the busy day is done,

I sit and watch the clouds,
With their crimson hues alight,
And ponder with anxious heart,
"Oh where is my boy tonight?"

Then four more verses about the soldier boy in the war, and a final stanza:

May God bless all our boys,
By the camp fire's ruddy glow,
Or when in the deadly fight,
They front the embattled foe;
And comfort each mother's heart,
As she sits in the fading light,
And ponders with anxious heart,—
"Where is my boy tonight?"

But Oliver Wendell Holmes, the physician, scientist and poet was doing the same. For the same magazine in March, 1864 Holmes wrote "The Last Charge," a heroic of the war.

In the spring of 1865, Horatio began slowly with prose pieces for *Student and Schoolmate.*

Alger's stock in the literary world was raised considerably when Publisher Loring decided to take on another Alger patriotic book for boys. With its backtracking and imperfections and schizophrenic character, *Frank's Campaign* had done well enough as a publishing venture to cause Loring to hope Horatio Alger might be the writer he wanted to equal Oliver Optic's success with boys. The new work was to be *Paul Prescott's Charge,* and despite its martial ring, and the decoration of later editions with cavalry sabres, the charge referred to in the title was the charge to Paul Prescott by his dying father. The book was, as Alger put it in the preface "written in furtherance of the same main idea, that every boy's life is a campaign, more or less difficult, in which success depends upon integrity and a steadfast adherence to duty."

Paul Prescott's Charge was a more sophisticated book than *Frank's Campaign.* The squire here was Squire Benjamin Newcome:

Justice of the Peace, Chairman of the Selectmen, and the wealthiest man in Wrenville... a man so dignified that... if the

President of the United States had called upon him, Squire Newcome would very probably have felt that he himself was the party who conferred distinction, and not received it.

Horatio had some conscious humor here.

In *Paul Prescott's Charge,* Alger was finding his way in boys' literature. He indulged in horseplay. The Irish were the butt of jokes in the America of the mid-nineteenth century, and Alger turned to an Irish joke. Hannah, the squire's Irish servant, did not appear immediately on being called by her master. She was making bread in the kitchen and stopped to wash the flour off her hands, while the Squire stood in the next room and shouted; then:

> At length she appeared at the door of the sitting room.
>
> "Hann-nah!" said Squire Newcome, fixing his cold gray eye upon her, "when you hear my voice calling you, it is your duty to answer the summons *immejiately.*"
>
> I have endeavored to represent the Squire's pronunciation of the last word.
>
> "So I would have come *immejously,*" said Hannah, displaying a most reprehensible ignorance, "but me hands were all covered with flour."
>
> "That makes no difference," interrupted the Squire. "Flour is an accidental circumstance."
>
> "What's that?" thought Hannah, opening her eyes in amazement.
>
> "And should not be allowed to interpose an obstacle to an *immejiate* answer to my summons."
>
> "Sir," said Hannah, who guessed at the meaning although she did not understand the words, "you wouldn't have me dirty the door handle with me doughy hands?"
>
> "That could easily be remedied by ablution."
>
> "There ain't any ablution in the house," said the mystified Hannah.
>
> "I mean," said Squire Newcome condescending to explain, "the application of water—in short washing."
>
> "Shure" said Hannah, as light broke in upon her mind, "I never knew what they called it before."

Here, Alger has introduced a device that he was to make famous and which was to delight millions of American and other boys around the world. He took the reader into his confidence with the remark "I have endeavored to represent the Squire's pronunciation..." in a way that could not help but endear the author in spite of the interjection of the aside. And, once he had had his joke at the expense of the ignorant servant and pompous employer, he was quick to get into action.

The story was quite different from *Frank's Campaign*, but many of the characters were, or would be, stock Alger figures. For instance, the squire's son, Ben, found drowning a cat in the rain barrel, said he was only trying to teach Kitty to swim, but the reader was not fooled, for Alger noted Ben's inner thoughts about drowning kittens:

> "O, I wouldn't drown her for anything," said Ben with an injured expression, mentally adding, "short of a three-cent piece."

The plot: Mr. Prescott, a carpenter, had fallen off a building, contracted internal injuries, languished and was forced to spend all the family savings in his illness. Paul, "a thoughtful looking boy" was about to start life as an orphan, dead broke and charged to pay off his father's debt of five hundred dollars. Paul was sent to the poorhouse where he met new characters: 1) Nicholas Mudge (coarse hard face, shock of red hair) "such an utter absence of refinement about the man, that Paul, was repelled by the contrast..."); 2) Mrs. Mudge (squint); 3) a gentle old lady named Aunt Lucy.

It was hard. Poor Paul had to get up at five and milk the cows and then go out and hoe the fields all day long, come home and chop wood and carry water. Paul ran away and at this point Horatio took the step that would bring him fame and fortune: he sent Paul to the wicked, fascinating city of New York.

In New York, Paul was first cheated by a street boy of most of the money he had: the boy "befriended" him, took him to a restaurant, where they both ordered oyster stew. "The Governor's son" as he called himself, then stepped out "for a minute" and Paul was stuck with the check.

That dastardly trick taught Paul and Horatio's readers the

pitfalls of the city. Paul, down to twelve cents, was not dismayed. He wandered around, fell asleep in a church and was discovered by the sexton. Moral: falling asleep in a church is a good thing for poor boys to do. He was befriended by the sexton's wife. Their son had died, so they took Paul in, and presto, he had a place to sleep and plenty to eat. Now, as Horatio had made quite clear in the preface, this stroke of luck was not such luck as all that, but the result of Paul's manliness and innate honesty, cleanliness and pleasant attitude toward his hard lot. Those attributes had attracted the sexton and his wife, so although Paul's "luck" seemed good, such luck, Alger said would only come to those with fine character.

In New York, Paul went to school. He was mistreated by George Dawkins, a "showy boy" who was first in his class and also the class bully. Poor Paul, not having had the benefits of much education started slow, but:

> At the end of the month, the master read off the class-list, and, much to his disgust, George Dawkins found himself playing second fiddle to Young Stupid.

This event occurred almost at the precise midpoint of the book: Paul had his first triumph, and even as the young reader savored it while turning the page, Chapter XVII whisked him back to the poorhouse and wicked Mrs. Mudge, bending over a tub. The Mudges quarreled because her husband, a shiftless character at best, was unsympathetic when the cow got out and ate her cabbages and she broke a broom. And then Squire Newcome got involved by appearing at exactly the wrong moment at the poorhouse and having the slops thrown on his dignified coat.

This whole chapter is an interleaf, it really adds very little to the plot, but it provides, in the Shakespearian manner, a few boffs for the audience while they prepare themselves to go on with the saga of Paul Prescott. Chapter XVIII returns to Squire Newcome and his constant demands for *"immejiate"* response. Another long joke makes its appearance here: as Ben Newcome was walking down the street, he was accosted by a stranger in a rig who asked the way to the town of Sparta; when Newcome pretended deafness, the stranger moved on to ask the question of old

man Haven, who really was deaf, and the disgusted stranger
drove off in a pet, insisting thereafter that all the people of Wrenville were deaf as posts.

Here again Horatio thrust an anecdote into the story to amuse
young readers. Horatio now gave one of the finest characterizations
in all his writings, that of Mrs. Mudge, mistress of the poorhouse.

Then Ben Newcome, the squire's son was back to his old
mischief, baiting Mrs. Mudge at the poorhouse, while delivering
to Aunt Lucy a letter from Paul. But wicked Mrs. Mudge, ap-
prised that Paul had sent a letter, was already scheming:

> Mrs. Mudge was bent on reading Aunt Lucy's letter. Knowing
> it to be from Paul, she had a strong curiosity to know what
> had become of him. If she could only get him back! Her heart
> bounded with delight as she thought of the annoyances to
> which in that case, she could subject him. It would be a double
> triumph over him and Aunt Lucy, against whom she felt that
> mean spite with which a superior nature is often regarded by
> one of a lower order.

Bad old Mrs. Mudge sneaked upstairs later in the day, rifled
through Aunt Lucy's meagre store of possessions and found the
letter. She sat down to read; was discovered by Aunt Lucy; and
they quarreled. The reader had the feeling that this incident was
going to amount to something, but it did not.

Was the chapter a waste? Well, in a way it was, and yet at the
end of it Horatio had completed a characterization of Mrs. Mudge
that was Dickensian in its thoroughness. No reader could fail to
believe that she was as scurvy a scullion as had ever disgraced a
poorhouse kitchen. Horatio had done it all through action.

Back in the city, Paul got a job at Smith and Thompson's
store and met Nicholas Benton, a boy who had just been promoted. Mister Benton, for now that he was promoted he insisted
on the honorific, launched into a dissertation on a subject dear to
every boy's heart:

> "I say," said Mr. Benton after a pause, "have you begun
> to shave yet?"
> Paul looked up to see if his companion were in earnest.

"No," said he; "I haven't got along as far as that. Have you?"

"I," repeated the young man a little contemptuously, "of course I have. I've shaved for a year and a half."

"Do you find it hard shaving?" asked Paul a little slily.

"Well, my beard is rather stiff," said the late *boy,* with an important air, "but I've got used to it."

"Ain't you rather young to shave, Nicholas?" asked Paul.

"Mr. Benton, if you please."

"I mean, Mr. Benton."

"Perhaps I was when I begun. But now I am nineteen."

"Nineteen?"

"Yes, that is to say I'm within a few months of being nineteen. What do you think of my moustache?"

"I hadn't noticed it."

"The store's rather dark," muttered Mr. Benton....

Paul Prescott was not taken in, but was only amused, as Horatio Alger wanted his young readers to be by the silliness of a boy's hirsute pretensions. And in four pages, Horatio established the character of Nicholas Benton, that of Mr. Smith, Paul's skinflint employer and the treacheries of the New York business world. The senior clerk, Williams, waited on a lady, and persuaded her to buy ten yards of a certain calico at a shilling (quarter) a yard on the assurance that the mayor's wife had been in the day before and bought similar dress goods. Then in came another woman, carrying a bundle of the same calico.

Seeing her coming, Williams hastily slipped the remnant of the piece out of sight.

"I got this calico here," said the newcomer, "one day last week. You warranted it to wash, but I find it won't. Here's a piece I've tried."

She showed a pattern, which had a faded look.

"You've come to the wrong store," said Williams coldly. "You must have got the calico somewhere else."

"No, I'm sure I got it here. I remember particularly buying it of you."

"You've got a better memory than I have, then. We haven't got a piece of calico like that in the store."

Paul listened to this assertion with unutterable surprise.

"I am quite certain I bought it here," said the woman, perplexed.

"Must have been the next store, Blake & Hastings. Better go over there."

The woman went out.

"That's the way to do business," said Williams, winking at Paul.

In the next chapter of this saga, Mr. Benton confided in Paul that he had fallen in love, had declared his love for the lady, Miss Hawkins, whose father was rich, and also persuaded Paul to accompany him to the Hawkins house, where Mr. Benton would serenade his love under her window as the clock struck nine. Paul went and watched as the lady in question came to the window in the middle of Mr. Benton's song and flung on him the contents of a pitcher of water. Again Horatio felt the need to interject low comedy into the action of the book.

Still, young readers had action apace in the next chapter, where Paul, asked by a lady if the calico would wash, told her honestly that it would not and got fired by Mr. Smith for his pains. He went home to the sexton's house.

"I am sure I have done right," thought Paul. "I had no right to misrepresent the goods to that lady. I wonder what Uncle Hugh will say."

"You did perfectly right," said the sexton after Paul had related the circumstances of his dismissal. "I wouldn't have had you do differently for twenty situations. I have no doubt you will get a better position elsewhere."

Paul went out looking, but virtue was not its own reward. He found no job. Then one day, while walking the street listlessly, he espied a team of horses running away with a carriage, a lady inside.

With scarcely a moment's premeditation, he rushed out into the middle of the street, full in the path of the furious horses, and with his cheeks pale, for he knew his danger, but with determined air, he waved his arms aloft, and cried "Whoa!" at the top of his voice.

The horses saw the sudden movement. They saw the boy standing directly in front of them. They heard the word of command to which they had been used, and by a sudden impulse, relieved from the blind terror which had urged them on, they stopped suddenly and stood still in the middle of the street, still showing in their quivering limbs the agitation through which they had passed.

The coachman, who had stepped off his perch to ring a doorbell, then came up to take the horses. Paul helped the frightened lady from the carriage and saw her home safely—to her Fifth Avenue mansion.

The lady, Mrs. Danforth, happened to be the wife of a rich merchant, and she sent Paul with a card to her husband at his place of business. Mr. Danforth liked Paul's forthright manner, and gave him a job in his counting room at five dollars a week, proving that any boy who is honest, thrifty, virtuous, ambitious and stops a team of runaway horses can get a job.

The perils of Paul grew more deadly page on page. Another office boy George Dawkins had fallen into the hands of fiends

> where he had learned both to drink and to gamble. In this way he had made the acquaintance of Duval, an unscrupulous sharper, who had contrived to get away all his ready money, and persuading him to play longer in the hope of making up his losses had run him into debt one hundred and fifty dollars.

Duval's conversation was larded with French phrases; he was obviously a villain left over from Horatio's French adventures. Duval tried to collect the debt, but George did not have the money. To get it, he laid a trap for Paul. Mr. Danforth was counting money, when he was called out of the room. George entered.

> Allowing himself scarcely a minute to think, he took from the roll four fifty dollar notes, thrust one into the pocket of Paul's overcoat, which hung in the office, drew off his right boot and slipped the other three into the bottom of it, and put it on again.

Half an hour later, Mr. Danforth returned. Paul was fired. Paul went out, Mr. Danforth puzzled over the matter but accepted the obvious. But Mrs. Danforth was not gulled. She suspected George Dawkins. She sent her husband out to shadow Dawkins, who of course headed straight for Duval to pay off the cursed debt, while Mr. Danforth watched from the shadows. Mr. Danforth then fired Dawkins and forced him to make restitution. Horatio was a little rough on Dawkins:

> Then came a storm of reproaches in which all the bitterness of his father's nature was fully exhibited. There had been no love between father and son. Henceforth there was open hatred.

So Paul got his job back with pleas for forgiveness from Mr. Danforth. Two years went by, and Paul got a Christmas present of $100 from Mr. Danforth; he had already saved $400. He paid off his father's debt and prospered, as did all his friends, the "good guys," while all his enemies got their just deserts in the last two chapters.

> The Mudges were discharged as poorhouse supervisors, and told to leave *immejiately* by our old friend Squire Newcome. Mudge took to drink and was found dead one night between his house and the tavern. Mrs. Mudge took to keeping a boarding house. Some time since, her boarders held an indignation meeting, and threatened to leave her in a body unless she improved her fare,— a course to which she was obliged to submit.

George Dawkins went west, unable to find a job in New York after his despicable conduct.

> Let us hope he may "turn over a new leaf" there and establish a better reputation than he did in New York.

Ben Newcome reformed completely at military school, and when the war broke out, he was unanimously elected Captain of the Wrenville Company, was promoted to major for bravery at Antietam and entered Richmond as a colonel in command of his regiment.

> I have heard on high authority that he is considered one of the best officers in the service.

The good sexton and his wife were happy. Paul continued to live with them and got a share in the Danforth business, which brought in a very handsome income. Horatio then summed up:

> And now we must bid farewell to Paul. He has battled bravely with the difficulties and discouragements that beset him early in life, he has been faithful to the charge which he voluntarily assumed, and his father's memory is free from reproach. He often wishes that his father could have lived to witness his prosperity, but God has decreed it otherwise. Happy in the love of friends, and in the enjoyment of all that can make life desirable, so far as external circumstances have that power, let us all wish him God speed.

There it was, the first of the stories of city life that would make the name of Horatio Alger, Jr. a household word. With all its imperfections, the pattern was drawn.

Chapter Seven

The Brewster Affair

In the autumn of 1864, Horatio Alger, Jr. was writing *Paul Prescott's Charge,* when he was invited by the Unitarian community to Brewster.

With all his clerical and extraclerical duties, Horatio was busier writing than ever. *Frank's Campaign* went into a third printing, Loring was very pleased with the manuscript of *Paul Prescott's Charge,* and Horatio was doing well with the magazine *The Student and Schoolmate.* He began writing the short stories Adams wanted and in the introductions was characterized as the author of the two aforementioned Loring books. One of his early contributions was "The Worst Boy in School," the story of Jim Bowers and how Mr. Bancroft, the teacher, turned him into a very good student by applying reason. Here was the ending:

> The boys were greatly amazed the next morning to find the teacher on such excellent terms with "the worst boy in school." From that time there was no better boy than Jim Bowers. Encouraged by the teacher, he made the most of his excellent natural abilities, and soon distanced all his school-fellows. He is now in a situation in Boston, obtained through Mr. Bancroft's

influence, where he is giving the best satisfaction, and I should not be surprised if in time he became a wealthy man. He is warmly attached to his old teacher, to whose forbearance and judicious management he owes his present good fortune.

"The Worst Boy in School" was a great success with the readers of *Student and Schoolmate,* and soon Editor Adams was asking Horatio for more. He wrote a dialogue: *Seeking His Fortune.*

Meanwhile, Oliver Optic was still producing the long serials that dominated the magazine, but Adams was shrewd enough to read his mail carefully and see that Alger had passed him. So Horatio was asked to write a three-part story, *Sam's Adventures,* which brought in even more favorable mail. This was followed in the spring of 1866 by "The Rivals," a two-part story of How The Prize Was Lost and Won. It began in a style that Alger had now perfected:

> "Attention, boys!"
> James Perkins, A. M. Principal of the Select High School in the town of Wrayburn, emphasized these words by a rap on the teacher's desk.
> There was a deep silence throughout the school room. All eyes were directed towards the speaker.
> "I have long been desirous," he said, "to do something to stimulate you to improvement in English Composition, and with that object in view, I have decided to offer a prize to be awarded to the writer of the best essay, which shall be handed to me a fortnight from today, on the subject which I shall assign...."

And, of course, the rivals were two boys, Gilbert Simmons, son of Squire Simmons "the lawyer of Wrayburn and a prominent citizen of the town" and Fred Bangs. Naughty Gilbert sneaked into the school house and blotted Fred's essay. But he was seen by another student, David Eaton, who recovered Fred's essay and took it to Fred, who recopied it. Next day, everybody agreed except Gilbert that Fred's was the best essay. Gilbert, fool that he was, suggested that a blotted essay was disqualified. But there was no blot, said the teacher. And then David Eaton presented Gilbert with the copy of the essay he had blotted.

Gilbert dashed aside with an ejaculation, and with a blush of shame pursued his way home.

Fred never intimated by word or look that he knew who had tampered with his manuscript, but it was long before Gilbert felt comfortable in his company. It taught him a lesson, however, that success is never worth purchasing by foul means.

Such tales of virtue sat very well with the elder members of the Reverend Mr. Horatio Alger, Jr.'s congregation, and boys seemed also to like them—and him—very well indeed. All that until the March day in 1866 when the bombshell was thrown into Brewster.

Whatever Horatio's crimes or his private sins, he kept them locked forever in his bosom after the Brewster affair; and they never came forth except in a painwracked poem he wrote in 1872, telling the legend of Friar Anselmo, a medieval priest who had committed a deadly sin, wanted to die and then found new life in helping the sick.

FRIAR ANSELMO

Friar Anselmo (God's grace may he win!)
Committed one sad day a deadly sin;

Which being done he drew back, self-abhorred,
From the rebuking presence of the Lord,

And, kneeling down, besought, with bitter cry,
Since life was worthless grown, that he might die.

All night he knelt, and, when the morning broke,
In patience still he waits death's fatal stroke.

When all at once a cry of sharp distress
Aroused Anselmo from his wretchedness;

And, looking from the convent window high,
He saw a wounded traveller gasping lie

Just underneath, who, bruised and stricken sore,
Had crawled for aid unto the convent door.

The friar's heart with deep compassion stirred,
When the poor wretch's groans for help were heard

With gentle hands, and touched with love divine,
He bathed his wounds, and poured in oil and wine.

With tender foresight cared for all his needs,—
A blessed ministry of noble deeds.

In such devotion passed seven days. At length
The poor wayfarer gained his wonted strength.

With grateful thanks he left the convent walls,
And once again on death Anselmo calls.

When, lo! his cell was filled with sudden light,
And on the wall he saw an angel write,

(An angel in whose likeness he could trace,
More noble grown, the traveller's form and face),

"Courage, Anselmo, though thy sin be great,
God grants thee life that thou may'st expiate.

"Thy guilty stains shall be washed white again,
By noble service done thy fellow-men.

"His soul draws nearest unto God above,
Who to his brother ministers in love."

Meekly Anselmo rose, and, after prayer,
His soul was lighted of its past despair.

Henceforth he strove, obeying God's high will,
His heaven-appointed mission to fulfil.

And many a soul, oppressed with pain and grief,
Owed to the friar solace and relief.

Horatio's announced interest, after he settled in New York City, was to devote his life to boys. His personal relations with boys never again came up for question, though there is certainly room for legitimate speculation about the vicarious motivations of a life that remained centered around boys. Whatever he had done, he learned the need for discretion, and perhaps the terrible shock of Brewster had really changed Alger's life style and character. His life at least certainly changed in the spring of 1866.

The Reverend Mr. Alger, Jr., trained for the ministry, abandoned it forthwith in 1866 and did not again seek a parish or association with his church. Instead, taking a little room downtown, Horatio threw himself into his writing. His father knew—he was too prominent a Unitarian churchman not to know—the dreadful content of that letter from Brewster parish to the Unitarian Assocation. Never again did the senior Alger ask his son about his ministry. Whatever private words passed between them went sealed in their hearts to the grave. But from this date on Horatio lived only for his writing—and for boys.

Chapter Eight

The Arrival of
Ragged Dick

Horatio Alger, Jr. had literary dreams as serious as those of any American writer, and they were heightened by his particular background and associations. Alger was just a generation removed from the literary greats of the Transcendental Period who had dominated the literary Boston of his college years: Longfellow, Holmes, Emerson, Lowell and Hawthorne.

Horatio wanted to be known as a great American novelist, and as he moved from furnished room to room in downtown New York he struggled to this end. He could make a living at writing tales for boys, and he did. He sold one story, "How Johnny Bought a Sewing Machine," to *Our Young Folks,* and he wrote a poem "John Maynard" which was based on an actual story of a shipwreck on Lake Erie.

'Twas on Lake Erie's broad expanse
One bright midsummer day,
The gallant steamer Ocean Queen
Swept proudly on her way.
Bright faces clustered on the deck,
Or leaning o'er the side,

JOHN MAYNARD AT THE HELM

> Watched carelessly the feathery foam
> That flecked the rippling tide.

The tragedy struck—fire broke out on the steamer—and the captain ran for shore. John Maynard, the pilot stood at the wheel.

> No terror pales the helmsman's cheek
> Or clouds his dauntless eye,
> As in a sailor's measured tone
> His voice responds, "Aye, aye!"
> Three hundred souls, the steamer's freight
> Crowd forward, wild with fear,
> While at the stern the dreaded flames
> Above the deck appear.

John Maynard stood fast as flames gathered around him, and he never gave up his post, though scorched and seared by the fire. Finally the ship grounded on the beach, and the passengers were saved.

> But where is he, that helmsman bold?
> The Captain saw him reel,—
> His nerveless hands released their task,
> He sank beside the wheel.
> The wave received his lifeless corse
> Blackened with smoke and fire.
> God rest him! Never hero had
> A nobler funeral pyre!

"John Maynard" gave Horatio Alger, Jr. the acclaim he had sought so long as a serious writer. Longfellow, his old Harvard teacher, wrote him a note of appreciation, which he cherished forever. He had letters from others of the literati and from many lesser lights. He was on his way it seemed, in the world of letters.

The major effort now was to crack through as a serious novelist. In the Brewster period, he had written two adult novels, and now he took them to Publisher Loring, hoping they would be as well received as his boys' books had been.

Loring was anything but enthusiastic. He agreed to publish these books only as a favor to the author. Horatio, who saw them as his breakout from a stereotype in which he already writhed, accepted a smaller royalty than on his boys' books, and also promised to deliver Loring a no-nonsense boys' story by the end of the year. Bringing out the two books in the same season posed a problem for Loring, so while the first, *Helen Ford,* was published under Alger's name, the second, *Timothy Crump's Ward,* bore no name at all save that of the publisher.

Helen Ford represents a distinct departure from the style Horatio was perfecting in his boys' books, as the opening, a very long paragraph for Alger indicates:

> Not many minutes walk from Broadway, situated on one of the cross streets intersecting the great thoroughfare, is a large building, not especially inviting in its aspect, used as a lodging and boarding house. It is very far from fashionable, since, with hardly an exception, those who avail themselves of its accommodations belong to the great class who are compelled to earn their bread before they eat it. Mechanics, working men, clerks on small salaries, seamstresses, and specimens of decayed gentility, all find a place beneath its roof, forming somewhat miscellaneous assemblage. It must not be supposed, however that perfect equality exists even here. It is often remarked that social distinctions are more jealously maintained in the lower ranks than in the higher. Here, for instance, Alphonse Eustace, a dashing young clerk, who occupies the first floor front, looks down with *hauteur* upon the industrious mechanic who rooms in the second story back. Mademoiselle Fanchette, the fashionable *modiste,* occupying the second story front, considers it beneath her dignity to hold much intercourse with Martha Grey, the pale seamstress, whose small room at the head of the third landing offers a delightful prospect of the backyard. Even the occupants of the fourth story looked down, which indeed their elevated position enables them to do, upon the basement lodgers across the way.

The story concerned a young woman, about fourteen at the time of the opening, who came with her sick and aging father to seek lodgings here. The father was an inventor. The girl was Helen Ford. Her adventures in the wicked city, where men and women alike try to prey upon her, were chronicled in nearly three hundred pages. Then her father got rich (not, however, through his inventions), and Helen began to live the life of a lady. She befriended Herbert Coleman, a struggling young artist, and Daddy Ford gave him a thousand dollars to go to Italy "the cradle of art" and get finished. He went, with the promise of four thousand more to come if Herbert would copy some Italian masterpieces. Herbert went off, but...

> Herbert's residence in Italy has been protracted somewhat beyond the three years originally intended. He has already sent home several paintings, originals, as well as copies, which prove conclusively that he has not mistaken his vocation. He has corresponded regularly with Helen, and she is eagerly expecting his return in the next steamer. They have tacitly dropped the old designations of brother and sister. Knowing what we do of their feelings towards each other, we need not be surprised if they are bound some day by a nearer tie. Mr. Ford, I am assured, will interpose no objection, feeling that genius and nobility of soul far outweigh the mere accident of riches.

So it ended. The villains had been dealt the blows they deserved and all was right with the world. But from Horatio's point of view, all was not right with the book; it did not sell well. Ten years earlier, during the period of the sentimentalists, it might have sold very well. In the 1850s Ann Sophia Stephens and other romanticists of the dime novel were hogging the fiction market, and stories about young women easily outdistanced the serious works of Emerson, Hawthorne, Melville and the other greats. Yet Horatio, whose tastes and observations had been sharpened during this time, was just out of it, and the market was changing rapidly. As far as books for young readers were concerned, the market had been tremendous for years. Broadened by the growth of public education and the expansion of libraries across America, the demand for books for young people, boys and girls, was nearly insatiable. Even in the middle 1860s the lady novelists dominated the scene. As far as sales were concerned, the best sellers of 1863 were Mrs. E.D.E.N. Southworth's *The Fatal Marriage* and Mrs. A.D.T. Whitney's *Faith Gartney's Girlhood;* in 1864 it was Mrs. Southworth's *Ishmael;* next year it was Mary Mapes Dodge's *Hans Brinker and His Silver Skates.* So Horatio, following what he thought were the trends, could hardly be faulted for not recognizing the basic change that was overtaking adult literature at the end of the Civil War.

In New York, Horatio Alger, Jr. had two concerns. The first was his yearning for immortality and the great novel; second, more prosaic but more demanding, was his need to support himself with his inkwell and pen. This latter problem was far easier for him to solve than the former, as the disappointments of 1866 proved. *Helen Ford* disappeared in the great public maw without much trace; *Timothy Crump's Ward*, the second adult attempt, sank even more quickly into oblivion.

In the juvenile market, Horatio met with far more success. Editor Adams of *Student and Schoolmate* was very pleased with the public reaction to Horatio's moral stories for boys and girls. In the summer Adams began serializing the long story, "Harry Lynch's Trip to Boston," which ran in the magazine in three parts.

Here was the Alger of the juvenile world, sharpening his pen, growing more adept at his line of exciting tales with each effort.

> "Where are you going to spend the Fourth, Harry?" asked Frank Benson, picking up a stone and throwing at a stray cow as he spoke.
>
> "I'm going to Boston," said Harry Lynch, with an air of importance. "You don't catch me staying around this little place. There ain't any fun to be had here. I'm going to Boston to see the balloon ascension, and the fireworks, and I expect to have a tip-top time."

But, as the reader learned soon enough, thirteen-year-old Harry was going off without the permission of his uncle and guardian, who had to be away on business. He went, he had misadventures, and when he came home, he was a chastened and sober young man.

The response to Harry's adventures was better than ever, and Horatio next turned to "The King of the Playground," the story of Sam Stockwell, the school bully, and George Fairbanks, the slender, sturdy hero, who fought with him only when forced to do so.

> At first George acted only in self-defense. He soon decided, however, that if this continued, the contest would be of indefinite duration. Accordingly, he struck a skillful and effective blow which felled Sam to the earth.

And, of course, this culminating fight, coming in the third and final installment, had the result desired by parents, schoolmasters and ministers of the Gospel.

> From that time a change came over Sam Stockwell. He had been beaten in a fair fight, and he knew if the fight should be renewed, he would be beaten again. Once or twice he tried to exercise his old sovereignty, but he saw that his subjects were no longer disposed to obey him, and he did not insist. George Fairbanks became a universal favorite. He showed no disposition to take advantage of his superiority, but set an example of quiet courtesy and consideration for others, which had the best influence on the other members of the school, even Stockwell, who ceased to be a bully and a tyrant.

So impressed was editor Adams with the mail he received on this Alger contribution that every month the magazine contained one or more Alger prose contributions. And in the fall of 1866, Adams made a heroic decision: he gave up his own position as lead writer of the magazine with the Oliver Optic serials and turned that spot over to Horatio for a new and even more promising story.

Horatio, in delivering the new exciting work he had promised Publisher Loring, had chosen another of what Loring was coming to call The Campaign Series: *Charlie Codman's Cruise.* It was, as Horatio said in his preface, "more adventurous than its predecessors, and the trials which Charlie is called upon to encounter are of severer character than befell Frank Frost or Paul Prescott."

The opening scene was Boston, home ground for Horatio in years past, and Charlie Codman, a fourteen-year-old boy from a poor family, a newsboy in fact, was just passing the Latin School as classes let out, and the encounter with other boys showed how manly and open Charlie was. Then came an encounter with old Peter Manson, the miser, whose character and adventures occupied several pages. A stranger came to Peter's hovel one night and accused him of being a bookkeeper who had ruined his master by stealing twenty thousand dollars in gold. Thus the master's daughter, who married a nice young man called Codman, was thrust into poverty. Codman died, leaving his widow, and the boy Charlie, who lived in a tenement owned secretly by the miser. The visitor came to blackmail Peter the Miser, and he agreed to pay only on condition that the blackmailer kidnap Charlie Codman and take him off to sea, thus eliminating one of the two witnesses who might testify to the miser's old crime. This villain, mate of a ship bound for San Francisco, had also been scorned by the beauteous Eleanor Codman in earlier years.

"I have done a good night's work" he said. "By working on the fears of the old curmudgeon I have made sure of a thousand dollars. He will be lucky if this is the last money I get out of him. He little thinks that I, too, have a revenge to wreak. He is not the only one that has been scornfully rejected by Eleanor Codman. Now to bed, and tomorrow shall see my work commenced."

So Charlie was to be trapped. He came home next day and told his mother of the kind man who had bought his papers and hired him to show him around Boston. He was to meet the man again the next day. Then the reader was introduced to Captain Nathaniel Brace and the ship *Bouncing Betsey,* both lying at one of the wharves of Boston port.

It is my privilege to know many sea captains who do honor to their calling, high toned, gentlemanly, and intelligent men; not learned in books, but possessing a wide range of general information. I am sorry to say Captain Brace was not a man of this class.

What sort of man he was, the reader would soon learn, if he kept moving through the story: "an unfeeling tyrant who did all in his power to degrade the profession which he had adopted, and add to the hardships which lie in the path of the sailor." The mate, Randall, schemed and Captain Brace acceded and Charlie Codman was shanghaied. bound and gagged, and held captive until the ship got out of sight of land.

Charlie, luckily, was befriended by Bill Sturdy, a behemoth of a man. "Probably there were no two men aboard the ship who would not have felt some hesitation in attacking Bill Sturdy."

Back in Boston, Miser Peter was mistreating Charlie's mother, raising her rent to two dollars a week and letting her know, obliquely, that Charlie had been shanghaied. But Mrs. Codman got a job as a governess (she had been well educated in her youth, though now fallen on evil days) and Alger, "leaving Mrs. Codman thus comfortably provided for," told the reader "we must now follow the fortunes of our young hero, Charlie, whom we left securely bound in the forecastle of the *Bouncing Betsey*."

A crew bully tried to take advantage of young Charlie, and Bill Sturdy came to the rescue, throwing the offender, Antonio, "down the stairs." Any reader with naval inclinations would wince at that lubberly phrase, but Alger had already pulled the teeth of his critics by noting in his introduction that he was unfamiliar with nautical usage and could be expected to make mistakes.

Alger digressed here to have Bill Sturdy tell a tale of piracy and adventure that fascinated Charlie Codman. Having been forced to join a pirate crew, Bill Sturdy subverted them all, blew them up and won the acclaim of a grateful shipowner.

But back to the plot: Antonio, vicious fellow that he was, decided to get even with Charlie Codman and Bill Sturdy. He stole a ring from the captain and hid it in Charlie's sea chest. It was discovered, and Charlie was nearly flogged, but Bill Sturdy, who had watched the wicked Antonio, told all and Antonio attacked him, showing his guilt. Even then, the captain and the mate conspired and decided that Charlie was *indeed* to be flogged, this time for "insolence," Bill Sturdy took the flogging himself and then took on the flogger (the wicked Antonio again).

Captain and mate conspired again to have Bill Sturdy shanghaied off the ship. Bill Sturdy and Charlie also conspired, to jump ship. Then the mate decided to have Sturdy murdered, and when the ship put in at Rio de Janeiro he went looking for a murderer. He found one, but the murderer mistook Antonio for Bill Sturdy and murdered him instead. Meanwhile Bill and Charlie escaped and signed aboard another ship heading for Liverpool.

Back in Boston, Mrs. Codman got on swimmingly with the uneducated girl she was tutoring and began to teach her a few things. The girl saw Charlie's picture and fell in love with it. The girl's father, Mr. Bowman, saw a letter from Charlie and offered him a job in his counting house.

The Wicked Mate now returned to Boston, saw Miser Peter and demanded more money to conceal the guilty secret. The miser refused. The mate attacked him. Just then, in burst Charlie Codman and Bill Sturdy. And so the miser was exposed as a thief, and Charlie Codman and his mother got their fortune.

Mr. Bowman, the banker, married Mrs. Codman; the miser went insane and soon died; the mate was killed by a sailor he had abused; evil Captain Brace died of a burst blood vessel in a fit of ungovernable rage; Bill Sturdy became a captain of a ship belonging to Mr. Bowman; and...

> It is not ours to read the future; but I should not be surprised when Charlie grows to manhood if we should find Bert's early choice of him as her husband prophetic.
> So we bid farewell to Charlie Codman. His trials and struggles have come early in life, but now his bark has drifted into smoother waters. The sky above him is cloudless. His character has been strengthened by his combat with adversity. Let us hope that his manhood may redeem the promise of his youth, and be graced by all the noblest attributes of humanity.

Charlie Codman was the most rootin-tootin Alger book yet, and Publisher Loring could hardly have been more pleased; but as he surveyed the manuscript, the unhappy sales records of *Helen Ford* and *Timothy Crump's Ward* were also before him. Even so, the young people's book market was booming, and Loring moved ahead to publish the new nautical book.

Horatio Alger, Jr. was already off on a different tack. In New York City, he had devoted himself to the homeless boys who inhabited the city. Some of them were runaways, some were orphans. Some were drummer boys and others who had served in the army and, discharged, found themselves far too sophisticated to go home again. Between them, Horatio and Adams contrived that Horatio's next work for *Student and Schoolmate* should be a long serial to replace the Oliver Optic leader and that it should deal with the adventures of these waifs in New York. Alger began writing a story about life among the bootblacks of New York. In the fashion of Dickens, he finished three chapters in a whirlwind of action and sent them off to Adams in Boston; Adams found them to be just what he wanted, and it was agreed that Horatio would produce the work in twelve monthly installments.

Adams' enthusiasm was welcome and very timely. Horatio was running out of money and after the disgrace of Brewster he dared not go home to Massachusetts. New York was expensive, and although he wrote for several publications and tutored young men on the side, he was finding it difficult to make ends meet. He moved from a house off lower Fifth Avenue to less-sumptuous and less-expensive quarters in Greenwich Village, but he still needed money badly and Adams proposed to supply part of it. Alger also needed a good strong success after *Helen Ford* and *Timothy Crump's Ward.* These works were producing no money for him whatsoever, and royalties on his earlier two successes for Loring were dwindling, while *Charlie Codman's Cruise* was as yet an unknown quantity.

The January, 1867 issue of *Student and Schoolmate* opened then, with a new face. There was *Ragged Dick,* or *Street Life in New York,* with a facing page drawing of a poor young bootblack.

> "Wake up there youngster," said a rough voice.
>
> Ragged Dick opened his eyes slowly and stared stupidly in the face of the speaker but did not offer to get up.
>
> "Wake up, you young vagabond," said the man a little impatiently, "I suppose you'd lay here all day if I hadn't called you."
>
> "What time is it?" asked Dick.
>
> "Seven o'clock."
>
> "Seven o'clock. I oughter've been up an hour ago. I know what 'twas made me so precious sleepy. I went to the Old Bowery last night and didn't turn in till past twelve."
>
> "You went to the Old Bowery? Where'd you get your money?" asked the man, who was a porter in the employ of a firm on Spruce Street.
>
> "Made it by shines, of course. You don't catch me stealing, if that's what you mean."
>
> "Don't you ever steal then?"

That very first page set the tone, and young readers of *Student and Schoolmate* could not wait to turn the leaf, and then, with the installment finished, could hardly wait for the next month and the next one. *Ragged Dick* seized the young mind as nothing had in several years. Not only the young, either, New York was the mecca of young America, and the struggles of this poor boy on the streets of New York caught the American fancy. Within a week Editor Adams knew he had a success on his hands. The mail began pouring in and did not stop. At a desperate moment of his career, Horatio had found the encouragement he needed.

RAGGED DICK

Chapter Nine

Lion Among
the Juveniles

In RAGGED DICK, Horatio Alger, Jr. distilled all the stylistic tricks he had been perfecting for a dozen years. He was now thirty-five years old, mature as he would ever be and free from scandal; he was the finished Alger. From this point on there would be no real progress. No nonsense about long descriptive passages ordering the beauty of the city or the character of the witnesses about him, no analytical frippery or dead weight of idea would cloud those opening lines; the action would be straight and pure. The language, coarse and ungrammatical, was a studied attempt to reproduce the language of the street boys of New York. The whole effect was recognized by the youth with their quick perception and by reformers and social workers who struggled with the problems of New York City every day.

Ragged Dick represented something virtually unknown to boys in the American countryside and totally unsung until this time: the street waif who made his living in the jungles of brick and paving stones:

> Dick's appearance as he stood beside the box was rather
> peculiar. His pants were torn in several places, and had appar-

ently belonged on the first instance to a boy two sizes larger than himself. He wore a vest, all of the buttons of which were gone except two, out of which peeped a shirt which looked as if it had been worn a month. To complete his costume he wore a coat too long for him, dating back, if one might judge from its general appearance, to a remote antiquity.

There was humor of a kind determined to appeal to boys:

> "Shine yer boots, sir?"
> "How much?" asked a gentleman on his way to the office.
> "Ten cents," said Dick, dropping his box, and sinking upon his knees on the sidewalk, flourishing his brush with the air of one skilled in his profession.
> "Ten cents! Isn't that a little steep?"
> "Well, you know 'taint all clear profit," said Dick, who had already set to work. "There's the *blacking* costs something, and I have to get a new brush pretty often."
> "And you have a large rent, too," said the gentleman quizzically, with a glance at a large hole in Dick's coat.

The gentleman did not have less than twenty-five cents, which he gave Dick, telling him to leave the change at his office. He was not at all sure that he would ever see the money, but as Alger pointed out, that showed how little the gentleman understood Dick. He had his faults; sometimes he played tricks on boys from the country, as a city boy had played a trick on Paul Prescott when that waif came to New York fresh from Wrenville. Dick was extravagant and spent his money at the Old Bowery Theater and in similar haunts, money with which he could have bought a new coat. Usually, as on this day, Dick started life in the morning without a penny in his ragged pocket or a cigar. Yes, he smoked cigars, which was very naughty—"No boy of fourteen can smoke without being affected injuriously," wrote Author Horatio Alger, Jr.

Dick gambled, and he frequented a gambling house where there was much drinking of "a vile mixture of liquor at two cents a glass."

Soon Dick, having given several shines, was befriending an acquaintance and staking him to breakfast. The acquaintance was a runaway from a farm, but as Alger explained, this poor boy's whole life was understandable:

> Johnny had but one tie to bind him to the city. He had a father living, but he might as well have been without one. Mr. Nolan was a confirmed drunkard, and spent the greater part of his wages for liquor. His potations made him ugly, and inflamed a temper never very sweet, working him up sometimes to such a pitch of rage that Johnny's life was in danger. Some months before he had thrown a flatiron at his son's head with such terrific force that unless Johnny had dodged, he would not have lived long enough to obtain a place in our story. He fled the house and from that time had not dared to re-enter it. Somebody had given him a brush and a box of blacking and he had set up in business on his own account. But he had not energy enough to succeed, as has already been stated, and I am afraid the poor boy had met with many hardships, and suffered more than once from cold and hunger. Dick had befriended him more than once, and often gave him a breakfast or dinner, as the case might be.

The pitfalls of the city opened before Alger's reader as crevasses before the arctic explorer. A gentleman, his shoes shined, gave Dick a two-dollar bill to change at a store nearby, and the clerk, seeing a ragged boy with a bill, tried to cheat him by claiming it was counterfeit. The gentleman came, and the clerk had to own up to his scheme and was fired; Dick was rewarded with fifty cents. Within a page or two Dick was befriended by a rich Mr. Whitney and his nephew Frank who gave him a whole new set of clothes because he offered to show Frank around the city. And good as his word he did: he showed him the clothes shops of Chatham Street, where traders gulled the public; the swindle shops, where boys and men were cheated if they showed the slightest cupidity; but he also showed him A. T. Stewart's store at Broadway and Chambers Street, the New York Hospital and Taylor's famous saloon at Franklin Street, where the boys met a stock swindler. Indeed, the book was a very thorough and direct guide to the places and people of New York City in the year 1866, and for that reason if no other it approached the realm of literature, a claim that will doubtless be gainsaid by critics. Literature or not, there had never been such a book: one swindle after another is exposed to readers who had never heard of such things: the pocket book dodge, where a man finds a pocket book stuffed with paper bills, turns to the country sucker, claims he must catch a train, offers the "honest citizen" the pocket book for twenty dollars and goes off with the cash while the sucker looks at the wallet padded with worthless paper. Dick was not fooled, he gave the city slicker an equally worthless bill and then showed Frank how it was done. The boys had an adventure aboard a Third Avenue horsecar, but adventure or not the description of the cars was as good as any ever given. They went to the Custom House and there encountered a country man who had been swindled by a city slicker who had sent him there telling him it was the Washington Bank. Dick found the swindler, retrieved the money and returned it to the sucker.

Rewarded by Mr. Whitney, Dick promised to reform his bad habits. He got a room for himself and opened a bank account. He repaid the fifteen cents owed the gentleman whose shoes he had shined at the opening of the book and was invited to attend the Sunday School, which the gentleman taught at the church at the corner of Fifth Avenue and Twenty-first Street. Then Dick found another street boy, come down in the world, and engaged him as a tutor to teach Dick to read and write properly.

Sunday School brought an invitation to the gentleman's house and a meeting with the gentleman's daughter. Dick then speeded up his campaign of reform, saved money, had it stolen, helped catch the thief—and in all of it Alger chronicled the everyday life of the middle and lower class in the city in a way it had not been done before.

Dick then found success through an accident: when a little boy fell off the ferryboat that Dick happened to be riding, Dick leaped into the water and rescued the child. The father in his anguish had shouted an offer of ten thousand dollars for anyone who would save the child, and he was suitably grateful. Dick was asked to come to the gentleman's counting house, was given a job at ten dollars a week (a munificent salary; his best friend, who was respectably employed got only six), and Ragged Dick became Richard Hunter, Esquire. The use of the unusual event to secure the success Dick needed was a ploy, of course, Alger simply had to keep the story moving and bring it to an end. But in it all there is a certain innate honesty—accepted by young America in the 1970s, in a different way. Alger said it was right to be decent, honest, reasonable, scrupulous and moral, but what really counted was luck. The youth of the 1970s discounted all else, even the luck factor, but were beyond Alger in another way. What he said—and hoped—and what they said and believed was something very old: to thine own self be true. The difference was that the youth of Alger's day needed the stimulation of money goals; the youth of the 1970s denied this.

The tremendous success of *Ragged Dick* in 1867 made an Alger enthusiast of publisher Loring. He brought out the story as a book and then found he had a national best-seller on his hands. All America wanted to read this revealing story of low life in New York City.

Horatio reveled in the success, but he did not give up his short stories or his other ambitions. He continued to write for *Gleason's Literary Companion.* This spreading of effort was a source of irritation to Editor Adams, who felt that he and *Student and Schoolmate* had created the Alger success—and in a way they had—but Alger's value to the magazine was now so great that in December, as the last chapter of *Ragged Dick* closed, author and editor added to the story. The story originally ended as Dick and his friend Fosdick were talking:

> "When in short you were 'Ragged Dick.' You must drop that name now and think of yourself as—
> "Richard Hunter, Esquire," said our hero smiling.

Alger and Adams added one final line:

> "A Young Gentleman on the road to *Fame and Fortune,*" added Fosdick.

For there was to be more of Ragged Dick—another twelve-part serial featuring the same characters with new adventures.

Alger and *Ragged Dick* seemed to have put *Student and Schoolmate* on easy street. As the year closed, Editor Adams noted in his editorial column, "Tangled Threads," that as the magazine entered its twenty-first year, "it had now passed its days of minority, and may assert its independence."

Having come so far, *Student and Schoolmate* proposed to put its circulation over the 100,000 mark. It would use two methods to do this: 1) a cash system of commissions for clubs that would secure subscriptions; 2) the presentation of the new Alger serial.

Horatio had the means to relax. In 1867 he continued to produce articles and stories for other publications. But in 1868 he agreed to write under his own name for no one but Adams, and he lived up to the agreement. He did, however, choose a number of pen names and write for other publications under those names, for Alger was a prodigious composer of prose. Like some of the pulp magazine writers of later years, Horatio was forever working on several stories at the same time. He would write a few pages of one, then tire of it and start another book or story, then come back to the first one. Sometimes this led him into the trap set for those whom the *New Yorker* magazine later described so neatly as "our forgetful authors." A character's name would change or a character introduced for some purpose would be forgotten and dropped without another word. Yet overall, the Alger stories continued to be eminently satisfactory to the audience for which they were written, the young boys of America.

As advertised, *Fame and Fortune,* carried on the adventures of Ragged Dick as Richard Hunter. Dick and his friend Fosdick moved to better quarters on Bleecker Street—coincidentally a street on which Alger himself lived at this time. The boys paid ten dollars between them for the room, breakfast, lunch and dinner. Richard Hunter had a bit of a problem with table manners and polite society, but he watched others and managed. He met his old acquaintance Frank Whitney (whom he had shown around the city in *Ragged Dick*), and Mr. Whitney was very complimentary:

> "It is always pleasant to see a young man fighting his way upward. In this free country there is every inducement for effort, however unpromising may be the early circumstances in which one is placed."

The Hunter course could not be smooth, in the Alger tradition of hard knocks. He ran afoul of a persimmony bookkeeper who just happened to be related to an old street enemy of Ragged Dick's.

But life at the boarding house was pleasant. Horatio carefully instructed his readers concerning this way of life, and his description must be regarded as largely autobiographical. A young woman named Miss Peyton paid particular attention to Richard and his friend. Someone had paid attention to Horatio.

The life of young business people—what in a later time could be called the way of the career girls and their friends—was delineated in the story of Miss Peyton, a young woman at the boarding house who had been laying her snares for a husband for nearly ten years. She caught Mr. Clifton, a friendly acquaintance of Richard's.

> Mr. Clifton with his wife's money bought a partnership in a retail store on Eighth Avenue, where it is to be hoped he is doing a good business. Anyone desirous of calling on them at his place of business is referred to the New York City Directory for his number. Whether Mr. and Mrs. Clifton live happily I cannot pretend to say; but I am informed by my friend Dick, who calls occasionally, that Mrs. Clifton is as fascinating now as before her marriage, and very naturally scorns the whole sisterhood of old maids, having narrowly escaped becoming one herself.

That last contained a private joke: Alger had been living in New York City for three years when *Fame and Fortune* was published, and yet his name still did not appear in the New York City Directory, nor would it until 1872, six years after he had moved to the city. It would be a matter of considerable annoyance to him for some time to come. As for the character Miss Peyton/Mrs. Clifton, she must remain a mystery; there is absolutely no information as to Alger's romantic entanglements, if any, except for the damning evidence of the Unitarian Church records from Brewster.

Richard began to frequent a polite society living on Madison and Fifth Avenues, where the rich and famous of New York dwelt. His Harvard College background made Alger at home in this milieu to a certain extent. Also, Alger had begun tutoring young college men and men preparing for Columbia College in particular. This, too, gave him entry into polite New York circles. So his stories of the balls and parties to which Richard Hunter went were based on the facts of the day.

But the world his readers preferred, that of the New York vagabonds, had its due toward the end. Micky Maguire, the boy hired by the persimmony Mr. Gilbert to get Richard in trouble, confessed all to Mr. Rockwell, Richard's employer, and in so doing aired his own conscience and grievances and hopes. Mr. Gilbert got his comeuppance, and Richard, long gone now from "Ragged Dick," was promoted to assistant bookkeeper with a salary of a thousand dollars a year. Soon Richard became a principal, in a manner Horatio was to make so famous:

> To this ($1000 annually) an annual increase was made, making his income at twenty-one, fourteen hundred dollars. Just about that time he had an opportunity to sell his uptown lots (bought with the money awarded him for the rescue of Mr. Rockwell's son) to a gentleman who had taken a great fancy to them, for five times the amount he paid, or five thousand dollars. His savings from his salary amounted to about two thousand dollars more.
>
> Meanwhile, Mr. Rockwell's partner, Mr. Cooper, from ill health felt obliged to withdraw from business, and Richard, to his unbounded astonishment and gratification was admitted to the post of junior partner, embarking the capital he had already accumulated and receiving a corresponding share of the profits. These were so large that Richard was able to increase his interest yearly by investing his additional savings, and three years later he felt justified in offering his hand to Ida Greyson, whose partiality to Dick had never wavered. He was no longer Ragged Dick now, but Mr. Richard Hunter, junior partner in the large firm of Rockwell and Hunter. Mr. Greyson felt that even in a worldly way Dick was a good match for his daughter; but he knew and valued still more his good heart and conscientious fidelity to duty, and excellent principles, and cheerfully gave his consent. Last week I read Dick's marriage in the papers and rejoiced in his new hopes of happiness.

Fame and Fortune was as satisfactory to *Student and Schoolmate* as *Ragged Dick* had been—or almost. But it did not, sequels seldom do, stir the readership of the magazine the way *Ragged Dick* had done. Familiar characters in a now-familiar setting did not have the shock value of a world newly exposed. Yet Horatio was too valuable a property to be trifled with, and so Adams arranged with him to write a new book for the 1869 volume of the magazine, this to be called *Rough and Ready: Life Among the New York News Boys.* Publisher Loring, having gotten on to a good thing, was reluctant to let it go, and he insisted that Horatio carry Ragged Dick further, which Alger agreed to do in a new book to be called *Mark the Match Boy: Richard Hunter's Ward.*

Such success called for celebration. Horatio celebrated by returning home, the triumphant and best-selling author whose grievous error of the past was now forgiven even by the Reverend Mr. Alger, Sr., who no longer said anything at all about Horatio's career. *Fame and Fortune,* indeed, was dedicated to the now venerable senior Alger "from whom I have never failed to receive *literary* sympathy and encouragement." All was well, Horatio had indeed found his niche, which was to "illustrate the life and experiences of the friendless and vagrant children to be found in all our cities, numbering in New York alone over twelve thousand." Fra Anselmo was justified.

Alger suggested that he might have done those books as nonfiction and that he was basing them very definitely on factual research.

> but the author has sought to depict the inner life and represent the feelings and emotions of these little waifs of city life, and hopes thus to excite a deeper and more widespread sympathy in the public mind, as well as to exert a salutary influence upon the class of whom he is writing, by setting before them inspiring examples of what energy, ambition, and an honest purpose may achieve, even in their case.

Yes, he meant it, every word. To prove it, he made a public offer. Loring was authorized to send, at the author's expense, copies of the two *Ragged Dick* books to any regularly organized Newsboy's Lodge within the United States.

The reason for this concentration on newsboys was that they, as a group, had come to the attention of social workers. The plight was brought to Alger by Charles Loring Brace, one of the most celebrated of New York philanthropists of the 1860s and 1870s. Brace's persuasion was to change Horatio's life and move an author's interest in poor young boys into a transcendental mission.

Chapter Ten

Rough and Ready

I<small>F ONE IS TO</small> understand the poor, emotional cripple that was Horatio Alger, Jr. as any more than a bad joke of the nineteenth century or a terrible monument to taste—as he has been described by several twentieth-century critics—it is necessary and only fair to put Alger in his own time and place. He was a bestselling author in 1867. That fact is indisputable. He slipped on that particular popular register the following year. Louisa May Alcott, another Loring author, took his place with *Little Women,* a saccharine, pristine tale of children in good society, as clear a delineation of the wanted world as Horatio's was of the unwanted. Never able to stomach reality for long, American tastes were embracing fantasy again.

Even if he knew that fact, by the end of 1867 Alger was completely immersed in his personal crusade against the plight of the poor waifs of the cities. He would at this point have been incapable of changing course, particularly with the aura of success still clinging so strongly to his urchin's tales.

He spent part of the summer of 1867 at the parsonage in South Natick, where his mother and father and sister Annie had been joined by Sister Olive Augusta and her husband Amos Cheney. Sister "Gusti" was a successful author in her own right; she was still contributing to *Student and Schoolmate* but had also published in a number of other magazines. Cheney was a big, lumbering man of no particular note, whose main claim to family affection was his amiability. The strain over Horatio's sudden dismissal from the Brewster parish had vanished by this time, and hereafter Horatio was to spend many of his summers in South Natick.

On return to New York, Horatio was introduced to Charles Loring Brace, a philanthropist whose special interest was the homeless boys of the city, and who had been working for their betterment for fifteen years.

Back in the 1850s New York had begun to recognize that poor children too often grew up to be prostitutes and thieves, if not worse. In 1852, Brace had found that in the eleventh ward of New York, of 12,000 children between the ages of five and sixteen, only 7000 attended school, only 2500 went to Sunday School, "leaving 5000 without the common privileges of education and about 9000 destitute of public religious influence."

Brace and others formed an association dedicated to the problems of vagrant children. The more they learned the more shocked they became. "I soon came to know certain centres of crime and misery, until every lane and alley, with its filth and wretchedness and vice, became familiar as the lanes of a country homestead to its owner," said Brace.

Brace visited the Rag Pickers Den in Pitt and Willett Streets, double rows of houses whose yards were heaped with bones and refuse. Cholera and yellow fever raged in summer, pneumonia in winter. Children were turned into outlaws and thieves. He tramped through the mud of Cherry and Water Streets, where crime was the watchword. Here little girls of ten became prostitutes. He saw the Thieves' Lodging House, where street boys were trained to become pickpockets and burglars; the immigrant boarding houses of the First Ward; the Rogue's Den in Laurens Street—more popularly known as Rotten Row—where a passerby could expect to have his head knocked in; and the area at Sixteenth Street and Ninth Avenue called Poverty Lane, where the murderous Nineteenth Street Gang hung out. He saw Dutch

Hill, near Forty-second Street, where the peddlars lived, and Corlear's Hook, where dwelt the thieves who beset the wharves and shipyards. He saw what was in some ways worst of all, the Sixth Ward, the Italian Quarter, where six-year-old children were apprenticed to crime.

Brace and his friends had tried several approaches to the poverty problem vexing society. They opened children's workshops around the city. These were unsuccessful. They gave money. No good. Finally, they hit upon a charity that brought at least some satisfaction to the people who would try to help the poor. In 1854, they established the Newsboy's Lodging House in a loft in the old *Sun* Buildings.

Heretofore these boys had been sleeping in boxes or under stairwells. Ragged Dick slept in a box in the beginning of Alger's story. But knowing, as Brace did after observation, that these youths were fierce spirits, the philanthropists did not seek to force their charity on the boys. They treated them as independent merchants and offered them a bed for six cents a night, with a bath thrown in, and supper at four cents extra.

Very early in the game, the boys decided to test the system. They were contemptuous of "do-gooders" and wanted to know Brace's angle. So they laid plans for a roughhouse on the premises, just to see what would happen. Someone turned off the gas (which meant the lights,) and then the boys began to set to it. But Superintendent C. C. Tracy was ready for them; his guards switched the gas back on, and the ringleaders were caught, identified and turned out of doors, where a policeman escorted them, pleasantly enough, to the lockup for the night. When boots began to fly, the boot throwers were dumped out of bed and left to contemplate their folly on the cold floors.

And so the lodging house was established. Brace described it all:

> The others began to feel that a mysterious authority was getting even with them, and thought it better to nestle in their warm beds.
> Little sleeping, however, was there among them that night; but ejaculations sounded out—such as, "I say, Jim, this is rayther better 'an bummin'—eh?" "My eyes, what soft beds these is!"

"Tom, its 'most as good as a steam-gratin' and there ain't no M.P.s to poke neither." "I'm glad I ain't a bummer tonight."

This was not Horatio Alger, mind you, making up his tales of the street boys, but the sobersided Charles Loring Brace, reporting facts.

> A good wash and a breakfast sent the lodgers forth in the morning, happier and cleaner, if not better, than when they went in. This night's success established its popularity with the newsboys. The "Fulton Lodge" soon became a boys' hotel, and one loft was known among them as the "Astor House."

In the 1860s, the Newsboy's Lodging House had grown in size and importance so that it was moved to larger quarters at 49 Park Place. Superintendent Tracy was succeeded by Superintendent Charles O'Connor, who with his wife as matron, oversaw the boys and tried to be a friend and counselor to them. Some 250 boys could be and were accommodated here nearly every night. In the year 1869, when a count was made, Brace said 8,835 *different* boys had lived in the house for various periods.

When Brace and Alger met, they talked about the problems and prospects of these waifs of the city. Brace later wrote down his own conclusions.

> They are an army of orphans—regiments of children who have not a home or a friend—a multitude of little street rovers who have no place where to lay their heads. They are being educated in the streets rapidly to be thieves and burglars and criminals. The Lodging House is at once school, church, intelligence-office, and hotel for them. Here they are shaped to be honest and industrious citizens; here taught economy, good order, cleanliness and morality; here religion brings its powerful influences to bear on them; and they are sent forth to begin courses of honest livelihood.

Brace introduced Horatio Alger, Jr. to the Lodging House and to Superintendent O'Connor. These two, guided by a common interest in boys—although not stemming from the same roots—got on very well. Alger soon had the run of the place. A

DAN, THE NEWSBOY

bed was put there for him, and he had a desk where he could write when he chose. For the next several years, Horatio would use the Lodging House in basic research for his tales of boys and the wicked world around them.

During the run of *Fame and Fortune,* Editor Adams left *Student and Schoolmate,* but Horatio continued with the new management. As scheduled, the serialization of *Rough and Ready* began in the first issue of 1869. For Alger, the short story was now almost a thing of the past. He did produce a three-part novelette, "George Conant's Terrible Adventure" for *Student and Schoolmate,* but his forte was now the serial story that would later in most cases be published as a book. The Alger method of working, juggling half a dozen stories at once, enabled him to produce four novels for boys for the 1869 publishing season. Two of these books were to be part of what Publisher Loring now called the Ragged Dick series. *Mark the Match Boy* was a direct sequel to *Fame and Fortune,* continuing with the respectable businessman Richard Hunter. Since Dick had grown up and achieved his fame and fortune, Alger had to have a new boy hero. It was Mark, drawn from life—one of the boys of the Lodging House who told Alger one day that he was "a timber merchant in a small way." He sold matches on the street.

The story of Mark opened with Richard Hunter at home. This was a Richard Hunter who was bookkeeper to the firm of Rockwell & Cooper. Horatio did not lose the chance to instruct youngsters in conduct *after* they had achieved that first rung on the ladder of success, as Richard had done.

> As Richard had a philosophy of his own, on this subject, I may as well explain it here. He had observed that those young men who out of economy contented themselves with small and cheerless rooms, in which there was no provision for a fire, were driven in the evening to the streets, theaters, and hotels, for the comfort which they could not find at home. Here they felt obliged to spend money to an extent of which they probably were not themselves fully aware, and in the end wasted considerably more than the two or three dollars a week extra which would have provided them with a comfortable home. But this was not all. In the roamings spent outside many laid the foundation of wrong habits, which eventually led to ruin or shortened their lives.

They lost all the chances of improvement which they might have secured by study at home in the long winter evenings, and which in the end might have qualified them for posts of higher responsibility, and with a larger compensation.

Not Richard Hunter. He and roommate Henry Fosdick spent their evenings at home by a cheerful fire, studying French and mathematics. They crammed for over a year, "and now were able to read the French language with considerable ease." They were go-getters, going.

> "What's the use of moping every evening in your room?" asked a young clerk who occupied a hall-bedroom adjoining.
> "I don't call it moping, I enjoy it," was the reply....
> ..."Are you studying for a college professor?" asked the other with a sneer.
> "I don't know," said Dick good humoredly, "but I'm open to proposals, as the oyster remarked. If you know any first-class institution that would like a dignified professor of extensive requirements, just mention me, will you?"

Mark the Match Boy opens with Fosdick getting a two thousand dollar inheritance of sorts—money lost by his father on the stock market which an honest stock broker, rehabilitated and in honorable work in Milwaukee, far from the wicked city of New York, repaid to the son. The broker, Hiram Bates, sought the boys' help in finding his lost grandson. Dick, who had once known most of the regulars among the street boys, could not recall a boy with the name—John Talbot—but that did not mean much. The boys had usually assumed nicknames in the streets:

> There was one boy I knew named 'Horace Greeley.' Then there were 'Fat Jack,' 'Pickle Nose,' 'Cranky Jim,' 'Tickle-me-foot' and plenty of others....

Dick and Henry accepted the commission, but not until after Mr. Bates took Henry out and saw that he invested his new-found inheritance in bank stock at eight percent per annum.

Fosdick's dividends would come to about one hundred and sixty dollars per year.

"One hundred and sixty dollars!" repeated Fosdick, in surprise. "That is a little more than three dollars per week."

"Yes."

"It will be very acceptable, as my salary at the store is not enough to pay my expenses."

"I would advise you not to break in upon your capital if you can avoid it," said Mr. Bates. "By and by, if your salary increases, you may be able to add the interest yearly to the principal, so that it may be accumulating till you are a man, when you may find it of use in setting you up in business."

And then Mark the Match Boy was introduced with one of Alger's apt and arousing descriptions of New York City and the New York poor.

Mark's wicked guardian, Mother Watson, sent him back out into the street, threatened with a beating.

"I'm so hungry," said Mark, "won't you give me a piece of bread?"

"Not a mouthful until you bring back twenty-five cents. Start now or you'll feel the strap."

Befriended by an Irish neighbor lady, Mrs. Flanagan, Mark was fed and then went out into the drizzly night to sell his matches. Outside he met Ben Gibson, an older boy of twelve, from whom he learned about the Newsboy's Lodging House and also how to spend the night riding a ferry for two cents. Mark was introduced along with the reader to the Fulton market in all its grandeur. Here was one of the Alger's fortes, his ability to evoke the sights and sounds and smells of the city in a manner that did not interfere with his story. After two adventures in the market area, one positive and one negative, and an aside that assures the reader that enemies will play an important part in the tale, Mark went off to the ferry and there encountered none other than Richard Hunter and his friend Fosdick. They each put fifty cents into Mark's pocket and left him sleeping on the ferry.

So Mark the Match Boy decided to run away from Mother Watson. Mother Watson found him, but he was protected by another street boy and a policeman and did not go back into his virtual slavery.

Now, Mark the Match Boy recalled what had been told him about the Newsboy's Lodging House. Here Alger made full use of the factual information he had gained from his conversations with O'Connor and his own pokings around the place. He used O'Connor by name. This portion of his book was purely nonfiction.

O'Connor was a genial soul, in fancy as well as fact. In Horatio's story the superintendent questioned Mark, and then Mark's friend Ben led him off to see the place and go to the gymnasium. A thousand boys had undergone this experience. Mark looked around and, like hundreds of others, discovered he had found a home.

Mark lived at the lodging house for three months. He did not do well financially. He did so badly in fact that one day he collapsed on the doorstep of Rockwell & Cooper, and was found there by the bookkeeper, who just happened to be Richard Hunter. Alger never let a miraculous coincidence stop him, and so Mark, who was very pale and seemed about to fall victim to some dreadful illness, became Richard Hunter's ward (the subtitle of the book) and went to live in Richard's spiffy room on St. Mark's Place.

Mark got a job as an errand boy while still living with Richard. In the pattern of Algerian coincidence, he worked in the same establishment where an envious, arrogant snob named Roswell Crawford worked. Roswell soon had Mark doing his work as well as the boy's own. Evil companions and a love of high life led Roswell down the garden path, and he made the decision to steal from his employer. It was the *Paul Prescott* story over again.

The opportunity soon presented itself:

> The next day, when Roswell was again alone, a lady entered the shop.
>
> "Have you got *La Fontaine's Fables* in English?" she asked. "I have asked at half a dozen stores, but I can't find it. I'm afraid it's out of print."
>
> "Yes, I believe we have it," said Roswell. He remembered one day when he was looking for a book he wanted to read, that he had come across a shop-worn copy of *La Fontaine's Fables*. It was on a back shelf, in an out of the way place. He looked for it and found his memory had served him correctly.
>
> "Here it is," he said, handing it down.

"I am very glad to get it," said the lady. "How much will it be?"

"The regular price is a dollar and a quarter, but as this is a little shopworn, you may have it for a dollar."

"Very well." The lady drew a dollar bill from her purse, and handed it to Roswell. He held it in his hand till she was fairly out the door. Then the thought came into his mind, "Why should I not keep this money? Mr. Baker would never know. Probably he has quite forgotten that such a book was in his stock."

Besides, as the price of a ticket to the Family Circle at Wallack's was only thirty cents, this sum would carry in him and his friend, and there would be enough left for an ice cream after they had got through.

The temptation was too much for poor Roswell. I call him poor because I pity any boy who foolishly yields to such a temptation for the sake of a temporary gratification.

Thus, Horatio set up the downfall of misguided, arrogant Roswell. Soon Mr. Baker returned to the store.

"Have you sold anything, Roswell." he inquired on entering.

"Yes sir, I have sold a slate, a quire of note paper, and one of Oliver Optic's books." [That was a private Alger joke.] Roswell showed Mr. Baker the slate, on which, as required by his employer, he had kept a record of sales.

Mr. Baker made no remark, but appeared to think all was right.

So the afternoon passed away without any incident worthy of mention.

Those last two paragraphs show why Horatio was boyhood's foremost writer of the day. Had Mr. Baker noticed something amiss, or had he not? Apparently, as Horatio was at pains to say, he had not. But the reader was not fooled; he knew that Horatio was playing a game—or was he? The delicious sense of involvement and excitement in the chase was all there, manufactured in Horatio's narrative skill.

To enliven the suspense, Horatio then jumped in the next chapter to the adventures of Richard Hunter which, of course, appealed to all boys who had read the previous two books about

Ragged Dick and his success. Richard was promoted in his job. Richard also introduced Mark to Sunday School. Richard met Roswell Crawford and his evil companion on the steps of the Fifth Avenue hotel. The two swells had cigars in their mouths and were pretending that this posh hostelry was their dwelling place.

Roswell joined the Madison Club, which was scarcely more than a gang. The initiation fee was five dollars to have access to the clubroom where these teen-agers smoked, told stories and "had a good time." The evil companion, who announced Roswell's election, suggested he steal the initiation fee from the bookstore. And so he did, laying plans as he did so to place the blame on Mark, thus revenging himself on Richard. Anyone who accused Horatio of simplicity in plots was certainly showing an abysmal ignorance of his work. And as for the material, Horatio drew these incidents from the tales boys told him. His familiar figure was forever moving about the Newsboy's Lodging House, and the youngsters considered him a part of the place. He was always ready with a doctor or a dinner, and his reward—at least one of them—was material for his stories. He got it. From such tales came the events he portrayed as fiction in his books.

Horatio took his readers to a meeting of the Madison Club, showing how carelessly members were selected.

> "Has he got five dollars?" inquired another member.
> "His father is a rich man," said Burgess. "There will be no fear about his not paying his assessments."
> "That's the principal thing," said Wilmot.
> "I second the nomination."

And then, the wickedness showed no bounds:

> A large flagon of hot whiskey punch was brought in and placed on a table. Glasses were produced from a closet in the corner of the room, and it was served to the members.
> "How do you like it, Roswell?" inquired Ralph Graham.
> "It's—rather strong," said Roswell, coughing.

Soon Roswell was three sheets to the wind, singing and indulging in speeches with the others, and then the cards were brought out, and the boys played euchre and other games *for money*.

This was the way in which members of the Madison Club spent their evenings—a very poor way, as my young readers will readily acknowledge. I heartily approve of societies organized by young people for debate and mutual improvement. They are oftentimes productive of great good. Some of our distinguished men date their first impulse to improve and advance themselves to their connection with such a society. But the Madison Club had no salutary object in view. It was adapted to inspire a taste for gambling and drinking, and the money spent by the members to sustain it was worse than wasted.

Next morning, Roswell arrived at work with a hangover and planted the key to the cash box on poor Mark the Match Boy. The plot then thickened in a marvelous Algerian manner: the five dollars that Roswell had purloined was counterfeit—and he had used it to pay his initiation fee.

Mr. Baker knew the money was counterfeit. Yet he was aroused. Roswell turned out his pockets. Nothing. Mark turned out his pockets. Aha, there was the accusing key.

"I have never opened the drawer, nor taken your money," said Mark, in a firm voice, though his cheek was pale and his look was troubled.

Mr. Baker was angry but fair. He wanted to get to the bottom of the affair.

"There seems to be a conflict of evidence here," said Mr. Baker.

"I hope the word of a gentleman's son is worth more than that of a match boy," said Roswell haughtily.

Then, in marched the secretary of the Madison Club to complain about the counterfeit bill Roswell had given for his initiation fee. Roswell was unmasked, fired, disgraced and forced to make restitution and apologize to Mark. Horatio really knew how to hurt a guy, even that was not the end:

It was only a few days afterwards that Mrs. Crawford received a letter, informing her of the death of a brother in Illinois, and that he had left her a small house and a farm. She had found it so hard to struggle for a livelihood in the city that she decided to remove thither, greatly to Roswell's disgust, who did not wish to be immured in the country. But his wishes could not be gratified, and, sulky and discontented, he was obliged to leave the choice society of the Madison Club and the attractions of New York, for the quiet of a country town.

Horatio always had pious hope:

> Let us hope that, away from the influences of the city, his character may be improved, and become more manly and self-reliant. It is only just to say that he was led to appropriate what did not belong to him, by the desire to gratify his vanity, and through the influence of a bad advisor. If he can ever forget that he 'is the son of a gentleman,' I shall have some hopes for him.

Roswell eliminated, Mark saved, Horatio devoted a chapter to reintroducing old friends. Mrs. Clifton, the former Miss Peyton of *Fame and Fortune* with her cap set for anything in pants, and Frank Whitney, who went all the way back to *Ragged Dick,* both appear. Then it turned out that Mark was really named Talbot and is the long lost grandson and heir of nice Mr. Bates from the beginning of the story. As usual, everyone got what was coming to him. Richard Hunter got $1000, which he turned over to the Newsboy's Lodging House, and Mark the Match Boy found his true home and was going to be happy ever after.

It was a busy year for Horatio. Mark was scarcely removed to his newfound splendor in Milwaukee, when *Student and Schoolmate* began talking about a new serial. Loring was talking about a new series. *Ballou's Monthly* was wanting a serial story of its own. Horatio spent much of his time at the Newsboy's Lodging House lounging around in carpet slippers and an old sweater. In the preface of *Mark the Match Boy,* he told readers he was dealing with a specific aspect of street life in New York and why:

> The author has observed with pleasure the increased public attention which has been drawn to the condition of these little waifs of city life, by articles in our leading magazines and in

other ways; and hopes that the result will be to strengthen and assist the philanthropic efforts which are making to rescue them from their vagabond condition.

So along came *Rough and Ready,* fourth in the Ragged Dick series and then *Ralph Raymond's Heir,* a story Horatio felt impelled to write, but which he published under the pseudonym Arthur Hamilton for *Gleason's Literary Companion.*

The editors of *Student and Schoolmate* were not pleased with Horatio's heavy productivity, no matter what names he chose to use. They were having their own difficulties. Horatio was their wheel horse and standby, particularly since Oliver Optic had gone his own way. But even at the height of Horatio's success with *Ragged Dick* and the following books, *Student and Schoolmate* was beginning to slip. First there was difficulty in collecting subscription money. Then the list began to decline despite valiant efforts on the part of the publishers to revive it. The editors began promoting, using the Alger name and the Alger books and boasting of the new authors they were attracting to their pages. As for Horatio, he was so busy now and so much in demand for serials that he scarcely had time to do anything but write.

Chapter Eleven

The Established Writer

ALL THE WHILE that Horatio Alger, Jr. was writing books, he was also tutoring boys for entrance into various colleges. Through Harvard friends he secured an introduction to banker Joseph Seligman and was soon put in charge of the two oldest Seligman boys, Isaac and George. He taught the sons of many other prominent New Yorkers. His credentials as a Harvard graduate, a minister—if one did not really inquire—and a writer of morality novels were as impeccable as those of any tutor in the world. The Brewster affair was sinking into the background in the anonymity of the big city as it could have nowhere else in America.

The past dimming, Horatio made trips home to South Natick when the writing and tutoring chores overwhelmed him. There were family problems. James, who had gone west to seek his fortune in the gold fields and ended up working in an optometrist's shop, had married, divorced and stayed in the West. Annie died of consumption, bringing a pall of sorrow over the South Natick house. Horatio went home to mourn and then returned to New York to plunge himself back into work.

He moved uptown from the Greenwich Village area to West Thirty-fourth Street, just off Fifth Avenue. His chores as tutor to the Seligman children were being taken seriously by the family. Horatio was, in fact, more than a tutor; he was a sort of governor who took the boys for walks and supervised their play as well as teaching them Greek and Latin and mathematics.

With four of the Ragged Dick series published, Loring still wanted more tales of street life in New York. Horatio undertook to write two more such books for publication in 1870. *Rufus and Rose,* which appeared first as a serial in *Student and Schoolmate,* was a continuation of the previous year's serial, *Rough and Ready.* The editors of the magazine were more than a little put out when Horatio insisted on producing still another of the Ragged Dick series that same year. They could not accommodate so much, and they knew they were losing the continuity of the series, but there was nothing to be done about it. Horatio was simply too prolific for them. Publisher Joseph Allen announced Loring's publication of *Ben the Luggage Boy* while *Rufus and Rose* was still running in the magazine:

> But while Mr. Alger has not fallen into the too common error of writing too much and publishing too frequently, he has not been idle. In gathering the facts connected with our serial, he has fallen in with a case which prompts to the publication of another volume independently of this magazine.

Then the editors offered this book, as well as the other Alger books of the Ragged Dick series at a low price. Already they were selling other Alger books for a dollar and fifteen cents, while Loring's published price was a dollar and a quarter. They were also selling a picture of Horatio for a dollar and a half, as a circulation stunt.

Ben the Luggage Boy tells the story of a youngster who runs away from home and ends up on the wharves of New York. It is a novel, but also a true story. Horatio said as much to readers in the preface. The book was finished early in the spring of 1870, and Loring brought it out a few months later. Horatio called it an exploration of a different aspect of street life than those he had undertaken before.

Well into the Ragged Dick series, Horatio had established firmly the style in which he would work.

There is a snapper to bring the reader into the tale:

> "How much yer made this mornin', Ben?"
> "Nary red," answered Ben composedly.
> "Had yer breakfast?"
> "Only an apple. That's all I've eaten since yesterday. It's most time for the train to be in from Philadelphy. I'm layin' round for a job."

Here, Horatio had identified the boys by speech and problems as poor street waifs in the shorthand to which his readers were totally accustomed. They could settle down knowing just what was going to happen, in outline, if without a clue to it in detail.

Description is used to set the scene and introduce the major character:

> The boy whom he addressed as Ben was taller, and looked older. He was probably not far from sixteen. His face and hands, though browned by exposure to wind and weather, were several shades cleaner than those of his companion. His face, too, was of a less common type. It was easy to see that, if, he had been well dressed, he might readily have been taken for a gentleman's son. But in his present attire there was little chance of this mistake being made. His pants, marked by a green stripe, small around the waist and very broad at the hips, had evidently once belonged to a Bowery swell; for the Bowery has its swells as well as Broadway, its more aristocratic neighbor. The vest had been discarded as a needless luxury, its place being partially supplied by a shirt of thick red flannel. This was covered by a frock-coat, which might have once belonged to a member of the Fat Men's Association, being aldermanic in its proportions. Now it was fallen from its high estate, its nap and original shape had long departed, and it was frayed and torn in many places. But among the street boys dress is not much regarded, and Ben never thought of apologizing for the defects of his wardrobe. We shall learn in time what were his faults and what his virtues, for I can assure my readers that street boys do have virtues sometimes, and when

they are thoroughly convinced that a questioner feels an interest in them, they will drop the "chaff" in which they com-
monly indulge, and talk seriously.

There is action. The book opens with Ben finding an old
lady on the slip from the ferry, having just arrived on the train on
the Jersey side of the river. Alger made one of his little jokes with
Ben's offer to carry her bag:

> "Who be you?" asked the old lady, suspiciously.
> "I'm a baggage smasher," said Ben.
> "Then I don't want you," answered the old lady, clinging
> to her bag as if she feared it would be wrested from her. "I'm
> surprised that the law allows such things. You might be in a
> better business, young man, than smashing baggage."

Then Ben began his "chaff":

> "That's where you're right, old lady," said Ben. "Banking
> would pay better, if I only had the money to start on."
> "Are you much acquainted in New York?" asked the old
> lady.
> "Yes," said Ben; "I know the mayor n' aldermen, 'n all the
> principal men. A. T. Stooart's my intimate friend, and I dine
> with Vanderbilt every Sunday when I ain't engaged at Astor's."
> "Do you wear them clo'es when you visit your fine
> friends?" asked the old lady, shrewdly.

The give and take established, Ben bargained with the old
lady, and after she had turned down several more-expensive
means of getting herself and her bag to her daughter's house on
Bleecker Street, some two miles from the slip, she accepted Ben's
way. Ben told the old lady a series of marvelous tales, all of them
manufactured from his vivid imagination.

> So Ben beguiled the way with wonderful stories, with
> which he played upon the old lady's credulity. Of course it was
> wrong; but a street education is not very likely to inspire its
> pupils with a reverence for truth; and Ben had been knocking
> about the streets of New York most of the time among the
> wharves, for six years. His street education had commenced at

the age of ten. He had adopted it of his own free will. Even now there was a comfortable home waiting for him; there were parents who supposed him dead, and who would have found a difficulty in recognizing him under his present circumstances.

The denouement occurs when after a series of adventures, in which good behaviour, strength of character and luck—which in the Alger morality comes only to those who deserve it—Ben the Luggage Boy is ready to go home. On Sunday evening he attended a sacred concert in Carnegie Hall with his sister, who had found him out. That showed how far he had come from the rude-tale-spinning street boy of the opening chapter. So Ben went home, which happened to be Philadelphia (a place to which Alger often consigned his young villains and their accomplices in earlier books) where his aged mother was still waiting for him after six long years.

> "Mother!" exclaimed Ben, and hurrying forward, threw his arms about his mother's neck.
> "God be thanked," she exclaimed, with heartfelt gratitude. "I have missed you so much, Ben."
> Ben's heart reproached him as he saw the traces of sorrow upon his mother's face, and felt that he had been the cause.
> "Forgive me mother!" he said.
> "It is all forgotten now. I am so happy!" she answered, her eyes filled with joyful tears.

The homecoming is as simple as that.

> They sat down together and Ben began to tell his story. In the midst of it his father entered. He stopped short when he saw Ben sitting beside his mother.
> "It is Ben come back," said his mother joyfully.
> Mr. Brandon did not fall on his son's neck and kiss him. That was not his way. He held out his hand, and said, "Benjamin, I am glad to see you."

There are no recriminations, no probing of emotions, no problems. It is hardly a Dostoyevskian treatment of human feeling, but then it was aimed at young men from the age of ten to about sixteen, who eschewed such weakness with the same horror that they felt at the prospect of washing or of kissing maiden aunts. Horatio knew his boys and he knew what they wanted. The emotional level of the scene was just proper for the market.

Then there is Alger's resolution. Ben was home. All other difficulties were solved. Ben's father suggested that now Ben stay home and enter the family business, which he would soon have for himself. Ben, suddenly shy, suggested that he did not know enough—which was certainly the case, since he had spent the last six years among streetwalkers, swindlers and bootblacks. But that was arranged easily enough; he was to stay home for a year and take private tutoring from the teacher of the academy. "You can learn a great deal in a year if you set about it," said his father. And of course Ben wanted to do just that. Alger left him studying at home with the prospect of next year assisting his father. And the father—a miraculous change had overcome him. Ben ran away from home in the first place because his father had been stern and hard; now he was so gentle and forbearing that Alger worried a little lest the family spoil the boy they had driven out six years earlier.

The adventures of Ben were received by the public with the same grand acclaim that the other New York street books had drawn. None of them, of course, quite matched *Ragged Dick* in terms of national attention, but that was natural. These later books were variations on the theme. *Ragged Dick* was selling out even then in edition after edition, and the other books, while not snapped up so eagerly were still produced and sold in the tens of thousands. Alger and Loring agreed that the Ragged Dick (or street) series, should end with six books. The final volume, *Rufus and Rose,* had already been written for *Student and Schoolmate* and would be published in 1870 so as neither to disturb the serial nor flood the book market. Horatio was already embarked on his new Luck and Pluck series, which took as its theme the triumph of virtue in small towns, or as Horatio put it in one of his prefaces:

> ...the best way to strive for success is to deserve it; and then, if it does not come, there will at least be a consciousness of well-doing, which in itself is a rich reward.

The street life stories would not die so easily; *Student and Schoolmate* insisted on another, basing their demands on the typical magazine editors' premise that success bears endless repetition. Loring, too, was perfectly willing to continue marketing a product for which there was a demand.

What was it to be? In the summer of 1870, Horatio was employed by the Seligmans as governor and tutor to the children at the summer home in fashionable Long Branch, New Jersey. There, living in the mansion, he had a further opportunity to sharpen his observations of rich New York businessmen, few being richer than Wall Streeter Seligman. Horatio also became involved in the Seligman's affairs. When the banker encouraged the beginning of a new young people's magazine which would put its profits into the Hebrew Orphan Asylum, Horatio was asked to contribute because his name, so famous, would help launch the magazine. Then and later, Horatio had a sharp eye for the juvenile market. He assessed the possibility of *Young Israel,* with Seligman backing, as very good indeed. He was willing enough to turn pen to paper for prestige and cold cash. That was something Benjamin Seligman could understand. At this time, *Ballou's,* which had begun to take his serials, to the consternation of *Student and Schoolmate,* had now declined, and Horatio needed a new market. That summer of 1870, between romps with the Seligman children, strolls on the beach and Greek verbs, Horatio plunged into writing *Paddle Your Own Canoe: The Fortunes of Walter Conrad,* which would go to *Young Israel.* He wrote in the afternoons, and at tea time read his current day's chapter to the Seligman brood.

Paddle Your Own Canoe opens on a scene well-known to Horatio from his boyhood and his teaching, crafty Horatio showing the hero giving a rousing declamation before his schoolmates at Vernon High School:

> The speaker was a boy of fifteen, well-knit, and vigorous, with a frank, manly expression, and a prepossessing face. His dark chestnut hair waved slightly above a high, intellectual brow, and his attitude, as he faced his schoolmates, was one of ease and unconscious grace.

This was Harry Raymond, the hero a poor boy from a small town, in the Alger tradition, who triumphed in the end. When he turned his hand to the new book for *Young Israel's* serialization,

Horatio took a slightly different theme, obviously encouraged by the opulent surroundings in which he found himself that summer of 1870 at the Seligmans. His hero was Walter Conrad, a rich boy from a small town "where his father was the wealthiest and most prominent and influential citizen, having a handsome mansion-house, surrounded by extensive grounds." Nobody knew just exactly how rich the Conrads were, but it was rich enough, the father had a fortune estimated at two hundred thousand dollars, a great deal of money in the 1870s. And here was Walter, at Essex Classical Institute, which Horatio had drawn from his years at Gates Academy and his teaching at Deerfield and Potawomie.

But the rich boy hero was immediately plunged into adventure right up to the top of his head; that second chapter saw him scurrying home in response to a telegram advising that his father was desperately ill. On the way home he overheard a conversation that indicated his father had been swindled in a stock deal; he got home to find his father had died that morning, and Walter was left without a penny.

Walter's wicked relations, cousin Jacob Drummond and his spoiled son, Joshua, thought they could get something out of Walter's inheritance, so they offered him a place in their home. Walter accepted. In honor of the occasion, Mr. Drummond, usually a very stingy man, ordered his wife to serve up cake and two kinds of pie for supper:

> "Cake and two kinds of pie, and hot biscuit!" she repeated.
> "Yes," he replied. "I am not in general favor of such extra living, but it is well to pay some respect to the memory of my deceased kinsman in the person of his son. Being the son of a rich man, he has been accustomed to rich living, and I wish him, on his advent into our family, to feel at home."

Walter arrived, dinner was served, and all went beautifully. Next morning, there was steak and fried potatoes and more hot biscuit for breakfast, and then, after breakfast, Walter dropped his bomb: he told Cousin Jacob that he had no money, and the next the reader knew, Walter had a job in the Drummond store working for his board and room.

Walter was paddling his own canoe with a vengeance. His cousin's son lorded it over him. Dinner that second day was corned beef and potatoes, bread without butter and no pie at all. What a comedown! But Walter did not lose heart, even when his bag was removed from the guest room into a tiny little chamber "furnished with the barest necessities." The next morning's breakfast consisted of the remains of the corned beef and potatoes and a plate of bread and butter.

> "Do you take milk and sugar in your tea, Walter?" asked Mrs. Drummond.
> "If you please."
> "I don't take either," remarked Mr. Drummond. "It is only a habit, and an expensive one. If you'd try going without for a week, you would cure yourself of the habit."

In the big sunny rooms of the Long Branch house, the Seligman children gaped as Horatio read his chapters, the opulence of their teas so much in contrast with that of poor Walter.

More, far more poor Walter had to bear. Joshua, his second cousin, insulted him and lorded it over him and finally drove Walter into striking him and defeating him in physical combat.

The fighters were disentangled, but the Walter-Joshua conflict became the central theme of the book, and soon Joshua, a slippery type if there ever was one, had his hand in his father's till just as Roswell Crawford had put his hand in the bookstore till when Horatio described the adventures of Mark the Match Boy.

The result was even worse. Walter was called a thief by the impetuous Drummond. Walter was cleared, for strangers saved his name, but he was furious and left for his old hometown.

Then Walter got a job as a book salesman for the publishers Flint & Pusher, an enterprising firm—and presto—he was in New York on page 164. But in a trice he was in Cleveland—for this was not a New York book—having had his pocket picked on the train. The conductor had seen the pickpocket take money from a wallet and throw the wallet away:

> The pickpocket turned pale. "You are mistaken in the person," he said.
> "No, I am not. I advise you to restore the money forthwith."
> Without a word the thief, finding himself cornered, took from his pocket a roll of bills, which he handed to Walter.

"Is that right?" asked the conductor.

"Yes," said our hero, after counting the money.

"So far so good. And now, Slippery Dick," he continued, turning to the thief, "I advise you to leave the cars at the next station or I will have you arrested. Take your choice."

Slippery Dick, whose name was to become a boy's gibe, hardly even waited for the train to slow down before he leapt off like a gazelle. The Seligman children gasped when Horatio read that incident, where else could youngsters of 1870 find a two-chapter exposition of pickpocketry?

The enterprising Walter was soon in Buffalo, visiting the Niagara Falls—an exercise in self-improvement that Horatio had himself undertaken. Sent on the road to sell books, Walter sold a copy of *Scenes in Bible Lands* on the first day, exchanging it for his room rent, and soon, after several little adventures, he had sold three copies and cleared three dollars and seventy-five cents for himself.

In a nutshell, Walter made a grand success of the book-selling business and learned a good deal about humanity in the process. Then at the end, his father's lawyer wrote him and announced that there was more money in the will than he had thought, that Walter was going to get at least two thousand dollars out of his father's estate.

And that was the end of the story, with a promise that Walter would be back in a new book soon, *Strive and Succeed: The Progress of Walter Conrad.* Having carried Ragged Dick and his friends through six books, Horatio was willing to try a more rural note.

Chapter Twelve

The Saga of
Tattered Tom

Horatio Alger, Jr., growing balder and a little tubby, recounted nightly to his young charges of the Seligman family the adventures of Walter Conrad in the wide world of which they knew nought, having been brought up in a close-knit, protected and wealthy Jewish family. Little Isabella Seligman began to object. Why was it, she asked her tutor, that he always wrote stories about boys? Were there not any little girls on the streets of New York. What was wrong with writing about girls?

There were, indeed, little girls on the streets of the big city, and they grew up into big girls, but the subject had hitherto been regarded as too delicate for treatment in a children's book. Yet Horatio was impressed by little Isabella's argument in favor of girls' lib and responded by creating a book about a girl street waif. He called her *Tattered Tom.* The ambience was by and large the same as that of the boys.

Loring was not much pleased with the whole idea. He considered Alger as his writer of books for boys and he wished Alger would leave books for girls to his girls' book author, Louisa May Alcott.

Student and Schoolmate was more charitable, not to the point of wanting *Tattered Tom* as a serial but when the book came out, the

109

SECOND SERIES

Tattered Tom

BOOKS.

by

Horatio Alger Jr.

THE YOUNG OUTLAW:
ADRIFT IN THE STREETS

editors of the magazine were generous in praise of their favorite writer:

> *Tattered Tom* is a story of girls' life in the streets of New York and it takes its place beside *Ragged Dick* as a graphic delineation of *outside* life in a great metropolis. It is not surprising that these books from Mr. Alger's pen have been so eagerly sought after, when we consider the fidelity with which he has studied the characters of those whose homes and social relations have been without the pale of moral or religious influences. His characters are always active, seldom overstrained, never unnatural. His boys are boys indeed, and now we have a girl— transformed in name and characteristics *almost* into the roughness of a boy-nature, it is true, and what wonder that it was so, but when the proper influence is steadily and kindly exerted, how rapidly does the original tenderness of the girl-nature develop itself, to bless and cheer the mother who has for so long a period mourned the loss of her stolen child. No mother can read this vivid story of street life without thanking God that *her* daughter has been spared a similar experience, and at the same time feeling a heartwarming sympathy for, and a desire to help those who, like "Tattered Tom" are apparently outcasts from society.

Student and Schoolmate offered *Tattered Tom* to its readers at a dollar and five cents, which was even cheaper than the old cut-rate offer. The magazine was far more interested in its current serial story, *Paul the Peddler,* where Horatio detailed the adventures of a young street merchant boy. Pure Algerphiles, who readily accepted *Paul the Peddler,* frowned on *Tattered Tom.*

> *Paul the Peddler* is well written [wrote one subscriber to the magazine] so lifelike, simple and affecting that it causes the sympathetic tear to start in behalf of struggling honorable poverty. My compliments to the author. His is the pen of genius. May he long live to adorn and embellish the pages of *Student and Schoolmate.*

For the lovers of the genre, there seemed to be no end to the demand for street stories. *Paul the Peddler* struck all the old familiar chords. But as always, with Horatio there was a difference.

Paul was a peddler. He made up little packages of candy with perhaps a half cent's worth of sweets inside, but also with a "prize." It might be a check for one cent or for ten cents. Then he sold them for five cents a package, hawking along the streets. By catching Paul in the act of unloading fifty packages in about an hour just off Wall Street, Alger also transmitted a feeling for New York's bustle and heterogeneity in the middle of the day.

Horatio's new hero was of a different type than the last run of city waifs. He lived with his mother in a tenement on Pearl Street—he was not an abandoned child, not a runaway, but one of the working poor. This Alger work, then, dealt with a different aspect of New York City's subterranean life, the life not chronicled in the daily or weekly press with its preoccupation on the lives of the Vanderbilts and their ilk.

Paul, his mother and his little brother were orphans of the storm of economic waste; the father, a cabinetmaker, had always supported them well, and they had lived for some years in a nice little cottage in Harlem. But the father had been run over by a dray, and on his death it was discovered that he had not saved anything. The result was movement to the tenement, where Paul was the sole support of his mother and little lame Jimmy.

Jimmy, with his bright eyes and inexhaustible cheerfulness, could have been drawn directly from the pages of Dickens' *Christmas Carol*. The comparison is not inept; in many ways Alger was doing in America what Dickens had done in London. To some extent the difference in their writings is due to their different styles, although Alger could adopt a far different and much more erudite style when he was not writing for a juvenile audience. The difference in characterization and plot is great indeed, but then Alger developed his characters and plots to meet the demands of American juvenile magazine and book publishers. Alger's work never rose above the popular level; there was no call for literature in the American juvenile market.

Still, for reportage of life in the nether regions of New York, Alger was unbeatable, and *Paul the Peddler* shows why. Other writers concerned themselves with the banquets of the Astors, Alger with the provender of the poor:

By the time the packages were made up dinner was ready. It was not a very luxurious repast. There was a small piece of rump steak—not more than three-quarters of a pound—a few potatoes, a loaf of bread, and a small plate of butter. That was all; but then the cloth that covered the table was neat and clean, and the knives and forks were as bright as new, and what there was tasted good.

Paul ran into hard times. Paul was out of business, but he found another. A man who ran a necktie stand on Broadway fell ill, and Paul took over the stand for half the profits.

Then Paul had a chance to buy out a necktie stand from a friend for thirty-five dollars—but thirty-five dollars was an astronomical sum. Paul and his mother together could raise only nine dollars. Mrs. Hoffman had a gold and diamond ring left over from better days, and Paul took it to a pawnshop. Horatio introduced his readers to the wonders of a New York pawnshop:

> Spider-like he waited for the flies who flew of their own accord into his clutches, and he took care not to let them go until he had levied a large tribute.

The broker then set about trying to cheat Paul, as he had already cheated three customers while Paul waited.

> The Pawnbroker eyed Paul sharply. Did the boy know that it was a diamond ring? What chance was there of deceiving him as to its value? The old man, whose business made him a good judge, decided that the ring was not worth less than two hundred and fifty dollars, and if he could get it into his possession for a trifle, it would be a paying operation.
> "You're mistaken, boy," he said, "It is not a diamond."

Paul refused to be gulled. The pawnbroker did everything from threatening to call a policeman to offering twenty-five dollars, but Paul saw that the ring was valuable and refused to sell or pawn it. Then Paul went to Tiffany's, but he had difficulty proving ownership of the ring and went to find a rich friend who would vouch for him. Enroute he encountered a vile swindler who entrapped him in a hotel room and stole the ring. Felix Montgomery, the evil one, seemed about to get off with his bottle of chloroform and Paul's ring. Paul tracked down the swindler, but the police interfered and took the swindler's side, and he escaped again. Finally after more adventures, Felix Montgomery was arrested and Paul got the ring, which he sold to Tiffany for two hundred and fifty dollars. He bought the necktie stand and was in business.

What the story of Paul the Peddler lacked in social significance it made up in adventure. Though a vast departure from the sociological overtones of *Ragged Dick*, it was eminently satisfactory to Horatio's youthful audience, and even as the author finished, he noted that he would use Paul again in two more books of this second street series. The second book would feature Paul; he would appear only incidentally in the third one, for that book represented another serious social study, one Horatio had encountered in his meanderings in New York.

Many Americans had begun to take an interest in city street boys. *Student and Schoolmate* reported on the newsboys of Philadelphia and their progress, even to a Christmas dinner given by Publisher George Childs of the Philadelphia *Ledger:* roast turkey, plum pudding, mince pie, ice cream, apples and Christmas candy. Yet in spite of their preoccupation with all the things that Horatio held dear, *Student and Schoolmate* was falling on bad times. Even the street series was failing to hold readership. By 1871 there had been seven such books, five of them serialized, and they had lost their power to draw readers to the magazine.

A. K. Loring had done so well with the Alger series and with Louisa May Alcott that he had moved his offices to larger and more luxurious quarters and, in true Algerian fashion, promoted one of his clerks to become his assistant and editor. This new editor, George W. Dillingham, was specifically given responsibility for handling Horatio Alger, Jr., and so a new relationship was born.

Chapter Thirteen

The New Crusade

Early in the 1870s a Newark department store owner named George Nelson Maverick encountered a particularly vicious system of exploiting street boys. The Italian and Sicilian community that had moved into New York and the other big cities of the middle Atlantic states was the culprit. Small boys, most of them orphans or unwanted children, were brought to the United States with a promise of the good life and were turned into the streets as musicians and beggars by adults who operated what amounted to beggar's rings. These adults did nothing for the children, they neither educated them, fed them nor clothed them. Maverick was outraged and began writing letters to the editors of various New York newspapers. But the papers were more interested in Van Rensselaers than vagabonds, and the letters aroused virtually no one. Horatio Alger, Jr. became known to the public as the expert on New York City street life and the defender of poor boys. Maverick turned to him.

Alger was interested. Out of his interest came the book *Phil the Fiddler,* which in its own way was a major exposé of a vile social ill. The book was published by A. K. Loring in the middle of 1872 and created a considerable stir in New York and other cities. The newspapers picked up the issue and began exposing the padrones. Charles Loring Brace and Charles Whitehead took up the cudgels. The public became aware of cruelty to children. In 1874 New York's legislature passed the first law protecting children. The Society for the Prevention of Cruelty to Children took interest. Half a dozen years after Horatio's book was published, the padrone system was outlawed and came to an end.

Horatio juggled three disparate commitments during 1872. He had to write the *Student and Schoolmate* serial—this year it was *Slow and Sure: from the Sidewalk to the Shop,* which chronicled the further adventures and successes of Paul the Peddler. Then he was writing *Strive and Succeed,* in which he brought to further glory Walter Conrad, the rich boy grown poor. Aptly enough, this book was dedicated to Isabella and Edwin Seligman, rich children staying rich, who had listened with so much interest to the original adventures of Walter Conrad.

Strive and Succeed represented something of a departure for Horatio. It put Walter, sixteen, into a detective's role to search out General Wall, who had operated the mining stock venture in which Walter's father had lost his fortune. To find out if the general had conspired to ruin other investors for his own profit, Walter adopted an assumed name while he studied General Wall and his schemes. Here, Horatio had new lines out representing his own past; Walter took on a class in Latin grammar since although he was only sixteen he had a firm foundation from his previous private school. Here Horatio devoted a full three pages to Latin grammar:

> John read the first line as follows, pronouncing according to a method of his own, *Cum esset Caesar in citeriore Gallia in hibernis,* and furnished the following translation:
> "He might be with Caesar in hither Gaul in the winter."
> "I don't think that is quite correct, Mr. Wall," said the teacher.
> "It makes good sense," said John, pertly.
> "It doesn't make the right sense. *Cum* is not a preposition, and if it were it could not govern Caesar in the nominative case."

There was more of this, quite a bit more. A young reader of the 1970s would find it hard going, Latin having fallen on bad times. But in the 1870s the references were not nearly so obscure. Still this was the first book in which Horatio had ventured to reveal his own scholarship and hint at his erudition. There was another change in the Alger approach. Loring had found that the sale of Alger books had begun to drop off in the East, but sales in the West were most gratifying. So Horatio located Portville in Wisconsin, which he regarded as the West.

Alger did a good deal of spoofing of country ways in *Strive and Succeed*, particularly in a scene wherein Walter in his teacher's guise was questioned about his knowledge by the local squire (who pronounced frigidity as frigg-i-dit-y, Philadelphia as Philadelphy,) who asked Walter if he knew where the Amazon mountains were located and was shocked when Walter forgot to mention Italy as being on the western boundary of Russia.

Among the excursions in this book, Walter explored letter writing. R.S.V.P. was revealed as "Respondez s'il vous plait" to the young readers. In responding to a flowery invitation Walter wrote:

> "Mr. Barclay and Mr. Howard are deeply indebted to Miss Melinda Athanasia Jones for her kind invitation, and will have pleasure in visiting her Amaranthine bower at the time appointed, and trust that they may be inspired by the muses, whose favorite haunt it is, to hold appropriate converse with the fair occupant, exchanging thoughts that breathe and words that burn."

Horatio had not spent his early years in the classroom for nothing. He described with fidelity the difficulties a young teacher had. There was the problem of Peter Groot, a red-haired, freckled-faced boy of fifteen or sixteen who looked as though he would be up to mischief:

> Walter was right in distrusting Peter. His idea of a teacher was, that he must be big enough to "lick" any of the boys; otherwise he had no right to expect obedience. Now, on examining Walter, he decided that he, Peter, could "lick him easy," as he expressed it in conversation with the other boys.

Some of the dialogue of this book is hilarious, and intentionally so. Alger introduced Miss Melinda Athanasia Jones, whose poetry had been declined by *Atlantic Monthly* and *Harper's Magazine*.

"It is because I am a Western *Literati*," she exclaimed to her brother with a lofty contempt for grammar. "If I were a Boston or New York *literati,* they would be glad to get my productions."

"I reckon you're right, Melindy," said her brother Ichabod. "Why don't you have your perductions, as you call 'em, mailed in Boston or New York? You could send 'em to somebody there."

"Thank you, I wouldn't stoop to subterfuge," said Melinda, reciting melodramatically:
"Breathes there a girl with soul so dead,
Who never to herself hath said,
Wisconsin is my native state?"

Or try this:

As Barclay and Walter entered the room, they beheld their fair hostess seated at the center table, with a volume of poems resting on her lap, while one hand supported her forehead, the elbow resting on the table. She had practiced this attitude during the afternoon before a looking glass.

She lifted her eyes slowly, appearing wrapt in meditation.

"Pardon my pensive preoccupation," she said, rising and greeting her guests. "I was communing with Milton. Do you often commune with him, Mr. Barclay?"

The scene improved:

"Do you ever provoke the muse, Mr. Howard?" asked Melinda.

A moment later she was admitting that she had dashed off a few rhymes that very day, and it took practically no coaxing to persuade her to deliver them.

". . . I cannot expect all to be so contemplative as I am [admitted Miss Jones]. My muse loves to dwell alone in primeval solitude. . . ."

But it is unnecessary to detail the rest of the conversation. Later in the evening some nuts, apples, and raisins were passed around, to which Melinda did full justice, notwithstanding her unsatisfied longings and the solitude of her soul.

Horatio included this scene for the delectation of Isabella Seligman. It is at once the funniest and most erudite passage in any of the books Alger had yet written, and it would have been absurdly recondite to any but educated youth.

But Horatio was soon up to his old tricks—on page 90 he began to chronicle the wayward path of Joshua Drummond, Walter's second cousin who had stolen six hundred dollars from his father's strong box and gone to New York. Anyone who knew Horatio knew Joshua would come to no good and could sit back to enjoy the gory details. Greenhorn Joshua was cheated of money right and left in the big city while Horatio gave his readers tastes of the delicious pitfalls of life in the wild metropolis. Joshua sought out an old friend, a slippery fellow named Sam Crawford, who had his eye on Joshua's six hundred dollars. Horatio stopped to describe a second-rate boarding house and a visit to Niblo's theater—no description of the play, just the place. He described a con game—how a stranger in Central Park found a "gold watch" and since he did not need it, agreeably sold the hundred dollar watch to Joshua for fifty dollars—no forty dollars—for Joshua was a sharp bargainer. Only at a jewellers did he learn that it was gold painted and worth about three dollars. Horatio was at his best when he fictionalized the wicked city. These anecdotes fascinated boys and girls—they were the high points of the books.

Meanwhile Horatio seemed determined to follow Joshua's villainous story more closely than Walter's virtuous one. But in time he shifted his reader back to pastoral Wisconsin, where that most uncivil Peter Groot was laying for the new master, Walter. Horatio described the conflict:

> He walked up to Peter's desk, eyeing him in a quiet determined manner.
>
> "You have defied my authority," he said, "and insulted me before the rest of the scholars. You believe me to be unable to enforce my orders. Come out on the floor and I will convince you to the contrary."
>
> "I'm comfortable where I am," said Peter, glancing about him triumphantly.
>
> "Then, as you don't accept my offer, I must force it upon you."

Walter, who now stood beside Peter's desk, seized him suddenly by the collar, and by a quick movement, jerked him into the aisle between the desks. Peter had not anticipated this. He was astonished and indignant beyond measure. The smile of triumph faded from his face and his features were distorted with rage.

"You'll be sorry for this!" he screamed, adding an oath which is better omitted. "I'll pay you up for it."

He knew how to fight after his style, and prepared to "pitch in" in his customary manner. Walter had drawn back a little, so as to be clear of the desks, and Peter followed him up. He aimed a blow at the young teacher's head, which would have been likely to give him a headache, but Walter had assumed an attitude of defense, and fended it off with the greatest ease. Peter quickly followed up the blow with another quite as vigorous. But this again was warded off. Walter did not immediately act offensively. He wished, before doing so, to show Peter that his own efforts were futile. In proportion as Peter discovered the ill success of his attempts to hit his opponent, his rage became more ungovernable, and he began to curse and swear. At length when he felt it to be time, Walter retaliated. One swift, well-planted blow, which Peter was utterly unable to ward off, and the troublesome pupil found himself lying upon his back on the floor of the schoolroom.

Here is Horatio at his worst. The stylized writing about the struggle is ridden with clichés and oversimplifications: the hero assuming a manly stance, guard up; the villain rushing and charging like a bull to no avail. Yet modern youth who have witnessed the cliché a thousand times on the television, relish it just as much as Alger's readers did when they read. There is something comforting about knowing the words and the rules and the outcome of the violence. If it was not literature, at least it was more appealing to his audience than were the literary parts of his book.

The three books of the year quite occupied Horatio's writing time. There were a few visits to South Natick and some trips with the Seligmans, but most of his time was spent in or about the Newsboy's Lodging House; when the house moved to bigger quarters, Horatio had his own room although he retained a place of his own uptown. With plenty of money these days, he played fairy godfather to the boys, helping them with their problems, finding some of them jobs, sending some to school, giving entertainments and parties for them, sending them out to the country or paying their fare to places where jobs had been found for them.

In the summer of 1873, Horatio planned a grand tour—a generous gesture to his mother and father and sister Olive Augusta Cheney and her husband, Amos. Since this trip would take a considerable investment of cash, Horatio redoubled his efforts in the winter and spring of the year. He wrote a series of short stories for *Gleason's Monthly,* most of them based on ideas either explored or touched in previous books. *Student and Schoolmate* had collapsed in spite of Alger's heroic efforts and the editors' reliance on them, but in Alger's life it had been replaced by *Young Israel* and *The New York Weekly.* Primarily, Horatio was still a serial author, with Loring coming in to take advantage of the previous publicity when the books were published. Both magazines were running his serials this year, and two more books would be published during the year, *Try and Trust: Abner Holden's Bound Boy* and *Bound To Rise: Up the Ladder.*

Try and Trust represents a geographical change in Horatio's writing; the change was not revolutionary, it had been in the making for two or three years, but a gradual emancipation of the books from the New York scene. "Our hero," as he called his principal character, did not arrive in New York until page 110, having come from Ohio by rail on a trip which included much skulduggery and a robbery. As always, there was juicy detail about the problems of a boy living in the big city, as when Herbert, the hero, went to get a job.

> "How much can you live upon economically?" asked the merchant.
>
> "I know little of the city," said Herbert. "You can judge better than I, sir."
>
> "You pay three dollars a week board. You'll need double that amount. Mr. Pratt, you may pay him six dollars a week. He will come to work tomorrow and you may pay him Saturday as if it was a whole week."

Bound to Rise is also bucolic in setting. It begins with the tale of a sick cow on a farm. It introduces Squire Green, a typical Alger squire:

BOUND TO RISE:
HARRY WALTON'S MOTTO

"Squire Green's a close man."
"He's mean enough, if he is rich."
"Sometimes the richest and the meanest."
"In his case it is true."

The squire of course drove a hard bargain with the man who needed a cow for his poor family. The story broke for a school episode, a prize contest in which Harry Walton, "our hero" won out, as a half dozen Alger heroes had won out in almost similar contests before, dating back to Horatio's very first stories for *Student and Schoolmate* in 1864 and 1865. But the cow problem persisted, Squire Green was a holdup artist who demanded sixty dollars for his cow, and so Harry went off to the nearby town and apprenticed himself to a shoemaker. Harry had all the usual adventures, worked hard, lost his money, which was found by his unscrupulous acquaintance. Then Harry got a job as assistant to a magician (what boy would not envy that?), and all seemed well, until Harry had more misadventures.

Finally, there came a day of reckoning. The note on the cow was due and Poor Mr. Walton had only two dollars, while his payment, with interest for six months was forty-one dollars and twenty cents— and Squire Green would demand every penny of it or back would go the cow. But then home came Harry in the nick of time. He had not only the forty-one dollars and twenty cents, but a hundred dollars in all, which he distributed among the family.

Bound to Rise is a really complete departure from the city life stories; it struck the chord wanted by *Young Israel,* and Loring put it in the Luck and Pluck series that was now taking over from the Tattered Tom series of street stories.

Horatio's fevered work schedule continued until June, when the Cheneys and his parents arrived from South Natick. After a few days of sightseeing in New York, wherein Horatio showed the relations up and down the Manhattan he knew so well, they sailed for Southampton. A stay in England, a visit to Stratford-on-Avon and some days in London, and they were off to the continent. They went to Vienna, then on to Venice, and spent the late summer weeks in Switzerland. For Horatio it was not all play, he took notes for future reference to work detail into new stories. While in Geneva he took time off to write the preface for

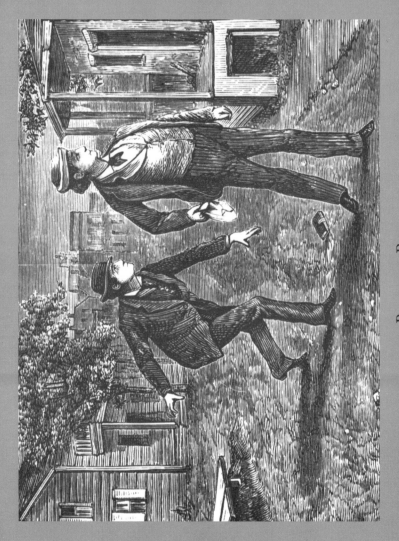

Bound to Rise:
Harry Walton's Motto

BOUND TO RISE:
HARRY WALTON'S MOTTO

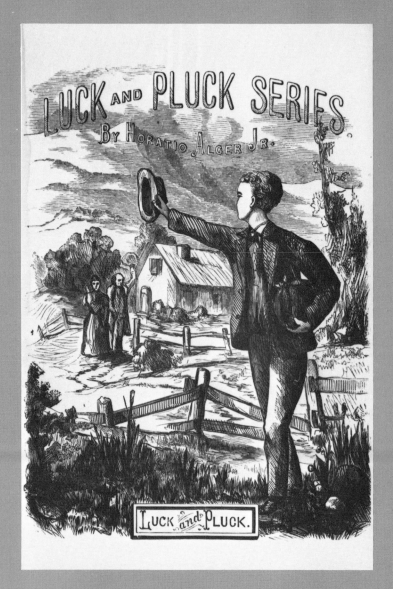

Luck and Pluck.

SINK OR SWIM:
HARRY RAYMOND'S RESOLVE

BOUND TO RISE:
HARRY WALTON'S MOTTO

Bound to Rise. The European trip confirmed what Horatio knew so well already.

> After having visited, for a second time, some of the leading countries of Europe, I am able to confirm what has so often been asserted, that nowhere here not even in the Swiss republic, of which I am a temporary resident, are such opportunities afforded to those who wish to rise, as in America. We hear, indeed, occasional stories of prominent men who have risen from the ranks; but what is rare and occasional in Europe is the rule with us.

Horatio had now found a new reason for writing and a new point of view. He had exhausted, to his own satisfaction, the crusade for the cause of the newsboys. Now he saw the larger picture: he must devote himself to proselyting the opportunity of America. Boys all over the country should see that in their own backyards existed the chance they should seek and that application, good character and earnestness would bring Horatio's old friends luck and coincidence popping out of the corners for them. *Ragged Dick,* the exposure of social evil, was long behind him.

Chapter Fourteen

Experimentation

It MAY NOT have seemed obvious to the naked eye, but Horatio's work had lost its steam by 1873. The world knew of the plight of city waifs. Legislators were now taking up the issue and commissions were being formed to study child labor and child abuse. Horatio served on such a commission at the behest of New York officialdom, but nothing much came of it; such things took time as the wheels of government ground on.

Horatio plodded along perhaps not quite knowing how to escape from his block, perhaps not realizing that he was in a block. *Young Israel* wanted a sequel to Harry Walton's adventures. Horatio promised *Risen From the Ranks*. Horatio reached out for new research material to write *Brave and Bold* for the New York *Weekly*. *Brave and Bold,* purporting to be the story of a factory boy, seemed to be somewhat of a departure for Horatio. There was one important change: *Brave and Bold* represented Horatio's flight into the rarified world of the international author; it was published in serial form by an English magazine, as well as by the New York *Weekly*.

In an attempt to bolster sagging sales Loring began a new Alger series with *Brave and Bold.* Boys had found Harry Walton's adventures rather tame and Walter Conrad a little too erudite for them. There were signs of a change in the literary market. Wild Indians and cowboys whooped it up through the pages of the magazines, and boys were avid for that kind of fare. So Loring and Editor Dillingham persuaded Horatio that he had to bring up the excitement in his books. Alger agreed to do this, but he drew the line at cutting down seriously on the moralizing. All that training as school teacher and minister of the Gospel could not be denied; if Horatio were to devote his efforts to boys' books, there had to be uplift.

Brave and Bold begins prosaically enough in the Millville Academy. When Robert Rushton, Alger's hero, presented a gold pencil case to Professor Granville, the teacher, on the occasion of the end of school, Robert's enemy snorted.

> "The professor made a bully speech," said more than one, after the exercises were over.
> "So did Bob Rushton," said Edward Kent.
> "I didn't see anything extraordinary in what he said," sneered Halbert Davis; "it seemed to me very commonplace."

Halbert, of course, was the son of the richest man in Millville. He dressed in expensive clothes and lived in the finest house in town.

> But something more than fine clothes is needed to give a fine appearance, and Halbert's mean and insignificant features were far from rendering him attractive.

And now, for almost the first time, and certainly for the first time in the beginning of an Alger book, *sex* rears its head: Halbert drew on his kid gloves and looked around for Hester Paine "the lawyer's daughter, the reigning belle among the girls of her age in Millville." Heretofore if there were any girls in the small towns where most of Alger's heroes originated, they were either the sisters of the hero or prop figures. In *Brave and Bold,* sixteen-year-old Robert Rushton had the temerity to ask Hester if he

could escort her home, right on the seventh page of the book!
More, the battle of virtue and vanity began right there, *over a girl!*

Scarcely had Hester accepted, when Halbert Davis approached, smoothing his kid gloves and pulling at his necktie.

"Miss Hester," he said, consequentially, "I shall have
great pleasure in escorting you home."

"Thank you," said Hester; "but I am engaged."

"Engaged," repeated Halbert; "and to whom?"

"Robert Rushton has kindly offered to take me home."

"Robert Rushton!" said Halbert disdainfully. "Never
mind, I shall relieve him of his duty."

"Thank you, Halbert," said Robert, who was standing by.
"I won't trouble you. I will see Miss Paine home."

"Your escort was accepted because you were the first to
offer it," said Halbert. "Miss Hester," said Robert. "I will resign in favor of Halbert, *if you desire it.*"

"I don't desire it," said the young girl promptly. "Come,
Robert, I am ready if you are."

With a careless nod to Halbert, she took Robert's arm,
and left the schoolhouse. Mortified and angry Halbert looked
after them muttering, "I'll teach the factory boy a lesson. He'll
be sorry for his impudence yet."

That last line evokes visions of Horatio's first juvenile *Frank's
Campaign.* Horatio was, alas, not capable of the complete change in
his approach to the boys' book, even after nine years of cranking
them out. *Brave and Bold* bears some study because it shows Horatio
in the middle of his career and in some ways at his worst again.

He had the cliché of conflict down pat. Halbert had stopped
Robert on the way home from the factory, to upbraid him for
escorting Miss Hester home and for thinking he was Miss Hester's
equal. Robert had told Halbert to mind his own business. Had
Miss Hester authorized Halbert to speak for her, he demanded?

"No but..."

"Then wait till she does."

Halbert was so incensed that, forgetting Robert's superior
strength, evident enough to anyone who ever saw the two, one
with his well-knit, vigorous figure, the other slender and small

of frame, he raised his cane and struck our hero smartly upon the arm.

In a moment the cane was wrested from his grasp and applied to his own person with a sharp, stinging blow which broke the fragile stick in two.

Casting the pieces upon the ground at his feet, Robert said, coolly, "Two can play at that game, Halbert Davis. When you want another lesson, come to me."

Thus, from the beginning the whole level of *Brave and Bold* hit a new "high." So did the skulduggery. Mr. Davis, the agent of the factory owner, had taken from Robert's father, a sea captain, five thousand dollars and used it to cover some dishonest speculations. He was *glad* when Captain Rushton disappeared.

The plot rushed on. To speed the excitement, entered an old miser, Paul Nichols, and his wicked nephew Ben Haley. After some preliminaries, Ben tried to steal Paul's gold hoard; Paul sprang on him "with a hoarse cry, like that of an animal deprived of its young ... and fastened his claw-like nails in the face of his burly nephew."

That ending to Chapter X certainly showed how hard Horatio was trying to please his publisher and his young readers by aping the dime novels. Next, Ben Haley tied up the old man and then went down the cellar to search for more gold. Robert Rushton happened by; he untied the old man, and they locked Ben in the cellar. The miser found a gun and gave it to Robert to use if necessary.

In a trice, Ben Haley had broken down the door and threatened Robert and the miser; Robert fired the gun, wounding Ben Haley. But Ben Haley was like a grizzly, one bullet in the shoulder would not stop him, and it would have gone badly for Robert except that just then a neighboring farmer burst into the room for no reason at all, and Ben ran off with gun and gold through the window, muttering imprecations:

> ... he shook his head menacingly at Robert, from whom he had received the wound.
>
> "There's a reckoning coming betwixt you and me, young one," he cried, "and it'll be a heavy one. Ben Haley don't forget that sort of debt. The time'll come when he'll pay it back with interest."

First, Ben Haley chopped up the boat—Robert had borrowed it from a friend—in which he escaped.

Horatio then had to move Robert to a larger scene. Robert was picking blueberries for a living. This proved to be a blessing in disguise, because he came across a tree fallen on the railroad tracks, as the train was barreling down on it—sheer disaster in the making. Robert tried to move the tree, but it was too big.

> There was one more thing he could do; and he did it.
>
> He took his station on the tree which was just in the path of the advancing train and waved his hat and handkerchief frantically. It was a position to test the courage of the bravest. Robert was fully aware that he was exposing himself to a horrible death. Should he not be seen by the engineer, it would be doubtful whether he could get out of the way in time to escape death—and that of the most frightful nature. But unless he did something, a hundred lives perhaps might be lost. . . .
>
> At first he was not seen. When the engineer at last caught sight of him, it was with a feeling of anger at the foolhardiness of the boy. . . .
>
> Reluctantly the engineer gave the signal to stop the train. He was only just in time. When it came to a stop there was an interval of only thirty feet between it and Robert Rushton, who, now that he had accomplished his object, withdrew to one side, a little paler than usual, but resolute and manly in his bearing.

Here was Horatio back at his old shorthand again, his hero well-knit, his bearing manly. Naturally, in the explanations that followed, Robert Rushton was acclaimed a hero. And there just happened to be on the train "a stout, good looking man, a New York merchant" who passed the hat, and presto, the passengers dug in and Robert had six hundred dollars, which at the current rate of family expenditure should have taken care of himself and his mother for two years; six hundred and thirty-five dollars to be precise. And, where the long green was concerned Horatio was precise.

In came a letter from the owners of Robert's father's vessel, who had found messages in bottles indicating that Captain Rushton might still be alive. And there was a letter from the captain himself, telling of the dastardly behaviour of a dissatisfied seaman, who had set fire to the ship and caused its destruction. And who was that villain? Why, none other than Ben Haley, the wicked nephew of the miser. Captain Rushton also informed his wife of the five thousand dollars he had entrusted to Superintendent Davis to invest for him. The plot really thickened.

Robert decided to work his way around the world and find his father. Robert went to New York, the scene of so much wickedness, and sure enough, a dishonest baggage smasher stole his carpetbag. But Robert chased him, discovered his name from another street boy, found him at his home and bearded the thief. Robert then went to a hotel "managed on the European system" which meant he did not have to take his meals there. That was good, because he went to call on the New York merchant who had been on the endangered train and was invited to dinner. And then he went to the handsome brownstone house on Fifth Avenue; with all of Tutor Horatio's experience in the homes of the Seligmans and other rich New Yorkers he might have outdone himself in a real description of an opulent New York mansion in the 1870s—but no, the reader learned of a servant in livery and then of a "sumptuously furnished parlor." That was that. And as for the dinner, again Horatio copped out: "I do not propose to speak in detail of the dinner that followed." And sometimes, Horatio wrote dialogue that could never have been spoken by mortal man.

> When the dinner was over, Mr. Morgan commenced: "Now, Robert, dinner being over, let us come to business. Tell me your plans..."

One problem with this book, from the reader's standpoint, is that when adventure was demanded of Horatio, he was so unfamiliar with the genre that the coincidence, the miraculous occurrence, was needed to explain every development. It just so happened that Robert called on Mr. Morgan. Fair enough, for he had been invited to do so on the day he prevented the train wreck. But it also just so happened that Mr. Morgan was sending a ship off to Calcutta on which Robert could ride as a passenger—free. Add those to the coincidence of Robert bursting in on the miser to untie him at just the right moment, of the farmer bursting in on the scene of violence just in time to save Robert and of the train threatened by the tree (Horatio never explained how it got on the track). Then, when Robert boarded the ship and the ship had sailed, who should turn out to be the mate: Ben Haley, the violent nephew of the miser, who had sworn revenge on Robert for shooting him.

Flashing back two years, an unusual device for Horatio, he took his readers to view an open boat "floating about in the Southern Ocean." In this craft were Captain Rushton and four sailors, starved and thirsty. One man drank seawater and liked it so much two others followed him. Soon they were gasping and suffering, as the Captain and Seaman Bunsby watched.

> "This is horrible," said the captain.
> "Yes," said Bunsby, sadly; "it can't last much longer now."
> His words were truer than he thought. Unable to endure his suffering, the sailor named Jack suddenly staggered to his feet.
> "I can't stand it any longer," he said, wildly. "Goodbye boys;" and, before his companions well knew what he intended to do, he had leaped over the side of the boat, and sunk in the ocean waves. There was a thrilling silence as the waters closed over his body.
> Then the second sailor also rose to his feet.
> "I'm going after Jack," he said, and he, too, plunged into the waves.
> The captain rose as if to hinder him; but Bunsby placed his hand upon his arm.
> "It's just as well, captain. We must all come to that, and the sooner, the more suffering is saved.
> "That's so," said the other sailor, tormented like the other two by thirst, aggravated by his draughts of sea-water. "Goodbye, Bunsby; goodbye, captain. I'm going."
> He too plunged into the sea, and Bunsby and the captain were left alone.

When Horatio set out about an action scene, no holds were barred; he decanted the seasick into the briny like lemmings, but even this last man, tormented by thirst, mouth and throat afire,

head spinning, did not forget his manners. In the Horatio Alger
lexicon, only the bad forget their manners, no matter what their
degree of desperation.

It just so happened that the ship *Argonaut*, bound for Calcutta,
picked up the captain's boat, and there was Bunsby dead in the
bottom and the captain scarcely alive. Poor Captain Rushton
had completely lost his memory, he had no identification papers
except the receipt for the money he had given Superintendent
Davis, and this remained hidden in a secret pocket and not
found, so when the captain recovered, he knew not who he was
nor whence he'd come. How he would have made out, a stranded
sailor on a foreign shore, was difficult to say, except that, naturally enough, a "large-hearted and princely American merchant,
resident in Calcutta" undertook to pay all the expenses of this
grimy, sick man he had never met and about whom he knew
nothing at all.

> "Leave him here; I will find him a home in some suitable
> boarding house, and defray such expenses as may be required.
> I am blessed with abundant means. It is only right that I
> should employ a portion in his service."

Small wonder, was it not, that American youths reading the
Alger books would aspire to greatness as merchants and men of
business? What could be nobler than the generous merchant,
putting his purse at the service of humanity in far-off Calcutta?
Many a stranded sailor of real life, pleading for aid at the American Consulates any and everywhere, would have delighted in
such a fairy godfather. Instead, too often they found the deadly
reality, forced to ship out on some leaking, rat and worm-infested
tub where the prospect of feeding on maggots was nearly as deso-
late as that of starving on the beach. These poor denizens of the
forecastle had never discovered Horatio's world, and sadly
enough most of them never would.

Back aboard Mr. Morgan's ship, bound for Calcutta, horrid
events were taking place. Captain Evans fell sick; in two sentences he was dead, and who was captain but Ben Haley, who in
a previous chapter had declared to Robert Rushton: "Think of
me henceforth as your relentless enemy."

Robert befriended the cabin boy, Frank Price, so Haley took his hatred out on Frank. On a pretended slight he decided to have him flogged. Robert interceded and was accused of inciting mutiny. Sailor Bates, who refused to flog Frank, was clapped in irons—and just then a storm slapped the ship and put an end to the flogging incident without a blow being struck or any harm to the vessel. The ship neared an island. Captain Haley went ashore with a party including Robert. Robert left the others and explored, but Haley came upon him, bound him to a tree with a stout cord he just happened to have in his pocket, and then deserted him to die. Sailor Bates, who had inexplicably gotten out of irons, sneaked back in the gig and untied Robert as the ship sailed away.

Robert and Bates played Robinson Crusoe aboard a deserted island in the South Seas. Boys and publisher wanted adventure, did they? Well Horatio was giving it to them with a shovel! Horatio, not long on south sea lore, soon had them building an Indian wigwam for shelter. They also found plenty of fruit (not specified) on the trees just outside the wigwam. Bates moreover just happened to have some cord and fishhooks with him, so they were able to rig up, and the sea around them was full of fish. It was no trouble at all to rub sticks together and make a fire. They lived very happily for six weeks until they were rescued by a passing ship, which was oddly enough also bound for Calcutta.

In Calcutta, almost the first person they encountered was Captain Rushton. Robert rushed up to him and called him by name; the captain was healed in a trice. He found the receipt for the Davis money, which had been kept in that same pair of trousers for two years without being noticed by anyone. Father and son went home on the ship that had saved Robert.

They arrived to unmask Ben Haley who now captained merchant ships. Haley acted as any Alger villain would:

> He rose from his seat, his face dark with anger, and smarting under a sense of defeat. "You have not done with me yet," he said to Robert, and without another word he left the office.

Any Alger reader knew what that meant—there was to be at least one more incident, although Horatio had already reached

BRAVE AND BOLD:
THE FORTUNES OF A FACTORY BOY

page 323. Then in twenty more pages, Horatio dealt with Superintendent Davis, who had to pay over nearly six thousand dollars, including interest computed at 6%, to Captain Rushton; auditors at the same time looked at the factory books and found that Davis had been embezzling for several years; Davis absconded leaving his wife and son nigh destitute; old Miser Nichols died and left all his money to Robert Rushton, which, including the farm and gold, came to ten thousand dollars; and Ben Haley got his desserts.

> when at Rio de Janeiro he became engaged in a fracas with the keeper of a low grog shop, when the latter, who was a desperate ruffian, suddenly snatched a knife from his girdle, and drove it into the heart of the unhappy captain, who fell back on the floor and expired with a groan. Thus terminated a misguided and illspent life. I should have been glad to report Ben Haley's reformation instead of his death; but for the sake of Robert, whom he hated so intensely, I am relieved that this source of peril is no more.

Robert went into business with Mr. Morgan as his sponsor. He prospered, "and promises in time to become a prominent and wealthy merchant." His father without any manufacturing experience became superintendent of the factory in the place of Davis. And, oh yes, Hester Paine continued to be attracted to Robert, not having appeared at all since page 176. Every boy knew what would come next, although, thank the Lord and Horatio, he was not to be inflicted with the treacly details:

> The mutual attachment which existed between her and Robert, when, boy and girl, still continues and I have reason to think that there is some ground, for the report, which comes to me from Millville, that they are engaged.

So ends this new grand adventure story, telling the fortunes of a factory boy. And in it all, in a fashion that was to become more and more pronounced, the title had virtually nothing to do with the book; the reader never saw Robert Rushton do a day's work in the factory, nor did he ever discover what kind of a factory it was. This was the new Alger.

Chapter Fifteen

Way Out West

I̲N̲ S̲L̲O̲W̲ A̲N̲D̲ S̲U̲R̲E̲, which tells the further adventures of
Paul the Peddler, there appeared a secondary character named
Julius, not a very pristine or admirable example of the street
boy—one who definitely was in need of reform. In this experi-
mental period, Horatio decided to take Julius and send him out
west for reformation, as he and others concerned with street boys
had been advocating for some time. So, Horatio put pen to paper
and wrote *Julius: The Street Boy Out West.* He gave full credit for
his facts to the Children's Aid Society, which had been working
with boys for a long time. He also gave credit to Charles Loring
Brace and his book *The Dangerous Classes of Society*—from which
Horatio drew an immense amount of material; and while *Julius* is
fictional, it is much less a story than a report on the adventures of
street boys as they were sifted out of the metropolis and moved to
better climates.

As the book opens, Julius is leaving New York to go with
Mr. O'Connor and other boys out west where he will work on a
farm. The parting was not without a certain nostalgia for him,
and this was heightened by his friend Pat.

"I don't think I'd like the country," said Pat, reflectively. "New York's a bully place. There's always something going on. I say did you hear of that murder in Centre Street last night?"

"No, what was it?"

"A feller stabbed a cop that was trottin' him round to the station house for bein' tight. There's always something to make it lively here. In the country there ain't no murders nor burglaries, nor nothing," concluded Pat, rather contemptuously.

Horatio is *so* much better when he wrote about the boys he knew and their open if not very admirable emotions, than when he described a shipwreck or a scene of violence. Here Pat indicated in one paragraph the young New Yorker's contempt of the boondocks—an attitude that would persist for a hundred years.

The city scenes, as always, had the stamp of authentic city. Horatio had a genius for showing his readers insights and opening doors that they never knew existed. For example, in the opening pages of *Julius,* the boy visits an amateur theatrical performance put on by other street boys. Horatio gave his reader a view of theatrical tastes of the 1870s on a low or Bowery level, that was not otherwise offered the young public.

The performance was held at "The Grand Duke's Opera-House." There were two musicians playing an accordion and a set of bones. The overture—representing the taste of the audience: "Squeeze Me, Joe," "Up in Avenue A" and "The Campbells are Coming"—opened a series of sketches. "Laughing Gas," which showed the effect of this new drug on various characters, was followed by a "robbery" in which two boys dressed as Tom King and Dick Turpin—notorious burglars of the day—appeared on stage with dark lanterns, attempted the robbery of a house and became so panicked that they sent the spectators into the aisles roaring with amusement. Then the most popular song of the hour, "The Mulligan Guards," was sung by all the audience, stamping their feet and shouting to the whine of the accordion and the roll of the bones.

From this scene, Horatio switched to the train that would take himself, Superintendent O'Connor and his charges out west to the town where the boys were to stay. A pickpocket on the train offered momentary excitement, and Horatio's detailed description of his *modus operandi* was precisely what boys liked to read.

Horatio's tales had the same tonic effect on the youth of 1874 that *Hawaii Five-O,* or *Mod Squad* would have on a considerably later generation. Julius, the hero of this book, was instrumental in apprehending the train pickpocket, who had just stolen a man's watch and was about to take his wallet. The pickpocket recognized Julius and vowed vengeance as he was hustled off the cars—thus neatly setting up the suspense never lacking in an Alger plot. The gentleman whose watch had been saved was, of all things, a wealthy merchant. He promised to be available to Julius in case of need, a ticket which the Algerian reader knew would be collected one day.

Then the train arrived at Brookville, and O'Connor and his boys descended. (This is nonfiction again.) They were met by a committee of citizens, and they marched to a public hall where they would stay—all fifty-two of them—until they could be sorted out and gotten places to live and jobs. It was very obvious from the manner of description that Horatio had accompanied O'Connor on this placement trip. Because *Julius* is in many ways far less a novel than a report, boys generally find the book rather slow going, unlike previous Alger works. But as the narrative progressed, Horatio picked up the tempo: Mr. Taylor, the man who decided to take Julius in, questioned him and discovered that he had been raised by a notorious burglar and robber:

> "It appears to me that you were brought up under bad influences."
>
> "Yes, I was," said Julius in a matter of fact manner.
>
> "Many would be afraid to take into their houses a boy who had been reared by a thief."
>
> "Maybe they would," said Julius.
>
> "They might be afraid that he had been trained to steal."
>
> "Yes," said Julius; "but what's the good of stealin' when you've got a good home?"
>
> "Quite true; but that isn't the highest view to take of stealing. It is wrong in the sight of God."
>
> "That's what they told us at the Lodgin' House."
>
> "I hope you believe it."
>
> "Yes, sir, I believe it."
>
> "And if ever you are tempted to take anything that doesn't belong to you, think first that it will be displeasing to God. After that you may consider that it is bad policy also."

During this period, the heavy religious overtone was quite unusual for Horatio. Particularly since Brewster days, God had not played a very large role in his boys' books, strong as they were on 'morality.' But background is not to be denied, and occasionally, as Horatio grew older, his ministerial proclivities reasserted themselves. Usually they were sternly suppressed as the story moved on, as when Julius learned to milk a cow, to drive a rig and to get along in rural family life with the Taylors and their five-year-old daughter Carrie. One day he was tempted; he found Mr. Taylor's wallet containing a thick roll of bills on the seat of the rig. Wild dreams flashed through his head, but he suppressed them sternly and returned the wallet to his employer.

Julius went to school, and in the chapters on the school, Horatio brought forth an ignoramus who had somehow secured the post of teacher, although he could neither add nor subtract. This low comedy appealed to boys of the age.

Mr. Slocum, the foolish teacher, having once visited New York and paused long enough to buy a fifty-cent handkerchief at A. T. Stewart's department store, launched into a travelogue, his descriptions almost totally inaccurate.

> "Did you go to the Grand Duke's Opera-House?" Julius asked, raising his hand.
>
> "To be sure," said Mr. Slocum, supposing it to be a fashionable place of entertainment. "It is an elegant structure, worthy of the great city in which it was erected. I have never visited Europe, but I am told that none of the capital cities of the Old World can surpass it in grandeur."

Mr. Slocum was a riot. He declaimed for them a rousing version of the Seminole's Reply:

> "I've scared ye in the city
> "I've scalped ye on the plain; ...

All this was done with gestures, scalping when scalping was to be done, swimming when swimming was to be done, fists shaken when anger came. And then Mr. Slocum told the story of his grand adventure with a bear in the woods of Maine where he grew up—and where Horatio sometimes summered. He had backed down an angry bear, telling him to go back into the forest, which the bear did. The state of Maine gave him a gold medal, he said.

A tame bear lived in the village, and the boys tricked poor Mr. Slocum by luring him and pretending the bear was chasing them.

Mr. Slocum saw the bear, started to run and ran half a mile before he stopped. He learned at the village store that he had been hoaxed and vowed to revenge himself on the boys. When he tried to take vengeance the next day, he was stopped by the biggest boy in school. Mr. Slocum then attacked the boy just as the Reverend Mr. Brandon, a school trustee, stepped into the room and that was the end of Mr. Slocum. This alarum is good clean fun that Horatio put in his book as a pace-changer. It was very much a part of his style by this time.

Now, into Julius' life came a drunken Indian, who came to the Taylor door and demanded two dollars with which he would buy supplies. At home were Mrs. Taylor, the maid Jane and four-year-old Carrie Taylor.

"What do you want the money for?" asked Mrs. Taylor.

"Buy rum—good."

"Then I am sure I shall give you none. Rum is bad," said Mrs. Taylor.

"It makes Indian feel good."

"It may for a time, but it will hurt you afterwards. I will give you some meat and some coffee. That is better than rum."

"Don't want it," said the Indian obstinately. "Want money."

"You'd better give it to him ma'am and let him go," said Jane in a low voice.

"No," said Mrs. Taylor. "Mr. Taylor is very much opposed to it. The last time I gave money he blamed me very much. If he is not satisfied with coffee and meat, I shall give him nothing."

"Ugh! Ugh!" grunted the Indian, evidently angry.

"I'm afraid of him, mamma. He's so ugly," said Carrie, timidly, clinging to her mother's hand.

The Indian repeated his demand for money, and getting none, said something unintelligible in Indian and went away.

"He's the worst looking Indian I ever see," said Jane. "I don't want to set my eyes on him again. He ought to be ashamed, goin 'round asking for money, a great strong man like him. Why don't he work?"

"Indians are not very fond of working, I believe, Jane."

This poor victim of the white man's calumny was even then plotting a revenge, which, in Horatio's words "would strike anguish into the heart of all the household."

At this point Horatio's familiarity with the noble redskin was not very great. It was drawn largely from touching a handful of Cheyenne, Kiowa and Apache warriors who had been persuaded by P. T. Barnum to come to New York and allow themselves to be exhibited at his American museum. Barnum had been around New York for a long time. He had retired to his mansion, Iranistan, in Bridgeport, in the late 1850s, but in the 1870s he was back again in New York, almost larger than life. He opened his circus in Brooklyn in 1871, although he lived in a mansion on Murray Hill in Manhattan.

Barnum and Horatio came to know one another through their mutual interest in the Newsboy's Lodging House. Barnum was a generous figure, a big fat man with bushy eyebrows and a large nose, who liked the boys and tipped them extravagantly for running errands and shining shoes. After the circus was opened, several times a year he would come to the lodging house and distribute free passes to Superintendent O'Connor. The boys would go to the show in gangs, and Horatio would go with them. Barnum shared with Horatio and O'Connor the belief that temperance, frugality and hard work would carry a boy far, and he was very much behind O'Connor's scheme to move the boys out of New York and to such western places as Horatio had set the story of his Julius. When Horatio moved uptown to Thirty-fourth Street, not far from the Barnum mansion on Fifth Avenue, old P.T. would come by the lodging house from time to time and collect Horatio and give him a ride home in his fancy carriage. Never one to miss a publicity trick, Barnum was ever after Horatio to set one of his books within the Barnum scenario, and eventually out of all this conversation came *The Young Acrobat,* which was first serialized by *Golden Argosy.*

Barnum and Horatio shared another interest—temperance, and Horatio frequently persuaded Barnum to come and talk about the evils of drink to the boys. Then either or both of them would bring up the Great American dream. Work hard, keep your health and your manners, and you will get rich. To prove it Barnum would flash his beringed fingers and finger the diamond stickpin in his tie. He was a persuasive arguer for the Alger dream.

With Barnum, Horatio had touched Indians and seen them in the flesh and heard tales of their derring-do from P.T. himself. He was perfectly capable of presenting the stereotype that red-blooded American boys wanted in these years as Americans sought justification for driving the Indian westward and toward extinction.

Horatio's Indian, as might be suspected, had not gone far from the Taylor house after muttering his threats.

> He had been greatly incensed at the persistent refusal of Mrs. Taylor to supply him with rum, or the means of purchasing it. Years before, he had become a slave to the accursed fire-water, and it had become a passion with him to gratify his thirst. But it could not be obtained without money, and money was not to be had except by working for it or begging. Of these two methods, the Indian preferred the last.
>
> "Work is for squaws!" he said, in a spiteful and contemptuous manner. "It is not for warriors."

John, as this ignoble redskin was known by whites, decided in a flash that he would kidnap the little girl he had seen at the Taylor door. Carrie, the child, grew sleepy and lay down on the couch in the parlor conveniently near the open window. Now in any well-ordered farmhouse, children who were sleepy went to their beds, but that would have meant the second floor and a ladder. If Horatio had a fault, it was always to eschew the complex in favor of the simple. So Carrie lay down on the prickly horsehair sofa, her mamma tenderly put a cushion under her head, and in a trice Carrie was in the land of Nod. Moreover, just to make sure that all went as ordered, Dr. Alger put her "in the deep unconscious sleep of childhood."

Mrs. Taylor left the room. Like a flash bad John was through the window, and in a moment he was out on the lawn speeding away with the little girl in his arms. Earlier Horatio had demeaningly described John as "a shabby vagabond," quite unlike James Fenimore Cooper's Indians, a ne'er-do-well who sniveled among the white towns, begging for strong drink. It must have agreed with him, because the action ascribed to bad John in Horatio's kidnap scene would have fitted the character of a four-minute miler. Carrying this burden, he sped across the lawn and out of sight.

Mrs. Taylor was meandering about the house, unnoticing, when suddenly she came back and found Carrie gone. She went upstairs, sensibly assuming that the horsehair had gotten to Carrie—but—no Carrie. Mrs. Taylor called and hollered—to no avail. Then the horrid truth struck her: " 'The Indian has carried her off!' she exclaimed in anguish, and sank fainting to the floor." Curtain. Begin Chapter XXIII.

Horatio had to admit at the outset that the Indian was fleet-footed, if nothing else, but he was swift to assure his reader that this was no attribute of character. Bad John was fleet-footed "like most of his race."

Little Carrie slept the sleep of the just. She might have been in the rum bottle herself, so heavily did she slumber as he ran and ran and ran. But finally, after a mile or so, a stray twig touched her face and immediately she awoke and began to yell. " 'Where are you taking me, you ugly Indian? I want to go to my mamma.' "

Horatio's was scarcely the best way for the girl to reason with an angry, thirsty Indian. John was obdurate, and they argued. He told Carrie what he thought of her Mamma. " 'Bad woman! No give Indian money.' " Carrie, sly and wise to the ways of the world, now cajoled, " 'Take me home and she will give you money.' "

John was not fooled. He knew the way of the white man with a redskin.

> "Not now. Did not give before. Too late."
> "Are you going to keep me here? Will you never take me home?" asked Carrie, overwhelmed with alarm.

With a fine disregard of linguistic distinctions, Horatio's John replied:

"Little girl stay with Indian; be Indian's pickaninny."
"I don't want to be a pickaninny," said Carrie.

That logical objection entered, Carrie subsided and began to question the Indian about his habits. She discovered that he slept under trees, but that he also had a wigwam at some indefinable place off in the distance. Tonight, however, bed was to be under a tree. Carrie objected and dragged her heels. Horatio, who had read James Fenimore Cooper as well as anyone, then sent John striding through the forest, dragging little Carrie behind, until they came to the Indian's old bivouac, a handful of leaves with a few branches arched over.

He turned to the little girl and said, "This Indian's house."
"Where?" asked the child, bewildered.
"There," he said, pointing to the pile of leaves. "Suppose pickaninny tired; lie down."

Carrie was so tired she did not even think to tell Bad John that he might, possibly, under the circumstances call her papoose, but he really ought to stop calling her pickaninny. She sat down, exhausted.

But being a woman, in a few moments she was once again nagging poor John with questions about his private life. " 'Are you married?' she asked."

Horatio, being a bachelor, had a tendency to make his little girls a bit precocious.

Learning that John's squaw was dead, Carrie was almost overcome by compassion for him; but there was a slyness in it too. She suggested that if he had a little girl, he would not like to have someone carry her off.

John tired of the dialogue. " 'Little girl no talk. Indian tired. He go sleep.' "

Carrie subsided—but only for a while. Soon, she prodded the poor sleepy Indian. " 'Are there any lions in this wood?' she asked."

Showing "a disregard of truth more often to be found among civilized than barbarous nations" John assured her that the wood was virtually alive with lions. He began to snore, while Carrie sat quaking and waiting for the lions.

It was not Leo who peeked around the big tree behind them, but Julius, who showed up at the exact end of Chapter XXIII.

Back at the farm, where Horatio took his reader to open Chapter XXIV, no one questioned Mrs. Taylor's wild story that an Indian had carried Carrie off. Mr. Taylor soon showed up and dispatched the hired man in one direction with a gun, while he took a second gun and went another way. Julius asked for a gun and got a pistol. Of course, Julius took the right path and found little Carrie.

Indian John must have been a very heavy sleeper, for Carrie slipped away and immediately she and Julius began a whispered colloquy that would have awakened a guard on Blackwell's Island—but not big John. Julius had to tell Carrie that there were not, in fact, any lions in the woods. She was not quite certain, even with his assurances, but they plunged on, lost and stumbling about so noisily that they awakened John who "sprang to his feet with a cry of rage and disappointment." He looked about him and knew all. " 'Boy,' he muttered. 'Small foot. Come when Indian sleep. No matter. Me catch him.' "

In practically no time at all, John had found Small Foot and his pickaninny, stealthily crept up on them and seized Julius before he could unlimber the pistol. Here was a lesson to any boy: those trained in the jungle of the city ought to stay in their own bailiwick. " 'Me got you!' exclaimed the savage, in accents of fierce exultation."

Little Carrie uttered a dismal cry at the prospect of becoming a pickaninny once more, but Julius stood up manfully and argued the merits of the Indian's case. Let Carrie go home, he asked.

"No go. Mother bad," said the Indian.

"She isn't bad," said Carrie, forgetting her fear in her indignation. "She's good. You are bad."

"Hush, Carrie!" said Julius, who foresaw that it would not be prudent to provoke the savage.

Off they went in Indian file, John leading and dragging Carrie, with the assurance that Julius was bringing up the rear. But Julius was thinking furiously. He wrote a note to Mr. Taylor promising to drop pieces of paper to show their trail so that even a white man could follow it. He dropped the note and then began dropping his pieces of paper.

But John had eyes in the back of his head. Pushing through the thick woods while dragging Carrie, he still saw that Julius was dropping papers. " 'What for drop paper?' he demanded, seizing Julius roughly by the shoulder." And Julius explained that he was trying to attract the attention of Mr. Taylor, whereupon John made him pick up all the pieces of paper.

They surged meaningfully through the forest but ended up only at John's pile of leaves and sticks, and John sat down. He was not really a very crafty Indian; Julius still had his gun and two dollars, which he offered the Indian sensing, by ESP perhaps, that John had a taste for firewater—he had not been in on the explanations back at the farm.

Poor John was torn with conflicting emotions. On the one hand he wanted that firewater. On the other hand he did not want his captives to escape. But the firewater won out, as Horatio knew it would, and John tied Julius to a tree.

How Julius had ever gotten along this far was hard to understand. Now he could not even remember, as John went hurtling through the woods for his firewater, what he had done with his knife.

> "Feel in my pocket, Carrie," he said, "and see if I have a knife."
>
> Carrie, who was not tied up, obeyed, but the search was unavailing.
>
> "How unlucky!" said Julius, "I usually have it with me, but I remember leaving it in my other pants...."

Carrie was capable of feeling in pants pockets but not of untying ropes, so there they sat, waiting for rescue. Meanwhile Mr. Taylor and Abner had run around wildly until they bumped into each other and joined forces. They entered the woods and found Julius' note, but no papers.

Mr. Taylor was nonplused, being more or less of a city slicker on the farm, but Abner knew the ways of the wild.

> "There is another way we can track them," he said.
> "How is that?"

"Noticing where the grass and sticks are trodden over.
That's the way of Indians. We'll fight the red man in his own
way."

So they went on into the woods, Mr. Taylor complaining that
since his eyes were not so good Abner had better lead the way. And
Abner found the waifs, still sitting there, Julius not yet having
discovered that Carrie could untie his knots. Carrie was saved and
carried triumphantly back to her mother. Julius was a hero.

An hour later, poor John was found, dead drunk, on the side
of the road. He was arrested, tried and sentenced to a month in
jail, and then warned to get away from this neighborhood.

> The savage endured his imprisonment with the stoicism of his
> race, and on the day of his release departed, and was not again
> seen in Brookville.

Mr. Taylor deposited two hundred and fifty dollars in
Julius' bank account and advised Julius to buy a farm. There just
happened to be one for sale, for fifteen hundred dollars by a man
who wanted to move to Minnesota. So Julius bought it and
rented it out—Horatio explaining the world of business again.

Julius got into a scrape. On a business trip he was accosted
by one of his old enemies from the city and had to frighten him
with a loaded pistol before the evil one went away. This pistolier-
ing was something new for Horatio's heroes, but it met the literary demands of the youth of the day. When Horatio began
writing he would not have dreamed of letting his boys react with
such violence, but times had changed. It was quite the approved
ideal for young men to be junior Matt Dillons.

In the end, Julius stayed in the West and seemed likely to
grow rich managing Mr. Taylors' farms. A niece of Mrs. Taylor
showed up handily at the right time, like a heifer in the barn, and
at the end of the book it appeared likely that Julius was about to
be married. He made one last trip to New York to talk to the
newsboys at the Lodging House, where he delivered a plea for
right, justice and the good life:

> "Boys," he said, "it is but a few years since I was drifting
> about the streets like you, making my living by selling papers

and blacking boots, ragged and with a dreary prospect before me. I used to swear and lie, I remember very well, as I know many of you do. If I had stayed in the city I might be no better off now. But in a lucky moment I was induced by Mr. O'Connor to go West. There I found kind friends and a good home, and had a chance to secure a good education. Now I carry on a large farm for my benefactor and second father, as I consider him, and I hope in time to become rich. I tell you, boys, it will pay you to leave the city streets and go out West. You may not be as lucky as I was in finding rich friends, but it will be your own fault if you don't get along. There are plenty of homes waiting to receive you, and plenty of work for you to do. If you want to prosper, and grow up respectable, I advise you to come out as soon as you get the chance."

Thus endeth Horatio's most serious and heartfelt sermon.

Chapter Sixteen

Painting America

Publisher A. K. Loring was asked one day to place Horatio Alger, Jr., in his niche in the American literary scene. "Alger is the dominating figure of the new era," said the publisher. "In his books he has captured the spirit of reborn America. The turmoil of the city streets is in them. You can hear the rattle of pails on the farms. Above all you can hear the cry of triumph of the oppressed over the oppressor."

"What Alger has done," he added, "is to portray the soul,— the ambitious soul—of the country."

By 1875 Horatio had almost entirely settled on writing his books for boys and given up his ambition to become a grand novelist in the manner of Mark Twain or Bret Harte, whose books had seized the imagination of adult America even as Alger's captured the youth of the nation. In 1874, following the trip to Europe, Horatio wrote a travel article on Venice for *Young Israel*. Other than that his work consisted almost entirely of the books and serials that became books and short stories that usually served as the grains or outlines of new books.

The years 1872 and 1873 had been most prolific. Alger wrote many stories for *Gleason's* in addition to his books, and he scarcely slacked off in 1874. He had nearly given up writing poetry. But long association with his sister Olive Augusta, "Gusti" to him, had brought about a renewed interest in verse. In 1875 Loring (who probably shuddered a little) brought out *Grand'ther Baldwin's Thanksgiving,* a collection of Alger poems, and the same year published *Seeking His Fortune,* which was a collection of the dialogues written by Horatio and Gusti for *Student and Schoolmate.* In fact, all but one of these dialogues were Gusti's. Horatio had only written one dialogue and it was included. He also wrote the introduction and lent his name to the enterprise. That these books were brought out is adequate comment on his importance to Loring as a "property." As with many other writers, when he achieved the pinnacle of success, his publisher would venture almost anything under the name.

Loring even dredged up *Timothy Crump's Ward,* the adult novel of so many years earlier that had failed. Horatio rewrote it slightly to conform to his present style and the book was published as *Jack's Ward.*

But Horatio was also busy on new work. *Young Israel* was now his primary serial market, and for serialization in 1875 he wrote *Herbert Carter's Legacy: The Inventor's Son.* Over the years, Horatio's measure of success had changed a good deal; during the Civil War years he had been preoccupied with service to country and family. Since that time he had observed that the national interest in fortune far surpassed any interest in fame, and he had acted accordingly. The heroes of that contemporary British author, G. H. Henty, were young men who followed great leaders and made names for themselves by engaging in derring-do. Money, when it was mentioned at all by Henty, was simply necessary so that a man could become a hero in proper fashion. But for Horatio and most Americans in the last three decades of the nineteenth century, money was an end unto itself. The important thing was to get rich. Horatio's boys had one additional obstacle, they had to get rich honorably, which gave them a certain obstacle in American society, but still richness was its own reward. *Herbert Carter's Legacy,* quite properly, was dedicated to one of the richest young men Horatio knew, Alfred Lincoln Seligman, the son of the banker, whose prospects were solid gold. The story was in many ways the prototype of the Alger stories. "These stories," Horatio said, "have been intended to illustrate the proverb that 'God helps those who are willing to help themselves.' Those who sit down and wait passively for fortune to shower her gifts upon them are likely to wait a long time."

It is the old story of rags to riches—Herbert was braced in the opening sentence by a sneering snob, James Leech, who ridiculed his ragged clothes. Herbert, game fellow that he was, stood his ground and acted with manly forbearance, squelching his desire to sock James Leech in the eye. Manly forbearance was an important part of the Alger syndrome; it was all right to fight, or shoot someone, but only after Horatio had made it clear there was no other course.

Money makes its appearance in this book on page 12 with a thorough discussion of the Carter mortgage. A small cottage on a quarter acre of land, having cost fifteen hundred dollars, was mortgaged to Squire Leech, father of James, for seven hundred and fifty. Herbert's father, having built the house and borrowed the seven hundred and fifty to do so, immediately collapsed in a fit of some kind. He died, leaving the widow with the mortgage and very little prospect of paying it off.

> Upon this, interest was payable semi-annually at the rate of six percent. Forty-five dollars a year is not a large sum, but it seemed very large to Mrs. Carter, when added to their necessary expenses for food, clothing and fuel. How it was to be paid she did not exactly see. The same problem had perplexed Herbert, who, like a good son as he was, shared his mother's cares and tried to lighten them. But in a small village like Wrayburn, there are not many ways of getting money, at any rate for a boy. There were no manufacturies, as in some large villages, and money was a scarce commodity.

Herbert earned a pittance by running mail around town for the postmaster. Then, one day he received a letter edged in black, which announced that his rich Uncle Herbert, a man of substance as Herbert soon learned from his mother, was dead.

"Uncle Herbert was rich, wasn't he, mother."

"Yes, he must have left nearly a hundred thousand dollars."

"What a pile of money," said Herbert. "I wonder how a man feels when he is so rich. He ought to be happy."

"Riches don't always bring happiness. Uncle Herbert was disappointed early in life, and that seemed to spoil his career. He gave himself up to moneymaking and succeeded in it, but he lived by himself and had few sources of happiness."

In fact, as Mrs. Carter added, Uncle Herbert was an old miser. She had tried to tap the money tree once for a loan, and Uncle Herbert had written her that she ought to have saved up her own money.

Having paid lip service to the philosophy of happiness, Horatio began to consider what Herbert and his mother could do with some of Uncle Herbert's hoard and then hopefully sent Nephew Herbert to the funeral to see what was going to happen. Herbert walked twenty miles to Randolph, where he met Cornelius Dixon, another relative, a fop who hoped to get the fortune.

But Cornelius got only a hundred dollars "to buy a new looking glass and a suit of clothes"—a nasty dig from the grave, that was. And Herbert and his mother got nothing but a musty old black trunk and a hundred dollars too. The old skinflint had left his fortune to the town of Randolph to build a new brick high school to be named Carter School so that Herbert Carter would go down as a public benefactor.

Herbert and the lawyer opened the trunk, which was full of old clothes. One coat had fifty-two dollars in it which the old miser had apparently forgotten to bury in the ground, but otherwise the trunk was empty of anything apparently valuable.

Back at home, Squire Leech was planning to turn Herbert and his mother out of their house. He knew that they could not pay the mortgage and doubted if they could pay the interest on it. But Uncle Herbert's fifty-two dollars paid the interest off. Then Squire Leech offered three hundred dollars for the house, and Mrs. Carter indignantly refused. The squire, a stock figure Horatio had been using for years, had become consistently more heartless in each book. Now he was downright devilish.

"I'll have that place yet," he muttered to himself as he left the cottage, "I won't be balked by an obstinate woman and an impertinent boy."

Time passed, and Herbert and his mother stayed poor, while the inexorable demands of interest continued. It appeared that they would be unable to pay the interest on the mortgage and that Squire Leech would get the property, either outright, or for some ridiculously low sum.

Down to twenty-five dollars, Herbert's mother worried, as well she might, about the mortgage. Herbert, however, had the confidence of his youth and firmly believed that something would turn up, although there was virtually nowhere in the village of Wrayburn that one might find a job. The only employment that seemed to exist in the area was in the service of Squire Leech himself, or of his "superintendent," Mr. Banks. But Squire Leech only wanted the Carter house because Banks had taken a fancy to it. The plot, in fact, depends on Mr. Banks.

> It may be asked why Squire Leech needed a superintendent. To this I answer, that his property, beside the home farm, included two outlying farms, which he preferred to carry on himself rather than let to tenants. Besides he had stocks and bonds, to which he himself attended. But the farms required more attention than he individually was willing to bestow. Accordingly he employed a competent man, who had the general supervision of them.

One apparent weakness in the structure of *Herbert Carter's Legacy,* which not many boys would allow, was Horatio's dependence on the stupidity of Squire Leech and the stubborn demand of Mr. Banks for the small and not very pretentious Carter cottage. It would have been easy enough for the squire to build a house for his superintendent, but no, for plot purposes, Mr. Banks must simply covet the Carter place and none other would do. Encountering Herbert one day, when the young man was looking for work, Mr. Banks suggested that the Carters sell out. His mother would never agree, said Herbert.

"I may as well say," said the superintendent, "that the squire has authorized me to hire you to work, in case your mother consents to sell."

"Is that the condition?"

"Yes."

"Then," said Herbert turning away, "I am afraid that I must give up the chance."

"That's an obstinate boy," said Banks looking after him; "but he'll come round after a while. The squire says he'll have to, or be turned out for not paying the interest."

Since there was absolutely no place to find work, Herbert invented it. He made arrangements with Mr. Crane, the local carpenter, to sharecrop his vegetable garden. Then he hired Farmer Kimball to plow the field in question with his oxen.

"Wait a minute," said the farmer, cautiously, who's agoin to pay me?"

"Mr. Crane. He tole me to engage somebody, and he would pay the bill."

"That's all right then," said the farmer, in a tone of satisfaction. "Crane's a man that always pays his bills."

"I hope I shall have the same reputation," said Herbert.

"I hope you will, but you're only a boy, you know, and I couldn't collect of a minor. That's the law."

"I shouldn't think anybody'd be dishonest enough to bring that as an excuse."

"Plenty would do it, so I have to be careful. What time do you want me to do the work for you?"

Cynics might say that Horatio was here showing boys how they could bilk the world, but that kind of mind would accuse television of showing boys how to rob banks. Horatio was concerned here with indicating the hard nature of business and the need for a boy to preserve his reputation for probity from the start. It is another of the little moral lessons that made Sunday School superintendents sit up and take notice every time an Alger book was published.

Herbert Carter's Legacy represents Horatio at far from his best, and he seemed to know it. Having plunked Herbert down in Wrayburn, so pastoral a community that one could hear the crickets chirp in the leaves of the book, Horatio was having a bit of difficulty—unusual for him—in speeding the plot along. The reader might well ask why there had been 150 pages of sweat and strain about the interest if it was as easy as all that for Herbert to pick up a sharecropping deal. Horatio felt the need to explain:

> The reader will perhaps recall the statement in our first chapter that there was a little land connected with the cottage, which was used for the growth of vegetables.

Horatio had obviously forgotten the vegetable patch as the book moved along, and now in the arrangement with Carpenter Crane he had to deal with it. It has the ring of a question asked him by an editor. Rather than go back, rewrite the manuscript and change the plot line, Horatio chose to try to pull himself out of the hole otherwise, but somehow his explanation seemed lame, and it grew more complicated:

> This, in fact, supplied nearly all that was required, by the widow and her son, and the probability was that Herbert would be able to send to market nearly all his share of the vegetables obtained under his new contract, and thus obtain payment in money, of which they were so much in need.

Two pages later, he had already forgotten. In conversation with James Leech, he explained what he was up to.

> "I am to have a third of the crops to pay me for my services."
> "What can you do with it?"
> "Part of the vegetables we can use at home, and the balance I shall sell."

Why Herbert stopped working long enough to even talk to James Leech was a mystery. That Leech boy was a dreadful snob and a bore as well. But he could have his uses, as to show the reader just what life was all about.

> "Don't it tire you to work?" asked James, with some curiosity.

"Of course, if I work all day, but I don't mind that."

"I should."

"You are not used to work."

"I should say not," returned James with pride. "I never worked in my life."

It was a strange thing to be proud of, but there are some who have nothing better to be proud of.

"I like to work," said Herbert.

"You do?"

"Yes, only I like to get something for my labor. You expect to work sometime, don't you?"

"Not with my hands," said James. "I shall never be reduced to that."

"Do you think it so very bad to work with your hands? Isn't it respectable?"

"Oh, I suppose its respectable," said James; "but only the lower classes do it."

"Am I one of the lower classes?" asked Herbert, amused.

"Of course you are."

"But suppose I should get rich some day," said Herbert.

"That isn't very likely. You can't get rich raising vegetables."

"No, I don't expect to. Still, I may in some other way. Didn't you ever know any poor boys that got rich?"

"I suppose there have been some," admitted James.

"Haven't you ever heard of Vanderbilt?"

"Of course I have. Father says he's worth forty millions."

"Don't you consider him a gentleman?"

"Of course I do."

"Well, he was a poor boy once, and used to ferry passengers across from Staten Island to New York."

Vanderbilt was in fact the precise epitome of the Horatio Alger hero. He had indeed ferried passengers from Stapleton, Staten Island, over to the Battery in his salad days. Thence he had risen to be a steamboat captain. By hooks and crooks to which Horatio shut his eyes, Vanderbilt had acquired a line of steamboats. By cheating passengers and often endangering their lives he had acquired a line of steamships in the California trade, hauling passengers from New York to Panama, carrying them across the isthmus in carriages and running another Vanderbilt wooden steamer on the other side to San Francisco. By selling rotting ships to the Union forces in the Civil War he had acquired a sizable fortune. By manipulating stocks and men he had acquired control of the rail lines that served New York from the north and west, and had combined them into the New York Central system. By this time Vanderbilt was the richest man in America, with more capital on hand than existed in cash in the United States treasury.

But a gentleman? Not on your tintype. Horatio might think that Vanderbilt had become a gentleman, but Mrs. Astor knew better, and as long as she lived he was not to grace the dining tables of the fierce little coterie of fur traders, land speculators, usurious bankers and indolent inheritors who called themselves New York Society. Vanderbilt's rough-hewn farmer son would aspire to be a gentleman, his grandchildren would claim they were gentlemen, and the great grandchildren would have acquired the patina of old money even as the basis for the fortune was destroyed. Horatio, however, never delved deeply into the social implications of money. He was content that his heroes should aspire to it, make it and enjoy it. The conversation with James Leech is the Alger philosophy boiled down to its essence; here was Herbert Carter, young American manhood, on the right track.

Considering the lightning speed with which Horatio moved his reader halfway around the world in *Brave and Bold* or whisked Harry Raymond out to the Australian goldfields in *Sink or Swim,* the action in *Herbert Carter's Legacy* moved at a snail's pace. Horatio seemed bound to rise to the attack on snobbery and to prove that poor boys could, indeed get rich, in spite of such obstacles as the Leeches.

> "Herbert says he hopes to be rich some time."
> "I dare say," said the squire, laughing heartily. "Everybody does, so far as I know."
> "Do you think there is any chance of it?"
> "About one in a thousand."
> "I shouldn't want the lower classes to get rich," said James thoughtfully, "They'd think they were our equals."
> "Yes, no doubt."

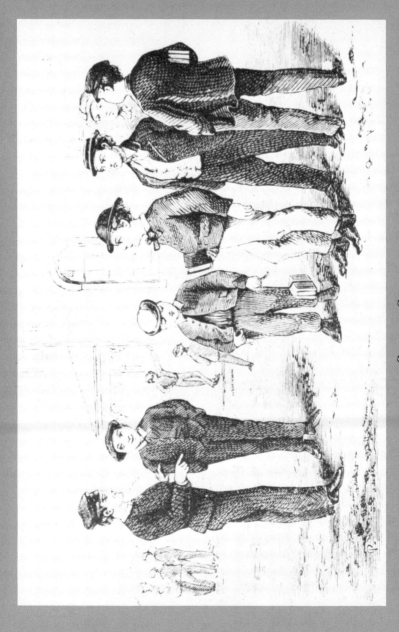

Sink or Swim:
Harry Raymond's Resolve

So, Squire Leech, whose own father had started life as a poor mechanic, made ready to foreclose on poor Mrs. Carter and take her home.

Squire Leech came to collect, and in spite of Herbert's good fortune, the Carters could fork over only fifteen dollars cash; the interest was twenty-two fifty. The squire refused to accept a penny less, and all seemed lost as he took his cane and left the house, but just then, Herbert remembered he had a letter from the post office in his pocket for his mother. He handed it over, she opened it, and out fell twenty dollars, a gift from an aunt she had not heard from for years; the squire, who was returning in a few moments to foreclose, was foiled again!

All the adventures of Herbert Carter are very low key. Much is made of a boatrace between Herbert and James Leech, much is made of the coming of a stranger to town to see Squire Leech, a very seedy stranger. Indeed, compared to other books, much is made of virtually nothing at all, and the biggest excitement comes when Herbert floors James Leech with a roundhouse punch.

The pallor of James Leech was matched by that of the plot James tried to get Mr. Cameron, a Yale man who had hired Herbert to read to him, to fire Herbert because of his rudeness. Mr. Cameron refused, but then he went off to see his doctor, who suggested a sea voyage for Mr. Cameron's eyes. Off he went to Rio de Janeiro, unaware of what happened to other Alger characters who found themselves in those dangerous waters. So Herbert was on his own again in the stagnant labor market of Wrayburn, and the interest on the mortgage was about to raise its ugly head for the third time in the book.

But there was a spark to come. The seedy stranger had persuaded Squire Leech to invest heavily in New York stocks, and the squire was counting his profits already. Herbert went to New York to seek a cousin and his fortune, and the street boys appeared to talk to him and liven up the tale.

> He kept on his way, attracting some attention as he walked. The city Arab knows a stranger by instinct.
> "Carry your bundle mister." asked a ragged urchin.
> "No thank you, I can carry it myself."
> "I won't charge you much. Take you to any hotel in the city."

HERBERT CARTER'S LEGACY:
THE INVENTOR'S SON

"I don't think I shall go to any hotel. I can't afford it. Can you show me a cheap boarding house?"

"Yes," said the boy, "What'll you give?"

"Ten cents."

"That ain't enough. It wouldn't keep me in cigars an hour."

"Do you smoke?" asked Herbert, surprised.

"Of course I do. I've smoked for four or five years."

"How old are you?"

"The old woman says I'm ten. She ought to know."

"It isn't good for boys to smoke," said Herbert, gravely.

"Poo bosh! dry up. All us boys smoke."

Herbert felt that his advice was not called for and he came to business.

"I'll give you fifteen cents," he said. . . .

That dialogue, with nothing at all to do with the tale at hand, is among the liveliest bits in the book. It rings with truth about the street boys, whose ignorance of virtue was as certain as Herbert's pretensions to it.

Then, Herbert shook the boy off and found Cornelius Dixon, the connection he had met at the reading of his uncle's will. He then became a New York newsboy and immediately ran into James Leech on the street—it seemed that all of Wrayburn had suddenly descended on New York. The fact was that Squire Leech had come to check on his investments and was not yet aware that he was being gulled by the mysterious seedy stranger who was in reality stealing his money. To support his new investments Squire Leech now had to sell or mortgage most of his real estate on the hope of doubling his money in a few months. The Squire had gambling fever, for sure.

Selling his papers, Herbert ran into old Mr. Cameron, the father of the Yale man. Now one of the last things the Yale man had done for Herbert was to take a funny-looking model of an invention and send it to his father for comment. Mr. Cameron had not looked at it yet, but now he promised to do so. The nature of the invention remained a deep secret all through the book; "I do not propose to give a detailed account of the invention. It would not prove interesting to my young readers, who will care only to know how far its value was likely to help the fortunes of our hero," said Horatio. The invention was something

HERBERT CARTER'S LEGACY:
THE INVENTOR'S SON

Herbert's father had been tinkering with all those years instead of paying off Squire Leech's mortgage, and it was of such little importance to the story that it was not even introduced until page 251—and then not mentioned again until page 306.

But of course, the invention turned out to be the key to fame and fortune for Herbert Carter. Herbert went to the Cameron house, and on the fourth day Mr. Cameron came to talk to him:

"Well, Herbert, I have made up my mind about your father's invention."

Herbert's suspense was great. His heart almost stopped beating.

The manufacturer went on.

"I consider it practicable, and am disposed to make you an offer for it. Are you authorized to conclude terms?"

"My mother will agree to anything I propose, sir."

"Then this is my offer. The model must be patented at once. I will see to that. Then make me over half the invention, and I will agree to pay you and your mother one thousand dollars a year for the next ten years."

So Herbert's future was assured. His mother could keep the house, and, of course, she no longer wanted it. They decided to move to a town where there was a fine academy that Herbert could attend.

As if the reader had not had enough of Squire Leech, almost immediately he was back again, nagging about the interest and pressing Mrs. Carter to sell her house for a paltry three hundred and fifty dollars. But as soon as he learned that Herbert and his mother were rich, he offered them their price, which was six hundred dollars above the mortgage, and they unloaded the place on him. Two years went by. Herbert finished the academy and had a job waiting as a clerk in Mr. Cameron's manufactory; Horatio promised his readers that soon Herbert would be a junior partner. The invention, whatever it was, turned out to be a whopping success and brought in lots of money to the Carters. Squire Leech, deceived by the seedy stranger, lost everything but a few thousands that would keep him out of the poorhouse. Poor James Leech had to get a job in a dry goods store and work with his hands—horror of horrors. But he saw how times had changed and was glad to be acknowledged as the companion of Herbert, who bore no grudges for all the mean things James had said about his mother. When one is rich it is easy to forgive a lot. Herbert had done all the things an Algerian hero need do, and he received his creator's benediction:

> For our young friend Herbert, we may confidently indulge in cheerful anticipations. He has undergone, the discipline of poverty and privation, and prosperity is not likely to spoil him. He has done his duty under difficult circumstances, and now he reaps his reward.

Vanderbilt was warned. Let him look out for Herbert.

Chapter Seventeen

Shifting With the Wind

A STRANGER to the works of Horatio Alger, Jr. coming across *Herbert Carter's Legacy* would wonder what all the shouting was about. It was an incredibly bad book, but the very factors that made it a bad book also made the story an incredibly good and successful magazine serial. Episode by episode, the serial had to stand on its own feet and thrill the young reader, and Horatio, being an old hand at serial writing, knew just how to do this, even in so limited a sphere as Wrayville. That is why the mortgage appears so many times, why every three or four chapters there is a climax—each climax ends a serial episode.

The first climax comes at the end of the will reading in which Herbert was left a tin trunk, others were left little bits which did not please them and the town of Randolph got the old miser's fortune, kit and caboodle. " 'That is all,' said the lawyer, and he laid down the will upon the table."

Chapter V picks up the action there and the next episode runs until the end of Chapter VIII, which has as its climax the offer of Squire Leech to take over the widow Carter's house for three hundred and fifty dollars cash and her refusal. As already reported, every boy reader is stirred by the ending of the chapter:

> "I'll have that place yet," he muttered to himself, as he left the cottage. "I won't be balked by an obstinate woman and an impertinent boy."

The demands of serialization also account for much of the awkwardness of the published book. Not only did the story ebb and flow like the tides around Rio de Janeiro, but once a chain of events was set in motion it either had to be completed or at least diverted. And the pressures on Horatio to produce the serial episodes in time for the next issue seemed to preclude the normal outlining process by which an author usually manages to keep track of his characters and their motivations and avoid inextricable situations or forgetful lapses. The problem of the vegetable garden is a case in point; Horatio seems to have quite forgotten that he gave Mrs. Carter a vegetable garden in Chapter I, so when he put Herbert in the vegetable business in Chapter XIV he had to do some tall explaining to his readers; he could not simply go back and make a change in the beginning because the beginning had already been printed.

For an optimum appreciation of Horatio's narrative ability and his impact on boys of the 1870s and thereafter, then, a reader should go back to the magazines, at least for the serial books. The other books, written truly as books, do not suffer from the same complaints.

Horatio's book for the year 1874, published by Loring, was a departure from his previous works in a significant fashion. Heretofore in his street stories, Horatio had in his words "endeavored to show that even a street boy, by enterprise, industry, and integrity, may hope to become a useful and respected citizen." In this new book, *The Young Outlaw: Adrift in the Streets,* Horatio wanted to show what happened to boys who did not exhibit these strengths of character. It was indeed, a different approach to life.

The Young Outlaw opens in a normal Alger fashion, the countryman coming to the city and asking a boy directions. The boy asked for ten cents to tell him anything, and then "chaffed" with the stranger, as they walked along, in search of Canal Street. The stranger handed over the dime:

> "There my boy, show me the way. I should think you might have done it for nothing."
> "That ain't the way we do business in the city, gov'nor."
> "Well, go ahead, I'm in a hurry."
> "You needn't be, for *this* is Canal Street," said the boy, edging off a little.
> "Then you've swindled me," said the deacon, wrathfully, "give me back that ten cents."

The street Arab was certainly not of the variety of Ragged Dick, who would never have cheated a stranger so brassily. No, he was Sam Barker, a boy from rural Connecticut. The venerable Deacon John Hopkins did not recognize him and was taken for another dime on a bet. Then Sam was off like a flash.

> "Stop you, Sam," he shouted.
> But Sam, with his head over his shoulder, already three rods in advance, grinned provokingly, but appeared to have no intention of stopping. The deacon was not used to running, nor did he make due allowance for the difficulty of navigating the crowded streets of the metropolis. He dashed headlong into an apple-stand, and suffered disastrous shipwreck. The apple-stand was overturned, the deacon's hat flew off, and he found himself sprawling on the sidewalk, with apples rolling in all directions around him, and an angry dame showering maledictions upon him and demanding compensation for damages.

As for Sam, he was around the corner, laughing until he thought his sides would split.

> "I never had such fun in all my life," he ejaculated, with difficulty, and he went off into fresh convulsion. "The old feller won't forget me in a hurry."

Here *was* a new kind of hero for Horatio. That first chapter gave promise of new directions; no moralizing, no good works, just a street boy taking a rube in the time-honored fashion.

Sam had been a street boy for nearly three years. The boy had been orphaned in the little Connecticut town where Deacon Hopkins lived, but he had no cause to regret his father's death.

> He had received many a beating from his father in his fits of drunken fury, and had been obliged to forage for himself for the most part, getting a meal from one neighbor, a basket of provisions from another, and so managed to eke out a precarious existence in the tumble down shanty which he and his father occupied.

Father dead, Sam could have gone on living as he was, but society decreed that he must go to the poorhouse if no one would take him as a worker. Deacon Hopkin, estimating that he could get a good deal of work out of Sam at very little expense, had taken him in as a gesture of Christian charity.

Sam was the trial of the household. His hero was Captain Kidd, the pirate. He had never read the Bible, and he balked at reading the catechism the deacon bought him for a dime. After dinner, at which Sam ate twice as much as anyone else and was refused the last piece of pie, the deacon put him on the catechism. But instead, Sam sneaked out for a walk in the woods.

When he came back the deacon asked if he had studied the lesson. Sam said he had, but he could not answer questions about it.

> "Then you told me a lie. You said you studied the lesson."
> "I didn't understand it."
> "Then you should have studied longer. Don't you know it is wicked to lie?"
> "A feller can't tell the truth all the time," said Sam, as if he were stating a well-known fact.
> "Certainly he can," said the deacon. "I always do."
> "Do you?" inquired Sam, regarding the old man with curiosity.

In the middle of the night, a hungry Sam went downstairs after that last piece of pie and broke some plates, then stepped on the cat's tail; the resulting noise was tremendous. A quaking Deacon Hopkin refused to go down and face "the burglars," but Mrs. Hopkin went down with her lamp. Sam had fled back upstairs and was feigning sleep, but she was a wise woman and guessed he had been after the pie.

Out hoeing potatoes, Sam was beguiled into wasting his time, to the anger of the Deacon. Then Sam hoed the Deacon's foot and hurt his corns, whereupon the deacon erupted in hurt rage. In all this low comedy Alger unmasked the deacon, a God-fearing hypocrite, as a most unadmirable character. What could Horatio be doing—abandoning his moral tales of righteous people? These people, including the deacon, were far more interesting than Alger's usual cast. They had shown no moral stature to which anyone could point with pride, and the young reader's sympathy was all with Sam.

Sam played sick, and the deacon's wife, who was no fool, fed him a cup of wormwood tea, a specific, she said, for what ailed him. When he tasted it and refused, she promised him a dose of castor oil instead. He drank the tea.

> "It was awful," said Sam to himself, as his nurse left him alone. "I'd rather hoe potatoes than take it again. I never see such a terrible old woman. She would make me do it, when I wasn't no more sick than she is."
>
> Mrs. Hopkins smiled to herself as she went downstairs.
>
> "Served him right," she said to herself. "I'll larn him to be sick. Guess he won't try it again very soon."
>
> Two hours later Mrs. Hopkins presented herself at Sam's door.

This time it *was* castor oil, and that prospect drove Sam back to the potato field, hoe over shoulder.

For a month Sam labored in the fields of the Deacon, eating heartily and making a bad impression on Mrs. Hopkins.

> "You'd better send him to the poorhouse deacon," she said more than once. "He's the most shif'less boy I ever see, and its awful the amount he eats."

Then one day came temptation. A man gave Sam a note for the deacon and when Sam got home late, after the deacon had gone to bed, he opened the letter in his own room and found ten dollars. Up before dawn, he took the money and headed for New

York. The deacon did not try to find him until he discovered that Sam had taken his ten dollars.

> "Bless my soul! I didn't think Sam was so bad," ejaculated the Deacon.
> "Didn't you go after him?"
> "No, he wasn't very good to work, and I thought I'd let him run. Ef I'd knowed about the money, I'd have gone after him."

So Sam went to New York, and Horatio told just how in detail. He took the train, accompanied an old lady, and they ate crackers and apples on the way. In New York he met a bootblack who blacked his shoes and showed him a cheap place to eat. In the manner of an Alger hero, Sam treated the other boy to a second helping of dinner and made a friend. But he had to find a bed, and in his searches he encountered a man named Clarence Brown who offered to help him. Brown took Sam to a humble room on Leonard Street, borrowed a quarter from him, bought some whiskey, tried to persuade him to play cards, and when Sam was lulled asleep by the drink, Clarence Brown robbed him of his fortune of six dollars and ten cents.

In the morning, not knowing he had been robbed, Sam went to a restaurant and ate a fifty-cent breakfast. Then he told how he had spent the night and how he must have been robbed, but the proprietor had heard such tales before:

> "A dead beat; but you don't play any of your games on me young man. I've cut my eyeteeth, I have. You don't swindle me out of a fifty cent breakfast quite so easily. Here, John, call a policeman."
> "Oh, don't call a policeman," exclaimed Sam, terror-stricken. It's true, every word I've told you. I'm from the country. I only got to the city yesterday, and I've been robbed of all my money, over six dollars. I hope you'll believe me."
> "I don't believe a word you say," said the restaurant keeper harshly.

One thing led to another; a regular customer of the restaurant said that Sam looked like a country boy to him, and the proprietor was unsure enough to drop the idea of calling a policeman.

"I won't give you in charge this time, thought I ought to; but I'll give you something to settle your breakfast. Here, Peter, you waited on this young man didn't you?"

"Yes, sir."

"He hasn't paid for his breakfast, and he pretends he hasn't got any money. *Bounce him!*

Whereupon Sam and Horatio's readers were introduced to an old Bowery custom—something that could not possibly have befallen one of those goody-two shoes heroes of previous Alger books.

If Sam was ignorant of the meaning of the word "Bounce" he was soon enlightened. The waiter seized him by the collar, before he knew what was going to happen, pushed him to the door, and then, lifting his foot by a well directed kick, landed him across the sidewalk into the street.

This proceeding was followed by derisive laughter from the other waiters who had gathered near the door, and it was echoed by two street urchins, who witnessed Sam's ignominious exit from the restaurant.

Humiliated and unhappy, for a time Sam wished he was back at the Deacon's. But he set out to make his way. Horatio had to stop here—page 135—for a little moralizing; one could not be Horatio Alger with his background and simply tell the tale of Sam the street boy without asides.

Boys who have a good home are apt to undervalue it. They do not realize the comfort of having their daily wants provided for without any anxiety on their part. They are apt to fancy that they would like to go out into the great world to seek their fortunes. Sometimes it may be necessary and expedient to leave the safe anchorage of home and brave the dangers of the unknown sea but no boy should do this without his parents' consent, nor then, without making up his mind that he will need all his courage and all his resolution to obtain success.

Trying to get work, Sam had to tell a lot of lies about his background; he still did not get the job he sought. A stranger asked him the way to the *Tribune* office; Sam did not know and asked a bootblack, who pointed to a building; Sam passed on the information and got a dime. He had, in fact, directed the man to the Tombs, the city prison.

Sam encountered Clarence Brown again and accused him of theft, but was talked out of the accusation. Brown gave Sam a cigar, which made him sick. When he recovered, Clarence Brown was long gone.

Sam then took up with another street boy and learned the ropes. They slept in an old wagon near the North River. The next morning they made their way to the river, and when a steamer came in, offered to carry baggage. Sam caught on quickly enough, and so he had a profession.

In its portrayal of city types, and in the reality of its action, *The Young Outlaw* is one of Horatio's truly superior books. Unhampered by the need to construct a series of stories within a story to keep serial readers amused and excited, Horatio was able to take his time and give a little thought to characters and situations. Because of this I feel there is no risk of boring the reader by giving more than a synopsis of the book. Had Horatio continued to write subsequent books as well as he did *The Young Outlaw,* his literary reputation would have been established.

Sam's life was the hard life of all the street boys Alger knew in the Newsboy's Lodging House rolled up into one. In *The Young Outlaw* Horatio gave his most impressive portrayal of street life since *Ragged Dick.*

> On the strength of his good luck, Sam provided himself with a good breakfast, which cost him forty cents. He felt pretty sure of earning something more during the day to add to the remaining thirty-five. But Fortune is capricious, and our hero found all his offers of service firmly refused. He tried again to excite compassion by his fictitious story of a starving family at home; but his appeals were made to the flinty hearted or the incredulous. So, about two o'clock he went to dinner, and spent the remainder of his money.
>
> Again he spent the night with Tim in the wagon, and again in the morning he set out to earn his breakfast. But luck was against him. People insisted on carrying their own carpet-bags, to his great detriment in the baggage smashing business. Tim was no luckier than Sam.

The hungry boys, then decided to approach an old apple woman and persuade her to trust them for a few apples to hold them until they were able to earn some money; or, rather Sam, with his green optimism about city character hoped to get credit.

"Wouldn't she trust?"

"Not much," said Tim, "You try her if you want to."

"I will," said Sam, desperately.

The two boys approached the applestand.

"I say," said Sam to the wrinkled old woman who presided over it, "how do you sell apples?"

"A penny a piece," she answered in a cracked voice. "Is that cheap enough for ye?"

"I'll take five—" said Sam.

The old woman began eagerly to pick out the required number, but stopped short when he finished the sentence,—"if you'll trust me till afternoon."

"Is it trust ye?" she ejaculated suspiciously. "No farther than I can see yer. I'm up to your tricks, you young spalpeen, thryin' to chate a poor widder out of her money."

"I'll pay you sure," said Sam, "but I haven't earned anything yet today."

"Then its that I can't be supportin' a big strong boy like you. Go away and come back, whin you've got the money." Here Tim broke in.

"My friend always pays his bills," he said. "You needn't be afraid to trust him."

"And who are you?" asked the old woman. "I don't know you, and I can't take your word. You're tryin, the two of you, to swindle a poor widow."

"My father's an Alderman," said Tim, giving the wink to Sam.

"Is he now? Thin, let him lind your friend money, and don't ask a poor woman to trust."

"Well, I would, but he's gone to Washington on business."

"Thin go after him and leave me alone. I don't want no spalpeens like you round my apple stand."

"Look here old woman, I'll have you arrested fer callin' me names. Come away, Sam, her apples are rotten anyhow."

Infuriated, the old woman began berating them. The boys went off, and only then did Sam discover that while he had been carrying the conversation, Tim had quietly been filching apples. Horatio, again, had to pay obeisance to his moral code, but it was much briefer than usual:

> Sam ought to have felt uneasy at appropriating the result of a theft, but his conscience was an easy one and he felt hungry. So he made short work of the apple, and wished for more.
>
> "I wish you'd taken two a piece," he said.
>
> " I couldn't," said Tim. "She'd have seen 'em stickin' out of my pocket and called a cop."
>
> "One's better than none; I feel a little better," said Sam philosophically. "I s'pose it's stealin' though."
>
> "What's the odds? She'll never miss 'em. Come along."

So Sam became a street boy for sure, and Tim taught him the ropes. Sam blacked boots for a while, paying half his receipts to the boy who owned the box. But he cheated his employer and was fired. He could have saved and bought his own box and brush, but whenever he had money he spent it on food. He learned about the Newsboy's Lodging House and went there. Interrogated by Superintendent O'Connor, he told a pack of lies about his background and his life, for he did not wish to be sent back to his home town in Connecticut. O'Connor knew, they were lies, he had had plenty of experience with street boys, but he was summing Sam up on quite different grounds. So Sam was admitted to the place, and for eighteen cents a day he had a bed and two meals. When he earned enough money he had lunch and sometimes a ticket to the old Bowery theater—and he was happy.

> It is hardly necessary to say that in a moral point of view he had deteriorated rather than improved. In fact, he was rapidly developing into a social outlaw, with no particular scruples against lying or stealing. One thing may be said in his favor, he never made use of his strength to oppress a younger boy. On the whole he was good-natured and not brutal. He had on one occasion interfered successfully to protect a young boy from one of greater strength who was beating him. I like to mention this, because I do not like to have it supposed that Sam was wholly bad.

Then one day as Sam was lounging against a building on Broadway, he saw a little old man stumble and turn his ankle in getting off the Broadway stage. Sam helped him up the stairs in the building to his office, and the old man, who turned out to be Dr. Felix Graham "the celebrated corn-doctor," offered Sam a job distributing fliers that said:

DR. FELIX GRAHAM
Chiropodist
Corns and bunions cured without pain
Satisfaction guaranteed
Broadway, Room 10

Sam would get ten cents a hundred for distributing the papers. Horatio indulged his sense of humor in describing Sam's attempts to unload the papers. Horatio's treatment of city types, though brief, is skillfully funny. First Sam approached a gentleman and lady. The gentleman was dressed like a dude, and from his tight boots and the way he walked, Sam judged him to be a candidate for Dr. Graham's services. But no, not at all, that was just the way the fashionable always seemed to walk. Then Sam came up to an old lady.

"Have you got corns, ma'am?" asked Sam eagerly.

Now it so happened that the lady was a little deaf, and did not understand Sam's question. Unfortunately for herself, she stopped short and inquired, "What did you say?"

"I guess she's hard of hearing," Sam concluded, and raising his voice loud enough to be heard across the street, he repeated his question:

"HAVE YOU GOT CORNS, MA'AM?"

At the same time he thrust a circular into the hand of the astonished and mortified lady. Two school-girls behind heard the question, and laughed heartily. The offended lady dropped the paper as if it were contamination, and sailed by, her sallow face red with anger.

"That's funny," thought Sam. "I don't know what's got into all the people. Seems to me they're ashamed of having corns."

Along came a countryman who allowed that he had two corns and that they hurt "like time." What did the doctor charge? Sam had no idea, but he had already assumed the superior wisdom of the street boy, who must answer every question as if he did know, so he said that corn removal cost ten cents a corn! The country fellow went up to the office and came down furious.

"Look here, boy," he said angrily; "you told me a lie."

"How did I?" asked Sam.

"You told me the doctor only charged ten cents for each corn. Jerusalem! He made me fork out a dollar."

Sam was rather surprised himself at the price.

"I guess they was tough ones, mister," he said. He cured 'em, didn't he?"

"Ye---es."

"Then its worth the money. You don't want 'em back do you?"

"No," admitted the other, "but its a thunderin' sight to pay," and he went off grumbling.

"Don't the doctor make money, though?" thought Sam. "He'd orter give me a commission on them two dollars."

Sam tried to collect his commission and convinced the doctor that the man had come up, not because of the circular, but because of Sam's sales talk. So he got an extra quarter and a hundred more circulars. Another fop came along, a foil for Horatio's low comedy.

A young dandy advanced, dressed in the height of fashion, swinging a light cane in his lavender gloved hand. A rose was in his buttonhole, and he was just in the act of saluting a young lady, when Sam thrust a circular into his hand.

"Go right upstairs," he said, "and get your corns cured. Only a dollar."

The young lady burst into a ringing laugh, and the mortified dandy reddened.

"Keep your dirty paper to yourself, boy," he said. "I am not troubled with those—ah, execrescences."

"I never heard of them things," said Sam.

"I said corns."

Sam was persistent and good natured, and he soon had nearly a dollar. But even better, he was given a job as Dr. Graham's office boy, with a weekly salary of four dollars. The doctor had a boy two years older, and he gave Sam a clean neat gray suit that fit and ordered Sam to wash more carefully than usual and become a creditable-looking boy. And then, one day when the doctor was out, in the manner of the Sorcerer's apprentice, Sam decided to become assistant doctor. He operated on a corn for a young Irishman and got into trouble.

> The knife slipped, inflicting a deep gash, and causing a quick flow of blood.
> "O murder, I'm kilt," exclaimed the terrified patient, bounding to his feet and rushing frantically around the room. "I'm bladin' to death."
> Sam was almost equally frightened. He stood, with the knife in his hand, panic-stricken.
> "I'll have you up for murder, I will!" shouted Mr. Dennis O'Brien, clutching the wounded member. "Oh, why did I ever come to a boy doctor? Oh, whirra, whirra!"

Sam was sent out to find a doctor, and just as he opened the door, in came Dr. Graham. The doctor was not pleased to learn that Sam had been playing chiropodist; Sam agreed that he had done wrong. All went well, then for several weeks, until Dr. Graham gave Sam a letter to take to his wife in Brooklyn. Unfortunately, the letter contained twenty dollars to pay a bill. Sam started out but fell in with evil companions. Soon the letter was open and the money removed. The boys went first to a pool hall and then to a saloon where they drank whiskey punches.

Sam was lightheaded and dizzy. He also had a fit of conscience, which his friend Jim tried to use to get the money away from him.

> "I guess not," said Sam, significantly. "Maybe I wouldn't find it any easier if you took it."
> "You don't call me a thief, do you?" demanded Jim, offended.
> "It looks as if we was both thieves," said Sam, candidly.

Sam went back to his employer with a cock-and-bull story about being robbed, and Dr. Graham almost believed him, until

THE YOUNG OUTLAW:
ADRIFT IN THE STREETS

his story was exposed by a man who had been on the ferry. But Sam, conscience stricken and afraid of being sent to Blackwell's Island, agreed to help get the money back from Jim, who had taken most of it. Sam was fired at the end of the week, but the doctor paid him off and bore him no ill will. He simply said they had to part company. "You are a little too enterprising for me," he added.

A hungry Sam was standing in front of a saloon a few days later, when Mr. Pipkin, the owner, took pity on him and gave him a chance to earn his dinner by distributing circulars. He had the job for a week, but his appetite was too much for Mr. Pipkin, so he lost the job.

Then two years went by in which Sam made his living by his wits, until the day he encountered Deacon Hopkins. That same day he was accosted by a four-year-old boy who was lost. The boy knew his name and that he had been playing in a park. Using his brains, Sam found a city directory, looked under the boy's name for an address near Union park and took the child home. And so the Daltons—for that was the name of the family— gave him a meal, and Mr. Dalton gave him a job as an errand boy in his office at five dollars a week.

> Sam's chance had come. He was invited to fill a humble but respectable position. Would he give satisfaction, or drift back after a while to his vagabond habits? Young outlaw as he had been, was he likely to grow into an orderly member of society?

Horatio alone knew the answer, but he proposed to share it with his readers.

> If any of my readers are curious on this subject they are referred to the next volume of this series, entitled
>
> SAM'S CHANCE:
> And How He Improved It.

Horatio Alger, Jr. had struck oil again.

Chapter Eighteen

Horatio Out West

In the last few months of 1875 Horatio was writing two more books; one was the serial for *Young Israel* in 1876 which would be *Shifting For Himself: Gilbert Greyson's Fortune,* and the other was the sequel to Sam's adventures that he had planned knowing his street boy books were the best he did.

The first book was a variation on an old Alger theme—the rich boy who goes down on his luck. Gilbert Greyson was rich but not stuck up about it. The mother of his friend John Munford, a simple carpenter's wife, summed him up for Horatio's readers:

> "I like Gilbert. Though he is rich, he doesn't put on airs, but makes himself at home even among such plain people as we are."

That statement, of course, is as unlikely a bit of dialogue as Horatio ever invented. It was odd how Horatio could capture the essence of New York street talk yet go all stilted and unbelievable when he wrote of the plain people among whom he had grown up. But the truth is that any elements of greatness in the Alger books exist in the street tales and nowhere else. This new book

had many of the faults of the other serial books. Chapter I introduces Gilbert. In Chapter II Gilbert lost his fortune; his guardian
Richard Briggs said the money was exhausted. Chapter III introduces Briggs' son Randolph, a young wastrel; Gilbert went to
stay with the Briggs family temporarily in their town house, met
a pretty rich girl whose fare he paid on the bus since she forgot
her money and seemed to be getting on well. He found a job, but
the boy whose job he took in a broker's office scowled at him on
page 35, and that meant evil portent for the pages to come.

This, then, became a tale of business life and boarding house
life in New York, with a lacing of upper crust society life added.
Mrs. Briggs, the wife of the guardian, was a social climber and
poseur of the worst kind. Horatio captured her. He knew the
type. Here, of course, Horatio was drawing on his own observations from the world of the Seligmans to create a new kind of
book dealing with a segment of New York that he had until this
time left generally untouched. But he fell back on old situations
and old ruses: in the business office the evil chief clerk conspired
with a boy who was a relative to frame Gilbert on a false charge
of dishonesty and get him fired.

In the absence of his employer, the plot succeeded and Gilbert was discharged as dishonest by the chief clerk–bookkeeper.
But the wicked boy, John, had been seen by a bootblack putting
the money in Gilbert's coat.

In a foray of a different nature, Gilbert was introduced to a
French count, Count Ernest de Montmorency, who spoke English
with an appropriate accent (I am most happy, Monsieur Jones,
to have ze honor of making your acquaintance) and larded his
conversation with French phrases (You have some fine water
places, N'est-ce-pas?). The count turned out to be an imposter
with virtually no relationship to the plot.

Gilbert, though troubled himself, still had the kindliness to
help a poor little flower girl and her poor father. He gave four of
his last five dollars to pay their rent for a month. Then, abused
by Mrs. Briggs in her husband's absence, he became a lowly
newsboy, and was mistreated again by the wicked bookkeeper
and his relative. But one of his rich friends (the father of the girl
on the bus) gave him a job tutoring his son in Latin and Greek,
and that held Gilbert until Chapter XXXIV, when Mr. Sands,

the broker, returned and found that Gilbert had been discharged by his bookkeeper. Mr. Sands was not pleased. In fact, he had been in the next stall in an oyster house and had heard the wicked bookkeeper and his boy relative plotting to do Gilbert in. So Gilbert got his job back, the bookkeeper and his relative were fired, and then Mr. Briggs came back from Europe.

Then Mr. Talbot, the father of the flower girl, turned out to be former bookkeeper to Gilbert's father, who had been a rich merchant in the West Indies, and Gilbert learned that Briggs had cheated him of his fortune of eighty thousand dollars. He braced Mr. Briggs about this, and Mr. Briggs confessed: "I have tried to be a villain, but I won't be one any longer. Your father left you a fortune and it shall be restored to you."

And so Gilbert became rich again. He first went to college and then into business, it was forecast. He helped the young man John, who had put the money in his pocket to get his job with the broker—which proved that evil did not always do a boy in. But it is most odd that Mr. Briggs, who had embezzled Gilbert's fortune when it was left in trust with him, did not even get a slap on the wrist—which was certain proof that there was a different standard of morality for Fifth Avenuers and for bootblacks. Horatio did not even chide Mr. Briggs for his despicable behaviour, and while a judge ought to have given Briggs ten years or so, the matter did not even get to court.

The readers of *Young Israel* were happy enough with *Shifting for Himself,* but Loring was not so pleased. And then came *Sam's Chance* (the sequel to *The Young Outlaw*) in which Sam made a long journey up to Boston and Cambridge and other places Horatio had frequented for years. Sam got mixed up by mistake with the students in Harvard yard and was given a freshman initiation. But Sam was not of the stuff of which Harvard men are made, so Horatio never got him into Harvard College. Sam did, however, go to live in Brookline with a rich family and got a good job in a Boston business house, and so, completely reformed, Horatio assured his readers that Sam was on the right track and would prosper in the years to come.

Loring was not overly pleased with *Sam's Chance* either; it, too, was one of the weaker of Horatio's books and certainly not up to the first book about Sam. Loring suggested that Horatio had grown stale and needed a change of scene. At about this same time, Horatio met Bret Harte and Edward Z. C. Judson, who wrote about the West under the pen name Ned Buntline. These two spoke excitedly of the West. Harte told Horatio he would find new material there for his stories. Loring talked of sales figures, which showed Horatio's books selling much better in the West than they had in the past and with more hope, he thought, than in the East.

That Horatio's brother was still living in San Francisco added to the argument. He decided to go west. Christian Tracy, the old superintendent of the Lodging House, was in town planning to take a group of boys to Kansas, and Horatio decided to accompany them.

The railroad took Tracy, Horatio and the boys to Kansas City. They crossed the Mississippi and then boarded another train for Independence where Horatio left his fellow travelers and joined a wagon train of settlers heading west. At Wichita he took the stage-coach to Scott's Bluff, Nebraska, which was then a jumping-off point on the Oregon Trail. At Scott's Bluff, Horatio joined a band of settlers and rode in a Conestoga wagon all the way to Fort Laramie, Wyoming. Horatio's destination was San Francisco, not Oregon, so he left the settlers there and took the Union Pacific Railroad cars to Salt Lake City. He stopped off there for a few days, visited the Mormon tabernacle and then moved on to California. He arrived in Oakland in Feburary, 1877.

The long trip showed in Horatio's literary output for the year. *Gleason's Monthly Companion* published several short stories, but that was work on hand. *Young Israel* had a new serial for the year, *Wait and Hope: Ben Bradford's Motto*. This last merely confirmed what Loring had been telling Horatio, that he needed a change in scene. *Wait and Hope* is the story of a mill boy who in the opening chapter was laid off at the mill. But he remained in the fashion of Horatio's heroes, undaunted: "There's lots of ways of making money, Aunt. Just do as I do—Wait and Hope."

In San Francisco, Horatio met his brother James, who was a successful optometrist. After a few days of reminiscence and sightseeing, he headed north for the gold country to meet miners and gather local color. But he was twenty-five years too late. After a month of searching for old timers Horatio headed for Oregon and for Washington, still in territorial status. Then he took a steamer from Seattle down to San Francisco. It is too bad that he never really used the material he garnered on this trip. In the Bay City, he made the intelligent decision to learn something about the sea, since he wrote about it occasionally, and he took passage on a four-masted schooner around Cape Horn. In late summer, 1877, Horatio was home again in New York with several manuscripts in hand.

Chapter Nineteen

The Unchangeable Alger

THE TRIP WEST was supposed to produce half a dozen books from Horatio's pen. But in hoping that it would give Horatio a new verve and point of view, Publisher Loring was as it turned out quite wrongly optimistic. As a later student of California put it:

> One looks in vain in any of his western stories for a gleam of genuine local color.... The vastness of the country, the grandeur of the Sierras, the impact of the desert crossing—all of this, though experienced by the author, is missing from his stories.

This analyst, John Seelye, suggests that Horatio was unable to give such description. The fact is that Horatio was quite capable of writing a distinguished sentence and making an apt description. But when he sat down to write a serial for the youngsters' magazines, he and the editors knew what was wanted: plenty of exciting adventures, one coming atop the other, and plenty of dialogue. Horatio, being a money writer, never overcame his concern for the obvious.

The year 1878 saw Horatio's serials in two magazines: the New York *Weekly* took *Joe's Luck*. *Young Israel* published *The Young Adventurer: Tom's Trip Across the Plains*. The latter was based on Horatio's own trip, and the former on what he had observed and read about the years of the gold strike miners in northern California. Indeed, in the next few years, Horatio published six different books which could be traced back to the trip to California. The effect of the Western adventure on Horatio is indicated, from the beginning, by *The Young Adventurer*. Here, once again the book begins with the ubiquitous Alger mortgage. "I wish I could pay off the mortgage on my farm, said Mark Nelson soberly."

The mortgage was held by Squire Hudson, the usual squire, "cold and selfish," who had additional reason to wish Mark Nelson ill—Mark had married the girl Squire Hudson was chasing.

Tom, his oldest boy, was now approaching sixteen, as were nearly all Alger heroes in the 1870s. Tom found the Squire's wallet on the road one day, and although it had six hundred dollars in it and he desperately wanted to go to California and dig for gold, he returned it to the squire; the squire, overwhelmed by his honesty, offered him a reward of fifty cents. Tom asked to borrow the money to go to California (some two hundred dollars) and the squire agreed on the condition that Tom's father increase the mortgage by that amount.

So Tom headed for California, having first met the squire's no-good son Sinclair, who, it was obvious, would somehow be a thorn in Tom's side. It was all so similar to what had gone before. Perhaps that is why boys like it.

On the train to Pittsburgh Tom met a young man named Milton Graham who flattered him and suggested they take a room together. Luckily Tom was warned by a friendly desk clerk at the hotel that Graham was not what he seemed, and he put his money belt in the safe overnight. Walking around the city, Tom met a drunk who was staying at their hotel, helped him home and then went to bed. Tom was asleep when Graham came in, but he woke up and watched Graham search for his money. Next morning Graham tried to get the money out of the safe, but the friendly desk clerk gave him short shrift and he departed angrily.

It is inconceivable that this adventure could have happened to Alger, but it is also conceivable and almost certain that he had heard of such an adventure somewhere on his trip. By and large, Horatio's books depend very heavily on reality of incident.

Then it was on to the *River Belle,* the steamboat that would take the western traveler to the West, and there, as the reader knew he must, Tom encountered the man he had helped, who was an Ohio legislator and a manufacturer. Milton Graham was also on the steamboat with a confederate, and together they plotted to rob Tom and his companion, Mr. Nicholas Waterbury. This incident most certainly did not come from Horatio's travels—he had gone by train, not by steamboat.

Tom met a girl, Jennie Watson and had a paragraph of conversation with her. After Graham made a play for Jennie and was rebuffed, he was angrier with Tom than ever, even angrier than when he discovered Tom had put his money belt in the safe. " 'Curse her impudence, and his too!' he muttered. 'I should like to wring the boy's neck.' "

That night, thieves entered the stateroom and robbed Mr. Waterbury—but the canny manufacturer had stuffed his wallet with green paper. Graham was so wicked he even tried to cheat his companion in crime of the money. Then the thieves tried to throw suspicion on Tom, but it did not come off because Mr. Waterbury saw them stuff the roll of bogus bills into Tom's pocket.

The result of all these shenanigans was that almost halfway through the book, the reader was still on the riverboat and in a manner unlike the Alger of New York, he had learned absolutely nothing about riverboats, the river or the surrounding countryside. In fact, he had learned nothing about anything except the shenanigans.

And there seemed little chance of their ceasing. Although Mr. Waterbury bearded the wretches and accused them of theft, Graham was so infuriated by Tom's refusal to be robbed that he determined he would chase after Tom and get his two hundred dollars. A real riverboat scoundrel would continue to ride the river—a little euchre here, a little pickpocketing there—but Graham was ready to sacrifice all for revenge. At Cincinnati, which was honored with a three-word mention, Jennie and her mother got off the boat. Her parting showed which way the wind blew with her.

> "I am sorry you are going to leave us, Tom," said Jennie; "I shall feel awfully lonely."
>
> "So shall I," said Tom.
>
> "What's the use of going to that hateful California? Why can't you stay here with us?"
>
> "Business before pleasure, Jennie," said her mother. "You mustn't forget that Tom has his fortune to make."

Naturally. And it would take him at least six months. Tom then parted from Mr. Waterbury, refusing with manly pride his offers of help. Then he went to a cheap hotel where he encountered a black bellhop who was straight out of a minstrel show.

> "Cato," called the clerk,—summoning a colored boy, about Tom's size—"take this young man to No. 18."
>
> "All right, sar," said Cato, showing his ivories.
>
> "When do we have dinner?" asked Tom.
>
> "One o'clock."
>
> Preceded by Cato, Tom walked upstairs, and was ushered into a small, dingy room on the second floor. There was a single window looking through dingy panes upon a back yard. There was a general air of cheerlessness and discomfort, but at any rate it was larger than the stateroom on the *River Belle*.
>
> "Is this the best room you have?" asked Tom, not very favorably impressed.
>
> "Oh, no sar," answered Cato. "If your wife was with you, sar, we'd give you a scrumptious room, 'bout twice as big."
>
> "I didn't bring my wife along Cato," said Tom, amused. "Are you married?"
>
> "Not yet, sar," said his colored guide, with a grin.
>
> "I think we can wait till we are a little older."
>
> "Reckon so, sar."
>
> "Just bring up a little water, Cato. I feel in need of washing."
>
> "Dirt don't show on me," said Cato with a guffaw.
>
> "I suppose you do wash, now and then, don't you?"
>
> "Yes, sar, sometimes," answered Cato equivocally.

That conversation is the last of Cato, a low-comedy character introduced simply to pander to the American taste—old transmitted to young—which demanded that the black be a buffoon. Horatio had no visible racial prejudice of any special strength, he simply did not regard blacks as human beings. In that he was absolutely the man of his time. Cato disappears for the water and is never seen again.

Out on the street, Tom saw Graham trying to fleece a poor German who understood neither country nor language very well. Tom saved him from the swindler, thus adding to Graham's account against him.

"I'll get even with you yet," said Graham, furiously; but our hero was not disturbed by this menace.

He ought to have been. Graham and his confederate managed to get Tom arrested for snatching a poor woman's pocket book but just then a quiet, well-dressed gentleman came along. For some reason, Horatio had an ambiguous attitude toward police officers; in some of his books they helped his street boys, and in others they roughed them up. He did not much like Cincinnati's policemen, that is sure, for he made the officer who arrested Tom a rough and cowardly brute. The officer was hauling Tom off to the jailhouse when the gentleman stopped him.

"Don't be in a hurry," said the quiet man.

"I know Mr. Waterbury, and I believe the boy's story is correct."

"It ain't any of your business!" said the officer insolently. "The boy's a thief, and I'm going to lock him up."

"Look out, sir!" said the quiet man sternly. "You are overstepping the limits of your duty, and asserting what you have no possible means of knowing. There is reason to believe that this man"—pointing out Vincent—"is the real thief. I call upon you to arrest him."

"I don't receive no orders from you, sir," said the policeman. "I'm more likely to take you along."

"That's right, officer," said Vincent approvingly. "This man is interfering with you in the exercise of your duty. You have a perfect right to arrest him."

"I have a great mind to," said the officer, who was one of the many who are puffed up by a little brief authority, and lose no opportunity in exercising it.

The quiet man did not seem in the least alarmed. He smiled, and said, "Perhaps officer, it might be well for you to inquire my name, before proceeding to arrest me."

"Who are you?" demanded the officer insolently.

"I am Alderman Morris."

A great change came over the policeman....

The policeman, chagrined and dressed down by Alderman Morris, took Vincent, Graham's accomplice, into tow and they all started to go downtown. But Officer Jones, in addition to being insolent and bad tempered, was also incompetent. Vincent escaped on the way. Tom went along to the station house, Mr. Waterbury showed up, and in a moment, Tom was freed.

Mr. Waterbury took him to a jewelry store and bought him a watch, the symbol of respectability in Horatio's world. A man or boy with a watch was not likely to be found in the company of thieves. It was only a silver watch, but that was to be expected.

"As you are to rough it, I thought it best to get you a hunting case watch, because it will be less liable to injury. When you become a man, I hope you will be prosperous enough to buy a gold watch and chain, if you prefer them. While you are a boy, silver will be good enough."

Roughing it? Here on page 147 Tom was still hanging around Cincinnati mooing over Jennie Watson. She condescended to kiss him goodbye because he was going away although she never kissed boys otherwise. This character trait was guaranteed to put Jennie high on the list of Horatio's thirteen-year-old audience, but not as high on that of the sixteen-year-olds. Indeed, Horatio's ambivalent attitude toward sex erupted quite frequently in these later Alger books. In seeking his kiss, Tom was first eager:

"Isn't it my turn now," asked Tom, with a courage at which he afterward rather wondered; but he was fast getting rid of his country bashfulness.

But after this kissing, Tom reverted: " 'She seems just like a sister,' said Tom. 'She's a tip-top girl.' "

Finally, on page 150, Tom got out of Cincinnati in the company of Donald Ferguson, a companion selected for him by Mr. Waterbury. If Horatio had encountered on his trip west the people he now wrote about, his journey must have been the vilest and most fraught with danger that had ever been conducted. For plodding along (Horatio, in typical Alger fashion, gave not a clue as to what manner of transportation they used), they arrived at a small tavern in a Missouri town and immediately were set upon by wild alcoholics.

> The barroom, which was the only public room set apart for the use of the guests, was the resort of a party of drunken roisterers, who were playing poker in the corner, and betting on the game. At the elbow of each player was set a glass of whiskey, and the end of each game was marked by a fresh glass all around. ... Presently at the close of a game, glasses were ordered for the party, at the expense of those who had suffered defeat.
>
> "What'll you have, strangers?" inquired a tipsy fellow, with an Indian complexion and long black hair, staggering toward Ferguson.
>
> "Thank you, sir," said the Scotchman, "but I don't drink."
>
> "Don't drink!" exclaimed the former, in evident surprise. "What sort of a man, pray, may you be?"
>
> "I am a temperance man," said Ferguson.... [But Ferguson was also a fool] "...and it would be well for you all if you would shun the vile liquor which is destroying soul and body."
>
> "...your impudence!" ejaculated the other in a rage. Do you dare insult gentlemen like us?"

In a few more sentences, Ferguson had mired himself in so desperately that he received a well-deserved poke in the nose, and then he would not fight because, as he said, the other was drunk. So he literally had his nose pulled. Thereupon he did fight. He won and thus acquired the respect of the drunks, proving perhaps for the delectation of Horatio's father, that a good temperance man is the match of a gang of drunks any day.

Tom and Ferguson got to St. Joe, which back in the 1850s was the jumping off place for the overland parties headed for

California. There they encountered a young Bostonian of the
Peabody clan who was out to make his fortune in fancy Boston
shoes that were already worn out. Their wagon train encountered
a pair of scalped bodies. The Indians were up to their usual
tricks. One of those they had killed, Horatio told his readers
mournfully was not even going to be able to go home to see his
lonely wife in Maine.

> "Poor woman," said Ferguson. "She will wait for her hus-
> band in vain. The mortgage will never be paid through his
> exertions."
> Tom looked sober, as he glanced compassionately at the
> poor emigrant.
> "He came on the same errand I did," he said.

The party buried the mortgagor and his companion, and
pushed on, but where only the Lord knew. Horatio gave no description of the terrain or the sounds of travel or the men of the
party or the animals or the smells or even the events—not one
person had character, save Horatio's hero and his immediate
companions, Ferguson, the Scot and Peabody the Bostonian, the
tenderfoot of a crowd.

Tom, out looking for a lost horse encountered

INDIAN CASUISTRY
in
Chapter XXVIII

Tom and Mr. Scott, a young man from Indiana, went out
alone, found their horse and were jumped by Indians. One old
brave spoke a little English. The Indians, whose attitude toward
horses on the plains was well known, said it was their horse now.
Mr. Scott quarreled with the braves; the Indians then decided that
the white men were trying to steal *their* horse, and they also
thought this would be a good time to pick up two more horses. So
they accused Scott of bewitching the horse to make it whinny for
him. The Lord only knew what they would do with the white men,
except that Tom and Mr. Scott lashed their horses and got clean
away. Then with a howl of surprise, the Indians were after them.

That Mr. Scott was a cool one. In the van of the Indians was a brave on the back of Dan, the lost horse, and Scott let him overhaul them:

> Scott wheeled around, took hasty but accurate aim at the Indian, and fired. The hapless warrior reeled in his saddle, loosed his hold on the reins and fell to the ground, while his horse, continuing on his course, his pace accelerated by fright, soon galloped alongside of Scott. There was a howl of rage from the main body of Indians, who saw the fate of their comrade, without being able to help him.

So they rode on, but the Indians were furious now. Charging on by their fallen comrade they saw the hole in his breast and the life blood gushing away, and they thirsted for vengeance.

> Should the two palefaces, one of them a boy, escape from them? That would be a disgrace, indeed; the blood of their brother called for blood in return.

Then Tom's horse stumbled. Tom was thrown and knocked unconscious; the horses and Mr. Scott sped on. After picking Tom up, the Indians decided they did not want blood but a body, and they adopted him into the tribe. Indeed, Tom was very lucky. Scott had shot the chief's brother and the chief now chose Tom to take the brother's place.

Tom suggested that it would be nice if the Indians would let him go home and help his father pay the mortgage. His new friends met that suggestion with stony eyes.

> Tom very sensibly concluded that it would be better to live with the Indians than to be killed, and signified his acceptance of the offer. Upon this the Indians formed a circle about him, and broke into a monotonous chant, accompanied with sundry movements of the limbs, which happened to be their way of welcoming him into their tribe.

Tom then played a magic trick on the Indians—among his hidden attributes was a working knowledge of conjury which had never come to light until this moment. The Indians then decided he was a magician, and twenty-four hours after joining the tribe, he was in charge. This makes it easy for him to steal a horse and escape. The Indians chased him, but Tom made his way back to camp. One member of the party wondered how Tom had gotten away. Tom pointed to a mass of broken flesh on the prairie behind him:

> "It is the Indians. They were pursuing me when they were trampled to death by a herd of buffaloes."
>
> "Wonderful!" ejaculated Miles. "I have heard of such things, but hardly believed them."
>
> "It was a terrible sight," said Tom soberly. "I wish I could have been saved in some other way."
>
> "It was you or they," said Miles sententiously. "It is well as it is."

This kind of problem obviously was very difficult for Horatio, who as a man of the gospel was supposed to have quarts of the milk of human kindness. But he was also a student of the penny press who knew how everybody felt about Indians. And, as with the morose and incompetent John, who had kidnaped little Carrie in revenge for her mother's refusal to give him rum, Horatio did not mind a bit.

The Indians are trampled on page 252. On page 255 the wagon train is virtually at the end of its journey, climbing through the Sierra Nevada. What did they see, these travelers in a land of great trees, magnificent rocks and clear cold air.

> They reached the summit, and, looking meagerly to the westward, they saw the land of gold at their feet.

That was Horatio, top to bottom. But then, perhaps he could not be faulted too greatly. The picture he painted was quite probably just what the original California gold rush prospectors saw too.

Chapter Twenty

More of the Same

IN ESSENCE, the new Alger was the old Alger living in a room in the thirties in New York, which was then far uptown, tutoring young bloods and writing his serials. He did lead a very active social life. He loved the theater and attended performances often in the company of boys or grown-up boys that he had once befriended. He still found jobs for dozens of boys and gave them money out of his own pocket. He traveled a good deal, mostly in New England, but also to Chicago and other middle western cities. He still frequented the Newsboy's Lodging House, for he and Superintendent O'Connor were the best of friends. Horatio continued to draw basic material from newsboys; in one way or another they appear in most of his books.

As for publishing, Horatio was going through a difficult change. Loring, his old publisher, was not doing nearly as well as he ought. Loring was the victim of overexpansion and changing times. He did not want to take on Horatio's secondary works. He was interested in the Pacific Series, which dealt with the far west, but was no longer interested in the street boy books, which were not selling enough in the 1870s to suit him. So Horatio's serial stories now had to have a new home. Street & Smith, the magazine publishers, arranged for the publication of *The Western Boy* in 1878. This book turned out to be one Loring should never have missed—it was tremendously popular. That popular acclaim came perhaps, because for once Horatio stuck to his plot and his characters and made them all come alive instead of rushing through his book as he was wont to do in the middle 1870s.

The western books told the story. *The Young Adventurer* was scarcely better written than the worst dime novels. Next came *Joe's Luck*—another serial for the *New York Weekly*, and it was no better as a book than any Alger serial.

As *The Young Adventurer* was a story of a trip across the plains, *Joe's Luck* was the story of a boy who took the sea route to California. It was the same old plot: 1) Joe Mason, poor boy, 2) lorded over by the son of his employer 3) Major Norton "a farmer and capitalist" and a stingy gentleman at that. Joe inherited some fifty dollars, went to New York, was bilked of his money, was befriended by a rich youth who, since he could not go himself to California, gave Joe his ticket on the promise that Joe would pay later, and arrived in California in a few pages with no discussion at all of the trip.

Horatio did have the names of his San Francisco streets and places right. If that was all he learned on his western trip, it is a sad commentary on his powers of observation. He could mention the Leidesdorff Hotel and the St. Francis, Montgomery and Clay Streets and Telegraph Hill, and do so with a sense of belonging. Further than that he would not go to bring a sense of place to his book. Joe rescued a man about to be robbed (Horatio made this departure in style to fit the rough western culture); the man slapped down $500 to buy Joe a restaurant, and in two days Joe had mastered the restaurant business. Joe wheeled and dealed, and bought three city lots on borrowed money. He had many adventures, but except for the setting, they could have happened anywhere—the pattern was the same as ever. The man who had bilked Joe of his ticket money in New York turned up in San Francisco and tried to rob the restaurant. He failed. Joe turned his restaurant over to a friend and went to the Yuba River country—which Horatio had visited briefly, years after the gold rush— did a little placer mining in the river; saved the life of the wicked enemy who kept trying to rob him—this time from a grizzly bear—and found a nugget, which the evil one stole. He joined a lynch party searching for the bad fellow and saw his enemy die by choosing to jump over a precipice rather than be hanged by vigilantes. So, Joe got his nugget back and found others; he became rich, went back to the East, lorded it over his old enemies, the farmer and capitalist, and then went back to San Francisco to live.

Horatio was now playing two themes—the city boy story and the western boy story. *The District Telegraph Boy* which was issued in 1879, is the tale of a young New York poor boy who became a telegraph boy and a detective of sorts and came out very well. There is one interesting character, a vile and violent blind man, for whom the hero, Frank Kavanagh, works for a time. Otherwise it is a New York tale of the old, familiar type about Madison Avenue and Fifth Avenue and the Newsboy's Lodging House. Another book published that year, *The Young Miner,* is the sequel to Tom Nelson's adventures—Tom was the boy who had gone across the plains to be kidnaped by Indians.

Next year, 1880, it was *Tony the Hero,* different from other Alger books in that the hero was a young tramp, forced into the tramp's life. The story is that of his escape from bondage; it is filled with squires and farmers, with evil Rudolph, Tony's "guardian" stalking him for pages at a time. There is, of course, a trip to New York. A rich English lady is looking for Tony—not to give him his rightful English estate, but rather to have him murdered by Rudolph so she could keep it. The Western series must have coarsened Horatio's morality, for the most dreadful things were now almost casually proposed and explored in the Alger books. Tony escaped death narrowly, and Mrs. Middleton, the lady villain, returned to England with Rudolph Rugg, the male villain. Tony was befriended by important people and educated. In six months he learned as much as some boys ever learn. And—toward the end of the book, Mrs. Middleton took a lover who was marrying her for her money, which was really Tony's money. Then Mrs. Middleton and Rugg fell out, and Rugg, possibly the best characterized of all Horatio's villains, decided he hated her more than he hated Tony and told all to the solicitors.

In a way, this is an international story. The second half is played in England, but it could have been New York or anywhere else except for the street names. Mrs. Middleton, at the last, had tricked her lover into marrying her.

> When, a week later, at Paris, the gallant Captain was informed of the trick that had been played upon him, there was a terrible scene. He cursed his wife, and threatened to leave her.
>
> "But Gregory, I have three hundred pounds income," she pleaded. "We can live abroad."
>
> "And I have sold myself for that paltry sum!" he said bitterly.
>
> But he concluded to make the best of a bad bargain. Between them they had an income of five hundred pounds, and on this they made shift abroad, where living is cheap. But the marriage was not happy. He was brutal at times, and his wife realized sadly that he had never loved her. But she has all the happiness she deserves and so has he.
>
> Rudolph drank himself to death in six months, so income he was to receive made but a slight draft upon the Middleton estate.
>
> And Tony! No longer, Tony the Tramp, but the Hon. Anthony Middleton, of Middleton Hall—he has just completed a course at Oxford, and is now the possessor of an education which will help fit him for the responsibilities he is to assume. His frank, offhand manner makes him an immense favorite with the circle to which he now belongs. He says little of his early history, and it is seldom thought of now.

The trouble with these later Alger books—or at least with this one—is the flighty sense of morality that the erstwhile Unitarian minister now displayed. Mrs. Middleton had hired Rudolph Rugg to kill Tony, and everybody of any importance in the story knew it. Yet Mrs. Middleton got off with no more than a bad husband. Rudolph—whose murder plot had failed only by a hair's breadth—was allowed to drink himself quietly to death. The law, in Horatio's books, had very little value to anyone.

The Young Explorer, which would be the last book published by A. K. Loring, was much the same as *Joe's Luck.* In 1880 poor Loring was on the rocks. He soon went bankrupt. This deprived Horatio of a publishing home, but not of a publisher. His old editor, George Dillingham, joined G. W. Carleton & Co. and now Street & Smith expanded to fill another part of the gap.

The new book was of a piece with all the old. Ben Stanton, the hero, was a New England boy duped of his money in New York, saved by a well-to-do lady and shipped to San Francisco. He headed for the mines, had adventures, struck it rich—all the old stuff. The best bit of the book was the insertion of a Chinese character who in spite of a Cantonese background was out prospecting for gold in California. One morning, two of the rough, tough miners came in hauling between them by his pigtail a Chinaman with eyes lolling around in his head, infuriated because he had been caught prospecting. This was Ki Sing.

> Mr. Patrick O'Reilly appeared to hold the opinion that gold-hunting should be confined to the Caucasian race. He looked upon a Chinaman as a rather superior order of monkey, suitable for exhibition in a case; but not to be regarded as possessing the ordinary rights of an adopted American resident. If he could have looked forward twenty-five years and foreseen the extent to which these barbarians would throng the avenues of employment he would, no doubt, have been equally amazed and disgusted.

That particular comment by Horatio was one of his very few references to public affairs of the day in which he was writing. Eight years before Horatio had gone west to California, The Burlingame treaty had given the Chinese the unlimited right of immigration—the railroaders needed cheap labor to build the lines and they were ready to welcome the Chinese then. But by 1876 and 1877 when Horatio was in California, the white residents were up in arms because Chinese, with their frugality and hard work, were out-Algering Alger, so to speak. The bloom was long gone from the gold fields, and work was not easy to find. As Horatio wrote *Joe's Luck* and *The Young Miner* and *The Young Explorer,* debate raged in Congress—and raged is precisely the word—as to what must be done to preserve the west from the incursions of the Heathen Chinese. The result was the Chinese Exclusion Act, which in the next few years virtually put an end to Chinese immigration, at least of the legal variety.

Ki Sing was a music hall Chinese, and he began life in Horatio's book as a comedy character.

"Me come flom Flisco."

It is well known that a Chinaman cannot pronounce the letter r, which in his mouth softens to l, in some cases producing a ludicrous effect.

Using that effect, Horatio proceeded to amuse his young readers:

"What are you going to do with your gold when you find it?"
"Cally it back to China."
"And when you've *called* it back, what'll you do then?"
"Me mally wife, have good time, and plenty money to buy lice."

But Ki Sing then took on, rapidly, a rather different character:

Of course Ki Sing's meaning was plain, but there was a roar of laughter, to which he listened with mild-eyed wonder, evidently thinking that the miners who so looked down on him were themselves a set of outside barbarians, to whom the superior civilization of China was utterly unknown.

The miners baited him:

"I say, John," said Dick Roberts, "are you fond of rat pie."
"Lat pie velly good," returned Ki Sing with a look of appreciation. "Melican man like him?"
"Hear the haythen!" said O'Reilly with an expression of deep disgust. "He thinks we eat rats and mice like him. No old pig-tail we ain't cats. We are good Christians."

And here, Horatio became absolutely literary, satirical in fact:

"Chlistian! Me don't know Chlistian," said the Chinaman.
"Then look at O'Reilly," said Dick Roberts mischievously. "He's a good solid Christian."
Ki Sing turned his almond eyes upon O'Reilly, who with his freckled face, wide mouth, broad nose and stubby beard, was by no means a prepossessing looking man, and said interrogatively "He Chlistian?"

"Yes, John. Wouldn't you like to be one?"

Ki Sing shook his head decidedly.

"Me no want to be good Chlistian." he answered. "Me velly well now."

O'Reilly was not very bright, but he made up for it in pugnacity. He sensed that he had been insulted. Richard Dewey—Horatio's subhero, who did not drink or smoke and who had a clear eye and was well-knit also—then lectured O'Reilly on the equality of man. Both O'Reilly and Ki Sing had come from foreign lands, he said. O'Reilly came from the ould sod to make his fortune, so they were alike. O'Reilly did not appreciate this line of thinking and the stage was set for a quarrel. The match that lit it was O'Reilly's suggestion: "I say, boys, let's cut off his pig-tail."

Now, it was well known, and Ki Sing confirmed it, that in the days of the Manchu, no Chinese could be allowed to roam in the celestial empire without a pigtail. So if Ki Sing's appendage were removed he could never go home. Richard Dewey and Ki Sing explained this to the miners, and most were sympathetic when Dewey spoke of home and mother—as Bret Harte and Mark Twain had already pointed out, the miners were a gang of insatiable sentimentalists. But O'Reilly was a "bad 'un" and he wanted the scissors to cut off Ki Sing's return ticket. O'Reilly pulled Ki Sing's queue, and Richard Dewey knocked him down and then proceeded to knock the stuffings out of him.

The rest was predictable: Ki Sing became the vehicle through which O'Reilly would be avenged on Richard Dewey. Ki Sing turned out to be hardworking and honest. Dewey saved Ki Sing's pigtail once more and then sent him away from this camp. Soon Dewey left the place himself. When he was injured in an accident, Ki Sing showed up to save him. Ki Sing was still used for low comedy, but his was a noble nature and it showed through. He became cook and steward to a group settling down to work a claim. Alger readers were promised that he would appear again in the next of the Pacific series.

Horatio continued to go back to South Natick with great frequency. He spent many summer vacations there, or traveling with his family. His mother had died in 1878. Brother James, in spite of family suggestions that he come home, had moved from

KI SING AND THE MINERS

San Francisco to Denver, which was undergoing the same kind of gold rush development that San Francisco had seen a quarter of a century earlier.

Horatio's markets had changed in the last two years, but little else had in his life. He was writing for Street & Smith, *Golden Days* and *The Home Companion. Gleason's* and *Young Israel* had run out their strings; but Horatio was writing the same old tales of boys and their fortunes, manners and enemies, and these were greeted with the same relish by what was now a whole new generation. As noted, Horatio's style had changed; in 1864 he would not have essayed the degree of violence or the openness in relations between generations or sexes that he now considered usual. The change had been gradual; it reflected the lessening grasp of the Puritan ethic on America. But in essence the Alger of 1881 was the Alger of 1864. Anyone who had read *Frank's Campaign* was likely to recognize *Ben's Nugget,* the last of the Pacific series. Loring was bankrupt, and so the book was published by Porter and Coates of Philadelphia.

The year 1881 saw one radical departure in Horatio's work. In the summer of that year, President James A. Garfield was shot by an assassin in Washington's Pennsylvania Railroad station. From the beginning it seemed that the wounds would be fatal. Book publishers were always looking for a way to capitalize on events. When John R. Anderson, a New York publisher, decided that Garfield was going to die, he looked around for a competent writer who could turn out a biography of Garfield in a hurry. He wanted to be first to hit a market he knew would soon be flooded. Horatio's productivity was well-known and often lamented in the publishing world, where prolific writers were detested as flooding the marketplace—except when a publisher needed one. Asked how long it would take him to write a biography of Garfield, Horatio said a few weeks. The contract was signed.

Horatio, at this time, was very conscious of his restricted status as an author. He had written to a classmate about literary life and his desire to do a lasting work of some kind. Publisher Anderson offered a new vehicle, the biography. Horatio repaired to his room in Manhattan and, working day and night as was his habit, he completed the manuscript of the Garfield book, using newspaper accounts, political biographies and all else that he could find. He finished the manuscript and on October 8, 1881, he wrote the preface to it and an apologia to his readers for its paucity of original research material. In a month the book was on the presses, and it was in the stores for the Christmas trade.

Was there to be a "new Horatio," a writer who could produce the lasting work he so dearly wished to write? If so it was obvious from the opening page of *From Canal Boy to President,* that this was not going to be the book. Horatio, the biographer, was very much like Horatio, the novelist.

> From a small and rudely built log-cabin a sturdy boy of four years issued, and looked earnestly across the clearing to the pathway that led through the surrounding forest. His bare feet pressed the soft grass, which spread like a carpet before the door.
>
> "What are you looking for Jimmy?" asked his mother from within the humble dwelling.
>
> "I'm looking for Thomas," said Jimmy.
>
> "It's hardly time for him yet. He won't be through work till after sunset."
>
> "Then I wish the sun would set quick," said Jimmy.
>
> "That is something we cannot hasten, my son." "God makes the sun to rise and to set in its due season."
>
> This idea was probably too advanced for Jimmy's comprehension, for he was but four years of age.

In the twentieth century, with all its electronic marvels, it is barely conceivable that some doting mother might begin recording the deathless words of a son she knew would grow up to be President of the United States, thus adding new burdens to the almost unbearable body of the printed word. But in 1835 in backwoods Ohio it was not possible at all. Undaunted, Horatio made up conversation after conversation. He also wrote chapters so that they began, rose to crescendo and came down with the grace of a serial installment. Having thus traced Garfield's career, and his death, Horatio summed it up.

> My task is drawing near a close. I have, in different parts of this volume, expressed my own estimate of our lamented President. No character in our history, it seems to me, furnishes a brighter or more inspiring example for boys and young men. It

is for this reason that I have been induced to write the story of his life especially for American boys, conceiving that in no way can I do them a greater service.

He closed the book with a long peroration by Chauncey Depew, President of the New York Central Railroad and a New York politician. Depew had made a stirring address on Garfield's life and public service. This tribute from a successful business man was Horatio's final estimate of the lessons of Garfield's life for young men.

Publisher Anderson was just right in his feeling for the market. *From Canal Boy to President* sold remarkably well. Its success gave the publisher the idea for a whole series of books by Horatio Alger on the great men of America. Immediately, Anderson commissioned Horatio to write a life of Abraham Lincoln. Horatio accepted and set about the task. Here, Horatio ran afoul of his own past. Back in the late 1860s he had conceived of the idea of a biography of Daniel Webster, and had written it as a story serial for Street & Smith. With the success of the Garfield book, J. S. Ogilvie and Company reached back and acquired the rights to the Webster biography, which they published under the title *From Farm Boy to Senator* to cash in on the vogue. Horatio produced the Lincoln book. Again he relied mostly on secondary sources, as he acknowledged in his preface, and again he wrote in the inimitable, but also unchangeable Alger style:

> Three children stood in front of a rough log-cabin in a small clearing won from the surrounding forest. The country round about was wild, and desolate. Not far away was a vast expanse of forest, including oaks, beeches, walnuts, and the usual variety of forest trees....
>
> "Abe," said the girl, addressing her brother, "do you think father will be home tonight?"
>
> "I reckon," answered Abe laconically, shifting from one foot to the other.

Horatio's preoccupation with wealth was also evident in his description of the homecoming of the father, Thomas Lincoln, with his new wife.

Mrs. Johnston considered herself a poor widow, but she was much better off than the man she had just married. She was the owner of a bureau that cost forty dollars; this alone being a value far greater than her new husband's entire stock of furniture.

It was not all conversation and speculation, not by far. Horatio produced here his best biography, but still it was not earth-shaking, even though he paused often to point up the morals applicable to a boy's life. He detailed the many exhausting chores young Abe had to perform such as bringing water from a spring a mile away because there was nothing nearer. Horatio philosophized: "But Abe is not to be pitied for the hardships of his lot. That is the way strong men are made."

Horatio's approach to biography was his own. On the chapter on Lincoln's nomination for the presidency, he devoted four pages to the struggle in Chicago, a page to the acceptance speech, a page and a half to the bitter election campaign, and three pages to anecdotes, on the theory that his boys would not care nearly so much about the facts and figures as about stories. And from what happened next, he seemed to be right; neither of the second two political biographies prospered particularly well. Anderson soon abandoned the historical figures field; Ogilvie said no more about the idea. Horatio had written his last serious work.

Chapter Twenty-One

In the Mold

Horatio was basking in the popularity of his new if short-lived career as a biographer in the fall of 1882. He had found biography exhausting, if rewarding in other ways, as he wrote a friend:

> The life of Webster was difficult to write. If you think I have succeeded in making it interesting, I am pleased. I wished to revive the memory of Webster and make the young people of today acquainted with him.

Horatio's father died in the fall of 1882, just after the author had finished *From Canal Boy to President*. With his passing Horatio lost his severest critic and the force that kept reminding Horatio of his own background and his responsibility to bring moral uplift to American boys. In time Gusti and her husband would have to move out of the white frame parish house and into a house of their own. It meant a change of only a few miles, for they removed to a big place in Natick. Horatio continued to visit them there, although, since this was not home, his summer travels often carried him further afield. In his fifties, when a man might be expected to slow down a little and reflect more while reaching whatever maturity he was to attain in his business or his life, there was absolutely no change in Horatio Alger, Jr.'s style or habits. He worked and he worked and he worked. From his pen came a succession of stories that, while different in names and places, were often almost the same. A squire was a squire, mean and pinchpenny, holding a handful of mortgages and nurturing a spoiled son. A hero was poor but honest and had lost one or both parents, and if the story was not actually set in New York City, there was almost always a New York scene where the street boys were brought in. Often, the hero was bilked of his life's savings or something valuable. Whatever the loss, it would only strengthen his determination to succeed.

The Train Boy was followed by *Dan the Detective.* If the plots were not precisely interchangeable, many of the characters definitely were so. Horatio's style had sharpened, but it had not changed. He began *Dan the Detective* with an exciting scene illustrated by dialogue, proceeded through a myriad of adventures, many of which had little or nothing to do with the plot, and ended with the triumph and wealth of the hero. Horatio's peculiar attitude that wealth had its perquisites above the law continued. In *Dan the Detective* the hero and his mother at the beginning of the book lived in such poverty that Dan sold newspapers on the street. When he went to buy a pear at a fruitstand he took one for three cents and refused to take two for five cents, because he could not afford so much. The reason for the misery was the default of his rich father's bookkeeper, Robert Hunting, who had absconded with the firm's funds. Dan's father apparently died of the shock, and Dan, who had been a student at an exclusive private school, was reduced to supporting his mother and living in a tenement. But, six years after the beginning of the story, when the last chapter was reached, Dan had a strange visitor, who appeared suddenly and acknowledged that he is Robert Hunting, the defaulting bookkeeper:

> Dan's handsome face darkened, and he said bitterly:
> "You killed my father."

"Heaven help me, I fear I did!" sighed Davis, to call him by his later name.

"The money of which you robbed him caused him to fail, and failure led to his death."

"I have accused myself of this crime often times," moaned Davis. "Don't think that the money brought happiness, for it did not."

"Where have you been all these years?"

"First, I went to Europe. There I remained a year. From Europe I went to Brazil, and engaged in business in Rio de Janeiro. A year since I found my health failing, and have come back to New York to die. But before I die I want to make what reparation I can."

"You cannot call my father back to me," said Dan, sadly.

"No, but I can restore the money that I stole. That is the right word—stole. I hope you and your mother have not suffered?"

"We had some hard times, but for years we have lived in comfort."

"I am glad of that. Will you bring a lawyer to me tomorrow evening. I want to make restitution. Then I shall die easier."

"You might keep every dollar if you would bring my father back."

"Would that I could. I must do what I can."

So in a way, Robert Hunting became a fairly respectable character after all those desperate years in the dens of Rio de Janeiro, whence went so many of Horatio's villains and where evil lurked at every corner. No thought of turning him over to the police entered anyone's mind. He had killed Dan's father, destroyed a family, wrecked Dan's education, ruined his mother's beauty and forced them to live in penury, but it was all made right by fifty thousand dollars. When Robert Hunting died a month later, Dan himself took charge of the funeral. Thus was the moral proved; it is all right to be rotten as long as you are rich.

Horatio's literary affairs became exceedingly complex in the 1880s. Past successes were heaped upon current successes. Publishers were bringing out edition after edition of his various books in hardcover and paperback. Old stories were republished here and there. Even his poetry was resurrected and included in anthologies for boys and girls. *John Maynard* was reprinted half a dozen times, became a favorite with elocutionists, and finally ended up in Bartlett's book of quotations. It was also listed as one of the anthology called *The Family Book of Best Loved Poems* published in the middle of the twentieth century. There, and perhaps in his other poetry which was painstakingly exhumed and published in Boston in 1964 by Gilbert Westgard II, lies Horatio's greatest claim to literary immortality. In his poetry Horatio transcended the sterile stock characters and breathless situations that marked all his later prose.

Late in life Horatio spent most of his free time with O'Connor and the boys of the lodging house; he gave them entertainments and he lectured to them about life. He kept his Harvard class contacts better than most and attended nearly all the reunions, writing odes and poems to celebrate these events, which brightened his sterile emotional life. Some of his classmates were preachers, some were judges, some were lawyers, and some were businessmen, but of them all Horatio was the most-famous national figure. He hobnobbed with Society and belonged to many clubs and associations. He knew all the newspaper and magazine editors, and any new juvenile magazine that opened its doors prayed for a serial or even a story from Horatio Alger's pen. An "Alger" assured the editors of attention from boys and their herders. Men who wished to help boys sought his advice on charities. According to Ralph Gardner, who studied his career for years and collected Alger works with a passion, Horatio was instrumental in the New York *Herald-Tribune's* famous Fresh Air Fund, which would take poor children from the city for summer vacations. Alger was lionized in Massachusetts and accepted by Harriet Beecher Stowe and others of the literary community as one of them.

By middle age, the professional tutorial relationship with the Seligmans had become one of his most lasting friendships. The Seligmans treated him as a guest. He came to visit them and stay with them in their various homes long after the children were grown. Through the Seligmans Horatio came to tutor Benjamin Cardozo, the scion of an important New York family who would one day become a United States Supreme Court Justice. Alger and the young man became friends, as Horatio did with most boys. He always showed interest in them and their problems. There was never again the slightest hint of scandal attached to his name, and it seemed that whatever had occurred back in those dim days on Cape Cod had been forgotten.

The family, in the broad sense, was the center of Horatio's emotional life. His brother James died in Denver, leaving a widow and daughter by his first marriage. Horatio went west again and brought the little girl back to Natick to live with his sister Gusti and her husband. They were the survivors of the family, all others had passed on by 1884.

Frank Munsey, the budding publisher, had made a success of *Golden Argosy,* a juvenile magazine. He was now competing successfully with Street & Smith in nearly every way—including for Horatio's writing. The constant flow of serials ended up in so many series that they became confusing. In addition to the Campaign series, the Ragged Dick series and the Luck and Pluck series, there was to be the Atlantic series, and the Way To Success series. Munsey was so pleased with the Alger material and its impact, that he invented a pen name for Horatio in order to double his impact. So Arthur Lee Putnam entered the field. Anyone who wanted to track him down would find him a small, stocky, balding man sitting in a dressing gown before a fire in a big room off Fifth Avenue, drinking endless cups of tea and writing, sometimes on Putnam's latest serial, sometimes on Horatio Alger's.

On the strength of Alger's work and reputation Street & Smith brought forth a series of paperbacked Alger books. One of the newer houses, the A. L. Burt Publishing Company started a Boy's Home Library, with Horatio at the backbone. His short stories appeared in collections. Altogether, the royalties added up, but they made very little change in Horatio's way of life. He bought a little property in Chicago, but he was not an investor. He gave most of his royalties away helping boys get out of the city, getting them started in a job, helping them finish their educations or buying them clothes so they could make a decent appearance. He set boys up in businesses. And whenever he traveled or went to a public entertainment or around the city, he usually had one or two boys with him as companions. Horatio, of course, paid all expenses. In all this interchange and familiarity with boys there was not one hint of scandal.

The work load kept piling up rather than decreasing. He published three, four, even half a dozen books a year, some of them old serials that he merely revised in part. Munsey wanted excitement and more excitement, so the stories ranged far afield. In the 1880s the frontier was the West, and then it moved to Australia. Horatio, who had never visited Australia, undertook to write about that continent and the gold rush there. There was scarcely any difference between Horatio's California and Australia books. Perhaps the most famous of the latter, *In A New World,* could as easily have been set in the Yuba River Valley. The story began in Melbourne, which never became more than a place name. The first character introduced was Professor Hemmenway, "a stout gentleman of middle age" who announced himself as "The Magician of Madagascar," though he freely confessed to friends that he had never seen the island of that name. If Professor Hemmenway was the magician of Madagascar, then Horatio was the magician of Australia. The two heroes of his tale were Harry Vane and Jack Pendleton, both sixteen-year-old American boys. In the opening, Horatio, wrote learnedly about eucalyptus leaves—he had met the euclayptus tree in California, and since it also grew down under, here was a way to give local color. Place names then gave whatever color he could manage—Bendigo, Mount Alexander—and the money was computed in pounds, but all else was the same. The boys encountered a villain who tried to lead them astray with drink and then fleece them. They saved an old man from robbery. He was Henry A. Woolson, and all Algerians knew that this was going to be a name to remember later in the story.

Then it was off to the gold fields, where the boys met precisely the kind of adventures that Algerian heroes had everywhere in the world. The adult Alger reader, after books and books and pages and pages of the same, might thirst mightily for an oasis of descriptive writing, of either character or place, but to no avail. The publishers and Horatio knew what young America wanted: boy hero, plenty of adventure, little or no discussion of girls, some good rugged violence, the turning of events against the villain, and wealth, if not always fame, to the young hero.

Having seen a cockatoo (local color) the boys were captured by bandits called bushrangers. They witnessed a murder (public taste grew bloodier every year), escaped, were sheltered by a shepherd and his daughter (no mention of the sheep or the way they lived) and made a claim. They found gold. Their claim, their gold and their lives were endangered by their first enemy (as usual), but they triumphed and came home to New York with a fortune of five thousand dollars each. Sure enough they met up with Mr. Woolson at the end of the book. But they saw neither wallaby, kangaroo, platypus nor Australian bushman in all the time they were in Australia. The only vegetation of any importance mentioned was that eucalyptus tree. The people involved spoke with American accents, and they lived and behaved just like Americans.

Horatio's personal life, in middle age as always, was filled with boys, but as to detail, very little was ever unearthed of much importance.

The Mayes hoax biography of Horatio spoke of a love affair in later life. Horatio was supposed to have fallen in love with Una Garth on another trip to France. Una was the wife of an American businessman who thought of nothing but business, and so was not even around to avert his eyes while the nimble Horatio lept in and out of Una's bed. Husband Russel Garth became aware of the lovers and whisked Una off to New York. Naturally enough, since he was coming home, Horatio followed. The affair waxed hot and heavy in Horatio's rooms for a time [wrote Mayes] much to the concern of Superintendent O'Connor, Horatio's true friend. O'Connor persuaded Horatio to buy a farm, but Horatio spirited Una away to the farm to live and there they dwelt in sinful dalliance. Mayes was very thorough in his fiction; he even invented an Alger novel, *Ray Radford's Reward,* which the author was said to have started but been unable to finish, so deep was his swooning passion. It all had the ring of Alger—one of the problems of Alger fiction is the similarity of names as well as characters, and *Ray Radford's Reward* was right in there with *Luke Larkin's Luck* or *Mark Manning's Mission,* which were real Alger books.

Una went back to Europe; Mayes' Horatio followed, panting. He pursued her all around Europe, then he had a nervous breakdown and was carried kicking off to the loony bin by the gendarmes. But here Mayes' Horatio was rescued by a boy for whom he had once bought a blacking brush. Given the best of care and a private room in the hospital, eventually the fictional

Alger (right), his brother-in-law Cheney (left), and a friend (ca. 1888)

Horatio recovered and came back to New York. Many years later, Ralph Gardner would write of a relationship with an Irishwoman named Kate Down, whose two sons were special friends of Horatio's. He had met one Down boy straight off the boat from Ireland, Gardner said. The boy came to stay at the Newsboy's Lodging House. Out of the friendship between middle-aged adult and boy had come a relationship in which Horatio bought a house for Kate in Brooklyn. He went to live there with her and adopted the boys.

Perhaps, but Horatio's correspondence for the period in question (1892–99), which is some of the very little of Horatio's correspondence saved, indicates that Horatio was living his usual life in various places: a room at 223 West Thirty-fourth Street, the next year at 227, Gusti's house at Natick and Old Orchard Beach, Maine.

Horatio was an enormously genial man. He loved the kind of puns and fun that boys adored as well. One day, for the delectation of the Sloss brothers, whom he was tutoring, Horatio sat down and wrote out a rhyme

"Strive and Succeed!" The world's temptations flee!
Be "Brave and Bold" and "Strong and Steady" be.
Go "Slow and Sure," and prosper then you must.
Win "Fame and Fortune" while you "Try and Trust."

The key words were all Alger titles, of course. He was so fond of conjuring with them that at one point he wrote an epitaph made up almost entirely of Alger titles and claimed he wanted it placed upon his tombstone.

His concern for the boys he loved was very real. He had brought one of them, Oren Trott, to Natick to stay with him during the summer. Later, back home, Oren fell in with evil companions and got into serious trouble. Here is Horatio's description of the problem as written in a letter of November, 1892 to another friend in Natick:

It appears that a boy named Hunt—a very bad boy, as Mr. Trott writes—followed him around persistently and as Oren is of easy disposition, managed to induce him to go about with him. This boy, *alone,* broke into some place and stole two watches and a ring. He prevailed upon Oren to sell the watches for him by offering him part of the proceeds. The sum realized was only a dollar and a quarter, but the fact that Oren sold them makes him an accomplice in the eyes of the law.

Both boys were arrested. Hunt is in jail now but Oren is at home going to school as usual. Still, he as well as Hunt will have to stand trial in January. A lawyer will be employed but whether the court will discriminate between Hunt and the boy whom he led into mischief is uncertain. Mr. and Mrs. Trott, who are excellent people, are very anxious and sad, and find the suspense hard to bear. If Oren knew the watches were stolen he was very weak and foolish to consent to sell them, and he realizes this now. I hope his previous good character will help him. He told me when he went home that he wished he had some boy companions at Peale's Island like the Natick boys....

Of course I shall stand by him whatever happens. I always do stand by a friend in time of trouble. I should like to have you show this letter to your uncle, as I want Oren's friends in Natick to think as well of him as they can. I should also like to have you say as little as possible about his trouble.

Horatio maintained friendships with many of his boys down to the end. Among them was Irving Blake, a poor boy he had helped, and who had now become a journalist. They were in frequent contact in 1894 and thereafter. When Alger was supposedly sojourning with Kate Down, he was also writing Blake to invite him to visit him at his rooms on Thirty-fourth Street on the special nights he kept open house. Through this correspondence, Horatio revealed a good deal of his own yearning to be remembered as a serious writer. He had undertaken the book on Webster, he said, to revive the memory of that statesman and make young people aware of his accomplishments, and from time to time he commented on other literary matters with the feelings of one who cared very much for that community. He was much saddened by the untimely death of Louisa May Alcott, for whom he felt a special kinship because of her writing field.

But above all in his correspondence, the feeling of a busy, satisfied bachelor comes through. He wrote about helping poor boys: one with money, one to find a place in a tailor shop, one for a lawyer's office, one for a business house.

In the summer of 1894 Horatio relaxed at Old Orchard Beach and with Gusti and her husband at Natick. He was working sporadically, for two months he had not touched pen that summer, but even on vacation he began to write. More serials and more boys' books were the result. At sixty-two he felt as vigorous as ever, and he wrote Blake "particularly because I have so many friends of your age with whom I sympathize."

Back at his digs at 223 West Thirty-fourth Street, he wrote Irving Blake about a poor boy he wanted to help, and then a few days later wrote again:

> I don't think he would be suitable for a lawyer's office, as his education is not sufficiently good, and he is only 14. I have a partial promise from my tailor to take him in the fall as [he] learned something of tailoring when an inmate of the Boys Catholic Protectory, and I will help him as he needs through the summer. There is another boy who would like the position in the lawyer's office. His name is Dennis Carlyle of 522 8th Avenue. He graduates this summer from the public schools. He is an orphan, but is better than Tommy Keegan, having older brothers who took care of him.

Horatio had grown far more tolerant than any of his relatives of the sins of the city, and he dined at the most fashionable places and houses in New York, not drinking himself, but no longer bothered by drinking when others imbibed. One day he and a friend dined at 122 William Street, at what was then the oldest public house in New York, which dated back 205 years and had been operated as a restaurant since 1764. "We got a fine dinner—table d'hote. If you are a temperance man, it won't do for you to go there," he wrote Irving Blake, knowing quite well that Blake was not a temperance man at all.

He wrote friends often about his work, which he took quite seriously, and yet without pretension. The titles of his books, heavy with onomatopoeia and alliteration, were not always his own doing. He wrote of a new book that it would be published in a small, dainty format, "similar to the books of Anthony Hope."

> I hardly thought the story worth such a setting, but my publisher proposes it. The title will be changed, as he doesn't like the one I had selected.

He was very much interested in literary doings, and read the literary magazines carefully. Dillingham remained one of his major publishers, although house after house was now bringing out Alger books, and he was in constant demand. When Frank Leslie planned a new juvenile magazine in 1895, he immediately turned to Alger for material, and although he no longer needed money or more work, Alger was agreeable; but Munsey was not, and Horatio was forced to decline such outside commitments. He was working in spurts. When he finished a story, he laid off writing for weeks or months, then started another and worked day and night.

Generally speaking, Horatio was pleased enough with his relations with Munsey not to worry about seeking commitments elsewhere. He wrote a friend:

> I learn that the circulation of Munsey's for July went up in spite of the reduced price of Cosmopolitan and McClure's. Munsey has the inside track.

Horatio was shy still. He was asked to do an article on writing for *The Writer,* of Boston, and declined because he was not sure of his own ideas, and because he did not want to get involved in controversy. He took a lively interest in politics and world affairs. He was basically quite conservative in his thinking, and certainly opposed to Free Silver, which was becoming an issue of the day. But boys still interested him most.

In August, 1895, he headed for a vacation in the Catskills, taking with him sixteen-year-old Frank Cushman, a distant cousin, who had just graduated from Boston's English High School. "You know I never travel alone if I can help it," he wrote Irving Blake, as he described his young companion:

> We are both descended from Rev. Robert Cushman, of Mayflower memory. He is as tall as you, and is a robust boy, weighing 150 pounds. He is quite able to pull me up the mountains, I may need such help.

That same letter mentioned two other boys, one of them living in Dartmouth, England, who had written recently describing an English election to Horatio. Without wife, and with little family left, Horatio reveled in his relations with boys. After two weeks in the Catskills, he brought young Robert Cushman down to New York with him on the steamer and then showed him the sights. He took him to the Statue of Liberty and to the theater. Robert was interested in sailing, so Horatio rounded up a friend who was a yachting expert and sent him off to see the *Valkyrie,* the newest of sailing yachts.

In the fall of 1895, Horatio was enjoying a good deal of leisure. He had only two serials a year to write, and by his standards this was almost like not working at all. H. T. Coates published *Adrift in the City* that fall, and he spoke of *Lester's Luck,* another story which had been published as a serial two years earlier. It was not actually published as a book for six more years, but sojourning with his sister and her husband in Natick, Horatio could hardly care.

> The country is still pleasant. Looking out the window I see on the lot adjoining the house a hundred oak and walnut trees. The leaves are beginning to change color. Every day a few children appear whom we allow to pick the nuts that have fallen. They are not of very good quality but the trees probably average 50 feet in height.

Back in New York in November, he was plunged into a busy social life.

> I have been expecting to see you here [he wrote Irving Blake]. I shall be absent Friday evening, Nov. 15, also Nov. 22, but shall be glad to see you some other evening. Next week I have dinner engagement on Tuesday and Wednesday and shall be at home on Monday and Thursday.

But if Blake or anyone else came on any given evening, they were just as likely to find Horatio out as in, for he seldom failed to respond to an invitation.

He was indefatiguable. He read nearly every magazine with special attention to the book notices, but did not like most of them because they were too vague. He wanted a précis of a book, not the comments of the reviewer. He was aware of all the markets available and passed the information along to other writers. He noticed an ad in the *Nation* by the Jewish Publication Society asking for short stories. He passed that on to Irving Blake, news-paperman and aspiring writer.

Editor Dillingham's death left Horatio considerably upset; it was hard at his age to make changes. But he was assured that the publishing house was in good shape and Dillingham's assistant, Mr. Cook, then took over and was able to convince Horatio that all would be well.

When *Adrift in the City* was published, it turned out to be more successful than any of Horatio's books had been for several years. He was pleased and related the tale of a book dealer he knew.

> Ehrich told a friend of mine that he sold every copy he had and had to order more. I think he had difficulty in obtaining them. While I did not care much for the book, I thought it would succeed.

Horatio was now regarded as a kind of fixture on the New York scene, and boys came to call on him seeking help. In fact, his popularity became a real nuisance and he moved down to 44 East Tenth Street, between Broadway and University Place, to escape the hordes. "I gave up my room on 34th Street because I had too many young callers who were unwelcome," he wrote, im-ploring his good friends not to broadcast his whereabouts.

When Louisa May Alcott died, he was truly upset.

> What a pity she died so soon! She had no competitor as a writer for girls. There are plenty of good writers for boys. If there were not, I should occupy a larger niche and have more abundant sales.

For a time during 1896, Horatio lived at the Hotel Imperial on Broadway at Thirty-second Street, then he moved back to his ancient haunts on Tenth Street, which was not far from the place he had lived when he first came to New York.

The markets changed again. He wrote for a magazine called *Pleasant Hours,* but it failed and *Leslie's* took over the editorial ma-terial. That spring he was tired, too much work he said, and he wished he could rally from the feeling of lassitude that overcame him. "I wish I had your youthful energy," he wrote Irving Blake.

In the late spring of 1896 Horatio traveled to Boston to meet A. K. Loring and spent a day with him at Marblehead talking over the old exciting days when the two of them were making literary history. Poor Loring had never recovered from the bankruptcy and was still living in virtual poverty. Horatio's existence was just the opposite; he had the money to do exactly as he wished, and he kept up a very active life. Staying in Natick in the fall of 1896, he visited the city of Boston, some twenty-five miles away, two or three times a week, attended the theater there, and when he was not going to the city went to entertainments in Natick itself.

Ever more time was spent these years in Natick and New England haunts, and ever less in New York, for with the departure of Superintendent O'Connor from the Newsboy's Lodging House, Horatio's relationships there had changed, and he no longer felt the same welcome.

There was, perhaps, something more than met the eye here. Perhaps the new superintendent was displeased with Horatio's relations with the boys. Perhaps he was suspicious of this old man who took such an interest in teen-agers.

But Horatio continued his friendships, undaunted by many failures.

> I don't know if you have heard that one of the boys who used to frequent my room—not to my satisfaction—is now at Sing Sing prison [he wrote Irving Blake]. Confined for burglary. I interested myself to obtain a mitigation of his sentence and was very successful. His prison term is two years, while it might have been ten or even more. I don't know the circumstances but he is not of the desperate type of which burglars are made. I don't think he realized what he was doing. I have sent him an autoharp to fill up his time as the prisoners are not now employed. I am on friendly terms with the warden, who is an admirable man.

He made the acquaintance of a young man named Edward Stratemeyer, who came to edit a Munsey magazine and later one for Street & Smith. Stratemeyer, who would later take over the accolade as the greatest volume producer of boys books in America, confessed that he had grown up on Alger's works and found them his literary guides. So no matter what happened to Horatio's own work, he had found a kind of immortality, at least.

In Natick, Horatio's interest in boys continued; he found jobs for them in Boston, he helped some get into business, and he helped some go to school. He had lost none of his old verve for writing, every year he brought forth another two or three books, trying to place his heroes in the areas that would appeal to boys. Occasionally he visited New York, but he never stayed for long. He had a Philadelphia publisher now, and New York seemed far less important to him.

Money was not a problem, but in these last years there was not so much of it as there had been in earlier years. Horatio looked forward to receiving his publisher's statements, hoping his books had sold well, but was not as happy as he had been with the results. He had capital, he invested some of it in a business in Boston, as a silent partner, to secure the income he was no longer receiving from magazines, for that revenue had fallen. Nor did he enjoy writing much now—he wrote Irving Blake that he looked back with longing on the days when work had been pleasant.

What the country wanted from him, still, was the story of the street boys, and he went hither and thither in New England lecturing, mostly to boys' groups.

In the spring of 1897 his old friend Adams—Oliver Optic— died, and Horatio had a sense of his own mortality strongly pressed upon him.

Horatio himself was feeling the effects of age. He frequently repeated himself in letters, and his handwriting had grown crabbed and sometimes almost undecipherable. In one letter he reviewed an article of Mark Twain's with the comment that he and Twain and the other old writers did not seem to improve with age. He was coming to terms with the failure of his ambition to produce that great American novel he had once wanted to write.

Chapter Twenty-Two

End of an Era

Horatio, in the evening of his life, still spent his time, money and emotions on boys. He was supporting several poor boys, in various ways, sending some through school and establishing others. He moved around New England giving talks to various boys' clubs on his visits to foreign lands and on the city and its street Arabs. And he was feeling the press of his years; in the winter of 1897 he wrote often in letters to friends about the cold and how it bothered him.

He took a lively interest in politics. One day while in New York he went to a meeting to hear Theodore Roosevelt, who was supposed to speak. For some reason, Roosevelt did not show up, and finding himself called upon to speak, Horatio delivered a very fair oration which was well received. He was a Republican, generally speaking, but not a hidebound one and he approached politics with a good deal of healthy skepticism. In 1896 he had predicted on the victory of William McKinley. "It will usher in an era of confidence and prosperity." When Tammany won the 1897 city elections:

227

> I am not sure but it is better to have Tammany win now. Before the next election it will have made mistakes enough to send voters in disgust to the Republican ranks. [Senator] Platt [the Republican leader] and [Richard] Croker [Tammany Democrat] seem to be "birds of a feather."

He felt impelled to explain to some of his correspondents his interest in writing. This year, *Walter Sherwood's Probation* was published by Henry T. Coates, his new publisher, as part of a new series called the Good Fortune series.

> I wrote it with a special purpose. Walter Sherwood is a type of a class to be found in all our colleges. I never feel as much interest in a rich boy as in a poor boy who has to struggle with circumstances. Walter had pecuniary troubles for a time.

In February he suffered a siege of bronchitis that really worried him. He wrote Irving Blake that "there was a strong *possibility* of pneumonia which to one of my physique would probably have been fatal."

In Natick he made speeches and whiled away his time. He went to South Framingham to address the YMCA on "Random Recollections of Foreign Lands."

He enjoyed publicity, when it came his way, but dreamed more of wealth.

> I recently bought a subscription book "Famous Authors of England and America" published in Philadelphia. Three pages are devoted to me, while curiously [J.T.] Trowbridge [another prominent boys' writer and an acquaintance] is not mentioned. He is not doing much, having made a small fortune by the sale of real estate in Kennebunkport, I should like to follow his example.

He was still preoccupied with literary markets.

> I suppose *Youth and Home* is dead, and I have heard nothing of it of late. Isn't it strange that juvenile magazines and papers don't seem to flourish?

He had adopted, informally, the two Down brothers and he worried about what was going to become of them.

> I think of giving Tommy a vacation from work and sending him to a commercial college soon. He will be 18 in March. He has been under my charge a little more than 3½ years. I sent John Down to the same institution at 18. I may not be able to leave Tommy much but I mean to leave him a better education at any rate.

He was lonely and often spoke of his lack of literary companionship, which he tried to erase by constantly reading new books and magazines. He had come to terms with himself about his unfortunate bout with the ministry and justified it as really no more than a literary excursion. Writing to Irving Blake, he explained that

> ... in 1860–61 and again in 1873 I went to Europe, visiting the principal continental countries, as well as Great Britain. At the later date I visited the Vienna Exposition. I have travelled considerably in the United States including two trips to the Pacific coast in quest of material for books. I studied theology chiefly as a branch of literary culture and without any intention of devoting myself to it as a profession. During my three years course, I was in the employ of various papers, chiefly the New York *Sun*, I acted as foreign correspondent for that paper during my first European trip.

His sense of humor was lively and boyish, and he took pleasure in poking fun at his friends, most of them old "boys" of his. Blake was one of the favorites, and Blake's rise at the New York *Tribune* gave Horatio considerable pleasure. The younger man wondered if he should not go on to college; Horatio told him no, the *Tribune* was his college and he would "receive a degree of Bachelor of Journalism" from it.

> If you want your picture in the paper, the best way is to get cured by some patent medicine. For instance it might be published that Irving Blake, a distinguished member of the *Tribune*

editorial force, has been restored to youth and health by Tompkins Rejuvenating Powders. So that while probably a man of middle age, he looks like a youth of 18.

Horatio always took a lively interest in the literary arts. When Bret Harte's new play, *Sue,* opened in Boston he took a young Natick friend to see it. Then he reviewed it for his friend Blake in a letter.

The plot is faulty but the character acting is good. Some of the minor characters are quite picturesque, especially those who take part in a lynching court scene. I don't think however, that the piece can on the whole be regarded as a success.

He bore reviews of his own work with more equanimity than most writers, as when *Frank Hunter's Peril* came out and the *Tribune* roasted him because all his books read alike.

As to the notice of my own books there is undoubtedly a family resemblance between them but I find this does not seem an objection to readers.

But in all, he did not envy his young friends so much as he admired them for their enthusiasms.

I wonder, Irving, how it would seem to be as young and full of life and enthusiasm as you are. I shouldn't dare to go back to 19 again, lest my share of success prove to be less than it has been. But you will have a chance to see "a strange new world" with many wonderful inventions and discoveries. If I could come back 50 years from now probably I should feel bewildered in reading the New York *Tribune* of 1947.

Looking back on his life, he took a certain satisfaction in having made the most of whatever abilities he had and in having achieved international fame as a writer.

Suffering frequent attacks of bronchitis and other ailments, Horatio lived in continual dread that he would contract pneumonia because he did not feel that he would survive it. The spring of 1898 was a particularly difficult time for him, and he felt his energy slipping away. A juvenile magazine suggested that he write a series of serials for them based on the lives of famous men, but he declined, saying it would take too much work—far more than the ordinary fictional serials he wrote—and he did not have the strength to do them.

Summer found Horatio little improved from his winter troubles. He had bronchitis still, and his heart pounded. By midsummer he was very weak and frail; Stratemeyer wanted to talk to him about writing a number of short stories, but he felt unable to make the trip to New York to discuss the matter. Yet he continued to write his books and the serials for Munsey. To keep up with the times, Horatio made his books much more violent than they had been in the past. *The Young Bank Messenger,* for example, deals with a young boy, unlawfully and unjustly deprived of his family fortune, whose guardian died at the beginning of the book. The boy was set upon by a tramp, who robbed him once and then tried to rob him a second time. A friend caught the tramp, knocked him down and threatened to shoot him. A bit later in the book, an outlaw robbed a farmer's wife, seized her by the throat when he became displeased and threatened to kill her. In an earlier time, violence would never have been perpetrated on a woman in one of Horatio's books, but boys demanded much more these days.

There were other changes. An Indian in this book speaks perfect English, but a black servant still speaks the patois attributed to all blacks: "Well, Massa Frank, what am you doing?"

This book has nothing to do with New York. The hero began life in Iowa and went to California, where he went into the gold fields, yet the lure was too great, and before the end of the book, the hero had to go to New York to see a lawyer and secure his rightful fortune. So it was of the same warp and woof of all the old Alger books, with but a few changes in detail. By this time, Horatio had written well over a hundred of them and had sketched out plots for many more. Indeed, the clue to his writing had always been the plot; he devoted scant consideration to characters, and when he considered the abilities of some of his young friends as literary aspirants, he spoke in terms of their ability to plot, not their ability to characterize or give a feeling for place and time.

By winter, 1898, Horatio was failing rapidly, and his writing showed it; physically he was scarcely able to carry on correspondence with his closest friends. He was suffering a certain financial stricture; his situation was not terribly serious, but for the first time in years, when Irving Blake suggested that he could use a loan for a time, Horatio felt unable to send him a draft until he had new royalty returns from his publisher.

The spring of 1899 found him no better. Asthma and bronchitis made him miserable and almost totally unable to work. He had planned once again to spend a little time at Old Orchard Beach with his sister and brother-in-law, for he found the sea air helped his breathing, but in July when they were about to leave, he came down with a severe attack of asthma and was put to bed. The family was so concerned about his future that his niece Annie was called from her home not far away, and she came to pay her respects. He lingered several days, and then on July 18, Horatio Alger, Jr. died.

But the literary Horatio lived on for many years. The publishers found the name too valuable to kill, and they employed Edward Stratemeyer to "finish up" various plots and half-done serials that Horatio had begun. So books continued to come out under the Alger name, and in the summer of 1901 the magazine *Golden Hours* serialized *Young Captain Jack,* which, the editors announced, was the last manuscript of Horatio, completed by Arthur M. Winfield (one of Stratemeyer's pen names).

In his personal will, Horatio left bequests of small amounts, ranging from $125 to $500 to half a dozen boys. To a niece in San Francisco he left a gold watch and $25 each for her children; to his niece Annie Andrews, he left a lot in Chicago. There were several other bequests, his library to Amos Cheney his brother-in-law, and then all the rest, the royalties and the manuscripts and the literary estate, he willed to his sister Gusti, his niece Annie, and the two Down boys he had informally adopted several years earlier.

For the next few years, Sister Gusti was busy placing books and serials, old manuscripts and some stories finished by Stratemeyer. The Alger vogue continued until nearly 1910 and then died out; soon Alger was famous only as the name for an American syndrome, the rags to riches story.

The Alger Family monument. Unitarian Church Graveyard, South Natick, Massachusetts

In the years that followed, the Alger books slipped away. Boys who grew up in the period before World War I were almost all familiar with his work, those after World War I too, until the mid-1920s, when he was more or less supplanted in his field, by Stratemeyer, who wrote even more books (*The Rover Boys, Tom Swift* among others) than Alger. In the 1930s and 1940s, librarians, taking on a social conscience they had not exhibited so sharply before, decided that the Alger books were trash and many libraries threw them off the shelves.

So Horatio Alger's memory languished until nearly midcentury, when social critics became concerned with the slippage and perversion of the old American dream and began delving into the psyche of capitalism. They discovered then that Horatio had been the high priest of the system, and they began counting the number of prominent men who had grown up on the Alger books and attributed some degree of their success to his inspiration. Among many others these critics found bankers, publishers and industrial giants who claimed that Horatio had been their ideal of an author and that they had drawn strength from his books.

In the interim years, Herbert Mayes had published the biography that attributed to Horatio the strange and sinful life, and from time to time various authors delved into this book to write a magazine article about a Horatio who never existed.

Meanwhile, however, Alger students and Alger collectors were trying to unravel the truth from the fiction. Ralph D. Gardner, the most indefatigable of Alger collectors, spent years studying the Alger story and collecting material. He published a book in 1964, *Horatio Alger: The American Hero Era,* which purported to be a biography, although Gardner made no mention of one fact he had discovered: the Brewster affair. While written in the Alger style, heavy with conversation, the book gave no sources at all for the conversations and very few for any other facts. Yet it was apparent that Gardner had researched heavily into the life of his hero.

Perhaps the most persistent student of Alger in America was Max Goldberg, who was for many years an active officer in the Horatio Alger Society, which was formed to preserve the name and fame of the author and celebrate his concept of the American dream. Goldberg never stopped collecting Algeriana, and had once intended to write a biography, but the Gardner book, he said, let the steam out of his engine. He continued to collect and as of the writing of this book, intended to leave his enormous accumulation of material to Brandeis University, where it will be available to Alger scholars.

Critics of Alger have never quite got the handle on him; it was hard for a mid-twentieth century critic to take Alger seriously because of the stick figures and stock types he used so many times in his books. Some critics tended at first to regard his influence as minimal and then reconsidered; while they refuse to take Horatio seriously as an author, they are willing to deal with him as a social force, a writer whose influence on the American scene has been so profound that it is hard to measure.

Publishing is a shadowy trade. The publishers of Horatio Alger, almost to a man, and company, have slipped out of existence over the years. Thus in 1974 there is no accurate record of the sales figures of Alger books, but estimates range from 100,000,000 to half a billion, in various editions, and this says nothing of the circulation of the magazines that carried his serial stories. Nor could anyone even estimate with accuracy the amount of money Horatio made from his work, except that he never cashed in on it the way twentieth century authors were able to do with only fleeting success.

In the 1950s, 1960s and 1970s Horatio came into a certain vogue, Macmillan republished his books *Ragged Dick* and *Mark the Match Boy* in a single Collier paperback volume, with some success, while Holt, Rinehart and Winston, Doubleday and Popular Library followed with some others. Collectors of the old Alger books came along in such number that the books are valued in first editions at around $25 on the average, with even the cheap editions selling at $4 and $5 a copy, while the rarest of all Algers, *Timothy Crump's Ward,* is estimated to be worth $1000.

Alger's persistence, above and beyond his critics, is a phenomenon of American life, a symbol of a dream that in the third-quarter of the twentieth century sometimes seems impossible of attainment; yet it is so much a part of the American manner of thought that it cannot be discarded. It *is* true, even in the last half of the twentieth century, that men came up from poverty and struggle, to become millionaires and live the good life; the Alger dream exists, and almost always when a man achieves fame and fortune, Horatio's name is invoked by newspaper journalists in describing the path to success. The emergence of big government, big business and conglomerates does not change that fact, and probably, as long as the American system continues it never will. Things have changed, but the dream has not died.

Chapter Twenty-Three

Horatio Alger
in History

Iғ one is to understand Horatio Alger, Jr. and his place in the American scene, one had best begin with a study of the America in which he grew up and reached maturity. This was in many ways the most exciting of all times in American history. As a boy he lived through the beginning of the western expansion; as a youth he lived with the struggle between slavery and freedom; as an adult he saw the burgeoning of an industrial giant in America. In other words, Horatio Alger, Jr.'s life spanned the maturing of the nation. When he was born it was a weak and spindly country just emerging from the depression caused by the War of 1812. When he died America was taking its place among the big powers of the world; it had shown its muscle in the Boxer rebellion and the settlement just afterwards, gone through the Spanish American war and become a colonial power, and Teddy Roosevelt was beginning to talk like a worldshaker.

So what Horatio represented in America was very real. The total approval of his books by ministers, educators and businessmen of his own day was also real. Alger's America was their America. They wanted boys to grow up with an appreciation of hard work, a strong character and good fortune. They loved money and power and saw nothing wrong in that. Debunkers of later years would sneer at Horatio Alger and the success syndrome, but without it, without the Vanderbilts and the other empire builders, the empire would not have been built. Of course in an energy-bedeviled and pollution-ridden time it could be argued that the world would have been a better place if Horatio and his heroes had never existed at all. It could also be argued that the Morgenthau plan would have made economic deserts of Germany and Japan at the end of World War II and prevented the Germans and Japanese from dominating the industrial world in the 1970s. And it could be argued that if only Alfred Nobel had never invented dynamite the world would be a safer place.

But the world is what it is, and Horatio was what he was because of it. The Alger books are strong medicine; they cannot be taken too often or too many at a time. The reader who can get through three of them without stopping has his head awhirl with wicked squires; wicked squires' sons; evil poorhouse managers; street boys; sweet and ineffectual mothers; dying fathers; strong, manly, robust heroes; delicate flowers of girls; evil roisterers and other bad companions; friendly, firm, helpful businessmen; and the rich, rich, rich. But the struggle, as Horatio said in a letter to Irving Blake late in his life, always counts for more than the reward. Alger was interested in the struggle, in the ability of young boys of no fortune, and maybe not even any education to speak of, to pull themselves up by their own bootstraps through courage, honesty, character—and yes, luck—for the Alger theory maintains that luck comes to those who deserve it. Alger needed no more justification than that for the miraculous coincidences that were a hallmark of his style.

In the America of the 1970s it is easy to poke fun at Alger and the Alger syndrome. But to do so is in a sense to deny our own history. Take some Alger heroes of real life: Daniel Webster was a poor boy, the son of a New Hampshire saloonkeeper, and he worked his way into the United States Senate and was Secretary of State and became a rich man. James Garfield grew up in backwoods Ohio and became President. Abraham Lincoln—everyone knows that story. And there were others. Alger was properly reverent toward Commodore Cornelius Vanderbilt, who came from a rawboned Staten Island farm family and became at least the second richest man in the world (one of the British royal family may have had more money, depending on how you valued land in the 1870s). Alexander Turney Stewart, who would be the greatest merchant of New York in his day, came over to the new world on a cattle boat from Ireland. Joseph Pulitzer, the newspaper genius, came as an immigrant from Hungary. Henry Ford, who lived in Alger's day, was a mechanic. Of course there was money and position in Alger's day, too. There were the Stuyvesants and Fishes and Astors and Roosevelts. But the opportunity of meeting these people on their own level existed for every boy, and that was precisely what Alger was talking about.

His books are weak in character. The flatness of the figures is so remarkable that it is almost impossible to remember a day after reading what was different about Walter Sherwood. What marked him from Ben Bradford? And what distinguished Tom Brace from Tom Temple or Tim Thatcher—all heroes of Alger books? But as Alger said, his boy readers did not seem to mind. They got an Alger book twice a year perhaps, and they read it avidly and were ready for the next one.

Alger was important as one of the first of the American travel writers, when he wrote about New York. He got more of the flavor of that wicked city in his books than any other writer. He did not do so well with California, the plains, the Midwest or Australia, but as far as giving a picture of life in New York is concerned, he was superb. The New York *Times* once called him "Prose Laureate" of that city. And he was also very good at picturing rural life in New England.

Paul Gallico, writer and critic, once gave Horatio credit for creating the "mortgage syndrome," that is, the deadly fear of mortgages or borrowing money that bothered many Americans and still bothers some. This is nonsense; Horatio was simply reflecting his own New England background, for New Englanders until very recently suffered under the Puritan conscience that despised debt and worshipped independence more than wealth. And this attitude exists in rural New England even to this day. Not long ago I visited with an old Vermont farmer, a man with 350 acres of land that he owns outright. No mortgage, no debt, no time plans for him. This old farmer started out small and kept on buying land from his neighbors when he had the money. He looks around him in the 1970s and is appalled by new neighbors who have 100 horsepower tractors, fancy station wagons, big houses and even *swimming pools*. And as we talked that day, he pointed a gnarled finger up the road, where a swimming pool was just being built. "And that feller doesn't even own his *own herd,*" he said. "It's mortgaged." The way he intoned that last word, it sounded as though the herd was cursed.

No, Horatio did not invent New England conservatism or the Puritan ethic, but he certainly did publicize them more than any other writer. Even as Horatio was working, other writers were using the same themes. *Bertha the Sewing Machine Girl,* a melodrama of the 1870s, deals heavily in mortgages and assaults on ladies' virtue. *The Drunkard* plays the same theme. The song *Heaven Will Protect the Working Girl,* very popular in music halls in the days of Horatio's youth, had two great Puritan lines:

> Beware of the upper classes
> With their villainous demi-tasses

Horatio had written in a letter that if he could come back in 1947—fifty years later—he would scarcely recognize the New York *Tribune.* How right he was—it was not even the *Tribune* then, but the *Herald-Tribune,* a marriage of a Democratic and Republican newspaper that were deadly enemies in every way in Horatio's day. And of course, even that marriage was not to last, for the parties died not too long thereafter.

In his study of Alger, Ralph Gardner makes an excellent observation on one aspect of modern America that almost precludes modern Americans from understanding Alger. The self-made man hardly exists any more. This author happens to know some self-made men, but I am fifty years old at this writing, and those men are in their seventies and upward; I don't know any of my own generation and only one of a younger generation. One day at the late Rube Goldberg's house on Long Island I met Howard Samuels, who later ran unsuccessfully for governor of New York, and was fascinated to learn that Samuels had made a fortune by the simple process of thinking up the plastic clothesline. I never really got into the matter of Howard Samuels' background, but I suspect from his demeanor that he was not really a self-made man in the old sense because he had too much of the veneer of civilization about him. I could not be a self-made man myself. My parents and the state of Oregon combined to give me a college education, which already lets me out. At times, when I am trying to impress my own children with the need for frugality and hard work and character and honesty, leading to luck—you know, all the old Alger virtues—I recall that I once had a job driving a wheezy truck for the Portland *Journal of Commerce* for five dollars a week and that later on as a college student I worked for the Eugene (Oregon) *Daily News* for seven dollars a week. They, somehow, are unimpressed. Or to put it another way, they are impressed, but much as children are impressed when someone takes them to the American Museum of Natural History and shows them the skeleton of the brontosaurus up on the second floor. It's nice, but it doesn't relate to anything. Still, I know for a fact something my children don't know and probably never will, given the world in which they live. Horatio was dead right about one thing: it is the game that is worth the candle, not the victory.

No, the day of the Alger hero is long gone and Walter Sherwood is just as much of a brontosaurus as I am; three generations have now passed since Alger's day, and he is quite right, if he came back to New York or New England he would never recognize either place.

Ralph Gardner mentions old Thomas J. Watson, who started out as a six dollar a week bookkeeper and became head of IBM in the Alger style. He is right, old Tom was an Alger hero; young Tom, who succeeded his father, was born when the old man was coming along and grew up in moderately wealthy circumstances. He was an airplane pilot in the service in World War II, and he seriously considered staying on in the service, but his father dragooned him out of that and into the company, which Young Tom turned into a multibillion dollar industrial giant. But he didn't accomplish this in the Alger fashion. His was the new way, the corporate merger and the manipulation of industrial strength and the wheeling and dealing and use of scientists to further industry. He wasn't an Alger type at all, but a super industrialist. And as for Young Tom's children, well, one of his daughters and one of mine went to school together (that's America for you!), and the last time my daughter ran into his daughter they were both living in about the same circumstances in Annapolis, Maryland, and nobody around those parts even knew Cindy Watson was young Tom's kid. New generation stuff.

Sure there were a lot of Alger heroes. I wrote a book years ago about a handful of them: Tom Watson; Alfred Fuller, the brush man; William Benton, the advertising man; and I have written about a lot more of them in another book called the *Idea Men:* old man Astor, who invented New York real estate; Westinghouse; and a dozen others. One thing they all have in common is that they are all dead, and that disposes of the Alger ambience too.

But just because Horatio and his pals, his heroes and the men who aped those heroes are gone, this does not mean that Alger has no further place in American society. He is an interesting relic, and his books are worth looking over once in a while to remember how things used to be. If nothing else, a reader must enter an Alger book with wide-eyed innocence and the understanding that everything Alger wrote about in his time *could and did happen,* for almost all of Alger's tales were taken basically from life. They might be bits and pieces worked together, but the squires and the villains and the businessmen and the heroes did exist, and Alger saw them day after day.

Alger did some social good in his time. He helped wipe out the child abuse system of New York, and he furthered the rehabilitation of New York waifs. Much of the success of the Children's Aid Society stems from interest he aroused. But primarily he was not anything more or less than a popular writer, and he saw himself in that role. As the years went on and the pain of the Brewster experience gradually died away, Alger preferred to think of his venture into the ministry simply as an exercise in literary skills of another kind; but everyone practices some form of self-delusion in older years, the object being to make the past a little easier to handle, and there is nothing wrong in it as long as a man's biographers don't take it too seriously.

Alger was the most popular boys writer in all American history, and his works sold millions and hundreds of millions of copies. In the 1970s, a younger, more sophisticated generation finds him unreadable in the same way that the Three Bears and Little Red Ridinghood are unreadable. But Horatio Alger's "success" syndrome remains a peculiarly American phenomenon, and the America of the 1970s has discovered in him another peculiarly American attribute—in the lionization of the homosexual. The information has come out that Alger was a homosexual. This may even serve to rekindle interest in him within the super-literary community and make of him an American folk hero to rival Oscar Wilde.

Chapter Twenty-Four

The Published Alger

As a youngster, when the first literary stirrings welled within his soul, Horatio Alger, Jr. thought of himself first of all as a poet. Poetry continued to be his greater interest for some time. In all, he published some 100 poems and odes; nearly all of them were written by 1875. In his twenties he began to discover that he had a real talent for narrative prose and *Gleason's Pictorial Drawing Room Companion* in 1853 was his first major market for short stories. He did even better in 1854 with *The Flag of Our Nation,* which ran twelve stories in that one year.

By Alger's own statement, he began to turn to children's literature because of the success he found in the pages of *Student and Schoolmate.* This is not strictly true. Long before his prose graced the pages of Oliver Optic's magazine, Horatio was finding markets. The various Gleason publications accounted for a hundred Alger stories before he published a line in *Student and Schoolmate.* So when he went to Oliver Optic it was not hat in hand, but as a published writer with a very fair record in the field.

Along with the books, Horatio continued to write short stories for many years. In 1859 he published twenty-seven stories.

A promotion piece by one of Alger's publishers

All through the 1860s he was a prolific writer of short prose, as he got his feet on the ground with his books. *Student and Schoolmate* did start him on one road: that of the serial story, and perhaps that is what he meant when he told Irving Blake that Oliver Optic had been responsible for his choice of the juvenile field.

One reason that Horatio's life was so dull was that in his adult years he had little time to do anything but write. Take the year 1872, for example. Horatio was forty years old that year, living in digs in New York and writing his head off. That year he published only two short stories, but he wrote another half dozen that were published by *Gleason's Monthly Companion* the following year. He also wrote a serial for *Student and Schoolmate, (Slow and Sure),* another for *Young Israel (Strive and Succeed)* and wrote separately *Phil the Fiddler* for Loring to publish as a book. This latter was the celebrated exposé of the Italian padrone system of child slavery.

Besides all this, Horatio spent a good deal of his time at the Seligman establishment, where he had been engaged as more or less permanent tutor to all the children.

Years after Horatio's death, Editor Harold Ross of the *New Yorker* would characterize another prolific writer, Alexander Woollcott, as the greatest self-plagiarizer in history. Ross was obviously not aware of Horatio's hidden talent: he managed to get one short story, "The Saracen Dwarf," published by *The Flag of Our Nation* in November, 1854. Somehow, he got *Ballou's Dollar Monthly* to publish it again in January, 1855, and *Gleason's Monthly Companion* to publish it again January, 1874. Presumably he was paid for the story each time it was published.

More than that, Horatio seldom let an idea go by without milking it. Thus a story "Five Hundred Dollars," which appeared in *Graham's Illustrated Magazine* in Janurary, 1858, became *$500: Jacob Marlowe's Secret,* as a serial story that ran in *Argosy* in 1888 and 1889. It was serialized in *Good News* in 1897. It was published as a book by the United States Book Company in 1890. Subsequently there were several other editions by other publishers. There is no real connection between the magazine article and the book, but the idea was there.

All through Alger, the ideas were repeated. Most Alger books, where the hero is in school at all, have a scene of confrontation between the hero and the bully. Quite probably this dates back to

Horatio's own boyhood, when he was unmercifully bullied by bigger boys in Revere. There are other set pieces that run throughout the Alger work: the poorhouse and its unfeeling managers is one; another is the heartless squire with mortgage in hand.

Boys and even girls never seemed to tire of these stereotypes, even as modern boys and girls never tire of the stereotypes of gangsters and western gunmen.

Horatio began his career as an author of books with *Bertha's Christmas Vision,* which must be accounted a publishing failure. His second book, *Nothing To Do,* was a publishing gimmick designed to take advantage of a momentary flurry of public demand. His third book, *Frank's Campaign,* was the beginning of the boys' books, and also the start of his long association with A. K. Loring. But it was only with publication of the fourth book, in 1865—*Paul Prescott's Charge*—that Loring considered Horatio successful enough as a writer to invest in a series of books by him.

This first series was the Campaign series. It was followed by the much better known Ragged Dick series, which had as its first book the best and most successful of all Alger works, that early story of a New York street boy.

By 1868 Horatio was successful enough and busy enough that he found it necessary to adopt a pen name. The first of these was Arthur Hamilton, which he used to write "Ralph Raymond's Heir," published that year as a serial story in *Gleason's Literary Companion.* The reason for the pen name was his relationship with Oliver Optic and *Student and Schoolmate,* who were bragging that Horatio was their literary property and were very jealous of anything he did for anyone else.

In these years, Horatio was still working on the Ragged Dick series of books and had begun a new series for Loring called the Luck and Pluck books, which had a wider frame than the New York streets.

Horatio had another pen name for quite another reason. The name was Caroline F. Preston, and it appeared on various short stories written by Horatio. But the name was also used by Horatio's sister Gusti, who wrote short stories herself. Ralph Gardner suggests that both Horatio and Gusti wrote some of the stories, one starting it and the other finishing it. The secret was revealed by the editor of *Young Israel,* who was a man with a sense of humor. When Alger took his family to Europe in the summer of 1873, *Young Israel* published a little note in the chat column of the magazine, noting that three of the magazine's contributors would be traveling abroad that year: Horatio, Miss O. Augusta Cheney and Miss Caroline F. Preston. It was a good joke of the private kind that magazine editors relish.

As time went on, Horatio moved his settings around the world. But he never did abandon the city scene, and most of his books, no matter what the actual setting, contain at least a chapter in which the young hero comes to New York and has adventures that involve street boys. Later he would adopt the name Arthur Lee Putnam for some of his books and stories—again to obviate a personal relationship and contractual commitment of the name Alger to some publication. Along came Frank Munsey, who found Horatio's work so compelling that he used the Putnam name so he might have two Algers running simultaneously in *Argosy.*

A third pen name, the most interesting of all, was Julian Starr. Horatio took time out from his boys' stories in the early 1890s to write an adult book entitled *The Disagreeable Woman* which was set in New York, but without a juvenile hero. The book was turned down for publication by Frank Munsey, who did not want anything but boys' books from Horatio, and by Porter & Coates, who succeeded the bankrupt Loring as Horatio's basic book publishers. So Horatio gave the book to George Dillingham, who had been Loring's editor years before and was now head of the G. W. Carleton publishing firm. Munsey still controlled Horatio's name, so he had to get the publisher's permission to put out the book at all, and Munsey insisted that a totally unknown pen name be used. For all this trouble, the book was a dismal failure and it soon disappeared from the world. In fact, as Gardner noted in 1964, the only copy extant is in the hands of the Libary of Congress, and if there are others, they are gathering dust in somebody's attic.

Horatio had many publishers, for several reasons. The first reason was the fragility of the publishing business. Loring went bankrupt and was followed by others of Horatio's friends. Porter & Coates, his second publisher, was succeeded by Henry T. Coates and Company. And then there was G. W. Carleton, to which Alger came through Dillingham, and J. S. Ogilvie, and John R. Anderson, who tried to start the Famous Lives series. Another Alger publisher of note was A. L. Burt, who took on a number of Alger serials from the *New York Weekly*. Late in the 1880s Frank Munsey went into book publishing, too, and brought out as books several Alger titles that had appeared in *Golden Argosy* magazine.

Penn Publishing did a number of Alger books in the last years of the nineteenth century and early years of the twentieth. Street & Smith published some. Then came M. A. Donahue and the New York Book Company, which published millions of copies of cheap reprints of Alger works. And finally, as the copyrights ran out, other publishers entered the field. In all, Gardner counted up more than sixty book publishers who had at one time or another put out an Alger book.

After Alger died, the spate of Alger books continued. Indeed, there were new titles. These were not books that Alger had finished and put away, they were books written by Edward Stratemeyer, who himself was one of the most prolific writers of boys' books in history. Stratemeyer and Alger had first met when the former was appointed editor of Street & Smith's *Good News* in 1890. Stratemeyer was carrying water on both shoulders—writing boys books and publishing. Alger had helped him get started as an author. Alger liked Stratemeyer and wished him well. As the young man changed jobs, he would come to Alger for stories, but Horatio was also a very canny man, a "money writer" in his last years, and he turned Stratemeyer down when he could not come up with an adequate payment for stories.

It was obvious that when Horatio died he would leave unfinished work behind him, for his work pattern was always to be laboring on several ideas at once. So either his employers or Gusti or both chose Stratemeyer to take on the Alger bottom drawer and make books out of what existed there to cash in on what was left of the Alger claim to fame. Stratemeyer published eleven more Alger books before he stopped mining that vein.

For those particularly interested in the ins and outs of Alger's literary history, there is no better source than Ralph Gardner's *Horatio Alger: The American Hero Era*. Gardner focuses on the collection of the books and the unraveling of the publishing stories around them.

The vogue for Horatio Alger continued until almost 1910, with some Alger stories published and republished, including many of Stratemeyer's. Then the vogue died out as times changed, and after World War I, although thousands of young Americans still read Alger avidly, fewer and fewer books were published. By the 1930s they had become very definitely dated, and librarians were removing them from the shelves as "trash."

In the 1950s and 1960s the Alger vogue was revived to some extent, and several New York publishers brought out various Alger reprints, including *Ragged Dick*. Doubleday and Co. even dredged up an original, *Silas Snobden's Office Boy*, which had been published as a serial by *Argosy* under the Putnam byline, but had never come out earlier as a book. Popular Library has since issued a paperback edition of this work. By this time, Horatio was published more as a curiosity than as an author. As with even the greats, style changes, language changes, ideas change. So the literary great of yesterday becomes the required reading of tomorrow and the forgotten figure of the day after. Horatio Alger, Jr. has come in for a very large amount of abuse from critics for his style and his use of language and his repetitions, but let these same critics go back and try Sir Walter Scott all over again.

But all of this is small talk. The fact is that Horatio Alger, Jr., super-author, was the best-selling author of all time in America. His name has come down to us and will linger on even after all the books are turned to dust. For Alger is the symbol of the American dream of success through steam and zest.

Notes and Acknowledgments

THE IDEA FOR this biography of Horatio Alger and his work was not my own, but that of Benton Arnovitz of Chilton Book Company to whom I am also indebted for the title. The primary research was done at Harvard University, which has more Alger material than any other source, including a very complete collection of Alger's works that contains all but the real rarities. From time to time Horatio Alger, Sr. and Horatio Alger, Jr. both donated books to the Harvard library, a number of them inscribed for one reason or another. I am in the debt of a number of librarians at Harvard's Widener and Houghton libraries. Max Goldberg of Natick was extremely helpful, showing me part of his Alger collection and answering a number of questions about Horatio's life. Librarians at the Marlborough, Massachusetts, public library, assisted me a good deal and showed me their collection of Alger books and biographical material they had accumulated over the years. Charles Holbrook of Yarmouth, Massachusetts, Walter Babbitt of Brewster and various ladies of the Brewster Ladies' Library helped me track down the information I needed about Horatio's stay there and the scandal that sent him away, and the librarian of the Yarmouth Public Library, graciously helped me with the files of the newspapers of Alger's day. Mrs. Marion Wiley of Brewster gave me some tips on other Alger material. Librarians at the Castleton, Vermont library were helpful. I am indebted to Professor and Mrs. William Patterson for the loan of Alger books.

Like many another who delved into the life of Horatio Alger, Jr., I began with the premise that the biography by Herbert L. Mayes, *Alger, a Biography Without a Hero,* was the authoritative work on the subject. But as I went along, I became aware of discrepancies and a lack of attribution in this book. Once I had got deep into the subject I found very little that could be verified in the whole work. Ralph Gardner's *Horatio Alger,* itself short on attribution, contradicted Mayes at nearly every turn. The Mayes book depended very heavily on a diary supposedly kept by Horatio, but the diary has never been seen by another writer. Max Goldberg, then President of the Alger Society, wrote to Mayes asking what had happened to his research material, Mayes replied that he had turned it over to the Children's Aid Society, but when Max Goldberg wrote that organization its officials had no recollection of ever having received any such material, nor was it found in the files. I wrote Mr. Mayes, but he did not reply.

Now comes an article in *Publisher's Weekly,* by William Henderson, quoting Mayes' admission that his book was a fraud. "Not merely was my Alger biography partly fictional, it was practically *all* fictional.... The project was undertaken with malice aforethought—a takeoff on the debunking biographies that were quite popular in the 20s.... Unfortunately—how unfortunately!—the book when it appeared was accepted pretty much as gospel."

I am very much indebted to the librarians of the Revere, Massachusetts Library for showing me their picture collection and helping me with details about that period of Alger's life. The officials of the Huntington Library in San Marino, California, kindly provided me with research copies of the greatest collection of Alger correspondence known, which consists of letters written mostly between 1892 and 1898.

In doing research for the Alger book, I consulted a large number of newspapers and magazines, but oddly enough, I found that most of them written in the 1930s and after depended on the Mayes book for basic material, and thus could scarcely be trusted. Harvard University's alumni archives possesses the most authoritative material on Alger extant. Very little was written about him in magazines up until his death, he usually refused to write anything about himself, as he noted in letters to friends, particularly to Irving Blake (one of his "boys"), and he often complained that most of the newspaper Sunday supplement articles written about him were inaccurate in whole or part.

Ralph Gardner's exhaustive study is the most complete book about Alger and his works known. Oddly enough it makes no mention at all of the Brewster incident and inverts in time several of the events of Alger's life. As a collector, Gardner was interested as much in the production, rarity and prices of the Alger books as he was in the author, and a large share of the book is devoted to material of interest to the collectors for whom it was obviously written. Frank Gruber, a collector and antiquarian, made an extremely valuable collation of Alger's works, separating the real ones from a number of fakes published after his death. Gardner used this and other materials to produce a book-by-book summary of Alger's publications, including the most complete list of Alger's published poetry and short stories.

Despite all the books that Horatio Alger, Jr. wrote, there are no manuscripts. As Max Goldberg told me, Horatio's sister Olive Augusta destroyed them all after his death because she had copies of the books and saw no reason to have musty old manuscripts cluttering up the place.

Above all, for research materials, I am indebted to Horatio Alger, Jr. himself. His books, as he so often said, were almost all based on facts or stories he had heard; this is particularly true of the street boy books and those that deal with American rural life. Where Alger went afield and described places and events that he did not know about first hand, there is a decided failure in the plausibility: the books about Australia and those that deal with the sea are totally unbelievable, and are thus very much weaker than such classics as *Ragged Dick*. Horatio's prefaces, dedications and sometimes the text give either information or excellent clues to facts about his life. The life itself, like that of most writers, was not very interesting. Writers tend to write, and being chairbound, do not have many adventures. Horatio's life up to Brewster tended to more excitement; after he went to New York, he became quite sedentary. If this book has a value, it will be to correct the record of a writer who influenced millions of young Americans over the years and whose own shyness and pristine personal habits in later years prevented his making much of a splash on the American scene.

Chapter One

The story of the Brewster affair comes from several sources. Primary sources are the old church records, unearthed for me by Walter Babbitt of Brewster. I am also indebted to the Ladies of the Brewster Ladies' Library and the libraries of the Yarmouth Public Library for letting me use the files of the *Yarmouth Register.*

Chapter Two

The notes about Alger's origins come from *Memorial of the Descendants of Thomas Alger, 1665–1875,* by Arthur M. Alger, Boston, 1876. The material on Horatio Alger, Sr. and his early life, comes from Harvard College records; Ralph Gardner's *Horatio Alger,* published in 1964 by Wayside Press, Illinois; librarians in Revere, Massachusetts; and this author's personal gleanings from letters, notes and stories. Herbert Mayes' *Alger: A Biography Without a Hero* confirms some of these details, but that work must be approached very gingerly. Horatio Alger, Jr. in various writings gives some mention of his early years, particularly in his own hand in the class notebook of 1832 at Harvard College.

Chapter Three

Harvard College's alumni records give most of the material about Horatio's undergraduate years. Gardner was consulted here. The note about the Boston *Advertiser* experience is from Horatio's later letters to Irving Blake (1894–98) in the possession of the Huntington Library in San Marino, California. The notes about Horatio's poems and stories come from an examination of their various publications, Gardner's biography and Max Goldberg, former President of the Horatio Alger Society and an avid student of Algeriana. Confirmation of Horatio's sojourn at Deerfield came from a letter to the author from David R. Proper, librarian, the Memorial Libraries of Deerfield, Massachusetts.

CHAPTER FOUR

The Deerfield experience was outlined in the Proper letter, as noted. The *True Flag* experience was mentioned by Gardner and confirmed to me by Max Goldberg. The story of *Nothing To Do* comes from Gardner, and the book itself, a copy of which is located in Harvard's Libraries. The story of life in Marlborough comes from the records of the Marlborough Public Library.

CHAPTER FIVE

The report on the Falls of Montmorenci comes from the files of the Marlborough Public Library. The tale of Horatio's European trip is culled from his New York *Sun* articles and later letters, and from Gardner. The report of the class reunion of 1862 is from the Harvard files. The material about *Frank's Campaign* comes from the book itself.

CHAPTER SIX

The material about Horatio's relations with *Student and Schoolmate,* comes from a study of the magazine during the period from 1864 to the end of the magazine's existence not quite ten years later. *Paul Prescott's Charge* was the source for the material about the book. Here and throughout the biography, I have quoted heavily from the books because Horatio's importance in the American scene was not the life he lived, a drab and sedentary life for the most part, but what he wrote and the view of America and the American dream that he imparted to millions of young people.

CHAPTER SEVEN

A portion of the material about the Brewster affair comes from Richard M. Huber's *The American Idea of Success,* New York, 1971. A visit to Brewster produced confirmation of this record from various people, including antique dealer Walter Babbitt. The files of the Yarmouth *Register* for 1864–66 yielded other information about Horatio and his activities in Cape Cod. The material about the stories that appeared in *Student and Schoolmate* is from the files of the magazine. The poem "Friar Anselmo" was originally published in *The New York Weekly* on August 5, 1872.

CHAPTER EIGHT

The poem "John Maynard" appeared originally in *Student and Schoolmate,* in January, 1868. It was reprinted a dozen times more in various publications throughout the years, and in a sense, is Horatio's most widely circulated work. The material about *Helen Ford* is from the book. The material about American literary lights of the period is from Richard Morris' *Encyclopedia of American History,* New York, 1953. The material about Horatio and *Student and Schoolmate* comes from the files of the magazine. Charlie Codman's adventures come from the book of the same name. The material about *Timothy Crump's Ward* comes from two articles in the *Antiquarian Bookman* by Alger collectors: one by Frank Gruber in the November 13, 1948 issue; one by Morton S. Enslin in the July 6–13 issue of 1959.

CHAPTER NINE

The study of *Ragged Dick,* this most successful of Alger's books in every way, is from the book itself. The study of magazine stories and other books here is self-evident.

CHAPTER TEN

Notes about Olive Augusta Cheney come from *Student and Schoolmate* and from Gardner. The material about Charles Loring Brace is from his own study of the *Dangerous Classes of Society,* his daughter's *Life of Charles Loring Brace,* New York, 1892, and his own *Short Sermons to Newsboys,* New York, 1866. The stories from *Student and Schoolmate* come from the files of that magazine, which was used extensively because in many ways it was the key to Horatio's success; later in life he wrote one of his young correspondents that he had decided to become a full-time author (after the Brewster disaster) because of his successes in that magazine.

The tale of *Mark the Match Boy* is from the book. Here as with *Ragged Dick* and several other stories, the author has extensively studied the book in order to bring forth elements of Horatio's technique.

CHAPTER ELEVEN

The Seligman story is mentioned in Gardner, in Horatio's

own writings and records and in the records of the Seligman family. Horatio's places of residence were so many that it became impossible to list them all; he moved around constantly, according to the New York City directories from 1872 to 1896, from one room to another, and although he spent a good deal of time at the Newsboy's Lodging House, he never claimed it as his place of residence. *Ben the Luggage Boy* is quoted extensively to show new aspects of Horatio's treatment of city life and his attitude toward family life. *Sink or Swim* contains a fine description of an Alger miser.

Chapter Twelve

The stories of *Tattered Tom* and *Paul the Peddler* come from the books, and the note about George Dillingham comes from the pages of Gardner who was an indefatigable researcher into the minutiae of Alger's life, particularly as it was concerned with the publication—not so much the writing—of the books.

Chapter Thirteen

It may be, as Gardner and Mayes have indicated in their books, that Horatio was the instrument of destruction of the infamous padrone system that had invaded New York in the middle of the nineteenth century, allowing heartless Italian and Sicilian men to exploit little children on the streets of the American cities. But the fact was that child exploitation, not just the padrone system, was just then under scrutiny by the legislators of America, and a great hue and cry was being raised throughout the land. I have played down the Alger part in the destruction of the padrone system because much of the material comes from suspect sources and Gardner's manufacture of conversations does not lend itself to total belief. Horatio was a shy man and primarily a writer, not a politician or public figure. He did make a number of speeches in New York and prided himself somewhat on his elocution, but since his basic impact was as a writer, I have confined myself here.

I was interested in *Strive and Succeed* because it showed a blossoming in a way; Horatio began to make some use of his classical education in his writing, not having dared to do so before. It may not have worked very well—later he did not repeat the experiment with Latin. His portrayal of Miss Melinda Athanasia Jones is one of the funniest in all the Alger books, and quite intentionally so, leaving a reader with the wonder as to what Alger could have done with the character had he ever really tried. The incident of the fight between "professor" Walter Conrad and Peter Groot represented something new in Alger, too. The mention of Horatio's trip to Europe with his family—it is scarcely more than that, represents one of the problems with writing about Horatio. His papers were not saved for the most part, and a biographer gleans what he can; Horatio later mentioned the trip in some of his few letters still extant, he wrote the preface for *Bound to Rise* from Switzerland; that is about all the basic information available. Gardner, who had several conversations with people who knew Olive Augusta Alger to some extent, has more, but unattributed, information on the trip.

Chapter Fourteen

Brave and Bold represents a departure for Horatio or a throwback to *Charlie Codman's Cruise,* and strictly as a book it is one of the worst he ever wrote. There is a good deal of humor here for the twentieth-century reader, but most of it is unconscious, as in the abysmal construction and writing of the scene where Captain Rushton's companions in the lifeboat leap into the briny and drown themselves like oysters performing for the Walrus and the Carpenter in Alice. Speaking in a literary sense, which it is very often hard to do with Horatio's works, this book is a fiasco.

Chapter Fifteen

In many ways, Horatio's books mirror his life. He became deeply involved in the Newsboy's Lodging House and in Superintendent Charles O'Connor's campaign to take boys out of the city and locate them in small towns and on farms. This is what *Julius* is all about; it followed fast on the heels of one of Horatio's trips with O'Connor to take poor boys out west. There is a nice scene here showing the kind of theater the boys made for themselves in New York, too. I have gone into some detail on the incident of the kidnaping of little Carrie because once again this shows Horatio at his worst, dealing with a subject he knew virtually nothing about.

CHAPTER SIXTEEN

Herbert Carter's Legacy is the prototype of a certain kind of Alger story which was to have such a tremendous impact on America, the tale of the poor boy, widowed mother and rich Squire. The theater of melodrama owes almost everything to Horatio here and by the turn of the century was making a mockery of the word mortgage. This period was one of such activity in railroads and business that it has been called the Era of Frenzied Finance, and Horatio's books, particularly this one, mirror the situation. Vanderbilt is invoked here by name, for at the time he was the most powerful financial figure in America and his name was actually trembling on the lips of all who involved themselves in New York financial matters. So here again, Horatio's story, in its time and place and ideas, represents more than is apparent.

CHAPTER SEVENTEEN

Looking about for a "new angle" to sharpen his work, Horatio came upon the reverse treatment of the street boy. *The Young Outlaw* began as a study showing what happened to the bad ones, but Horatio could not have an antihero, and so the young outlaw began to reform. But the interest here focused on the seamier side of Horatio's New York. In the scenes with Dr. Frank Graham, chiropodist, Horatio was at his best—he could be very funny when he set his mind to it.

CHAPTER EIGHTEEN

The jobs Horatio had teaching the Seligmans and other scions of rich families were naturally reflected in Horatio's books. This is especially true in *Shifting for Himself*, which studies a certain type of Fifth Avenue family in New York as much as it deals with Gilbert Greyson, the rich boy down on his luck. *Wait and Hope* shows how Horatio could drive a reader wild by overworking a theme, but the world is indebted to him for Professor Crane, the noted Phrenologist, and Mrs. Perkins and Ben's aunt make a pretty pair of harpies waiting for the world to come to an end.

CHAPTER NINETEEN

Horatio's California trip could have been a key to a whole new kind of writing, but he went there with the intention of creating not the California he saw, but the California that had existed twenty-five years earlier, and the result was zero—he might as well not have taken the trip. Gardner tells of his visit to the Mormon Tabernacle at Salt Lake City, but it affected him and his writing so little that its inclusion in a biography is simply a matter of collecting minute scraps of dross. If Horatio was touched and awed and educated by his trip west—and he must have been, for he was a very sensitive man—for reasons of his own he chose not to write about what he saw but about what he imagined he might have seen had he gone there with the Gold Rush. It was unfortunate.

Chapter Twenty

Home from the West, Horatio sank into his old lethargy of spirit, but he wrote as fast as ever. The Pacific series is dreadful, among the worst of Alger, surpassed in its aridity only by the books on Australia which came later. But Ki Sing was a character who would have delighted Bret Harte, and Horatio was relatively sympathetic to him. This chapter also deals with Horatio's experiment in biography and its failure.

Chapter Twenty-one

Horatio was definitely on the decline in these last years in New York, as the works he then composed very clearly indicate. More and more books were published and republished, but the returns grew slighter. The quotation from the Sloss brothers' manuscript and the references to correspondence come from the Huntington Library collection.

Chapter Twenty-two

I am indebted to Max Goldberg for showing me a copy of Horatio's will, which saved me a good deal of time working through the legal paper files of the Cambridge probate court. Mr. Goldberg was also the source of several other papers and stories about Horatio in his later years. The rest is self-evident.

Index

Abolition, 21, 27, 34

Abraham Lincoln, 209-210, 237

Adams, William Taylor (Oliver Optic), 27, 40, 49, 61, 69-70, 73-74, 80-81, 83, 90, 226

Adrift in the City, 223-224

Albee, Obadiah Wheelock, 14

Alcott, Louisa May, 85, 109, 114, 220, 224

Alger, Ann, 11, 35, 85, 99

Alger, Arthur M., 253

Alger, Francis, 11

Alger, Horatio, Jr.
  ancestors of, 7-8
  assessment of, 236-242, 249
  Atlantic series, 215
  birth, 9
  books for boys, 40-48
  campaign series, 70, 215
  critics of, 234
  death, 232
  Divinity school, 24, 26
  education, 10, 14-23, 35
  first book, 27-28
  first novel, 40
  first writings, 18-19, 22-25
  at Harvard, 17-23
  homosexuality of, 4-6
  Luck and Pluck series, 104, 123, 215
  as minister, 1-7, 60, 62
  Pacific series, 199, 201, 205, 207
  poetry, 18, 30-32, 49-50, 62, 64, 154, 213-214, 243
  pseudonyms, 98, 215, 246-247
  Ragged Dick series, 90, 98, 108, 215
  teaching, 24-27, 34
  travels, 36-39, 123, 128, 187-190, 195, 200, 203, 222, 227, 258-259
  Way to Success series, 215
  will, 232
  youth, 9-11, 14

Alger, Rev. Horatio, Sr., 2-3, 8-11, 15-16, 18, 21, 24, 26, 33-35, 41, 63, 84-85, 121, 211, 250, 253

Alger, Israel, Jr., 8

Alger, James, 8

Alger, James II, 8

Alger, James, III, 9, 11, 35, 99, 187, 205, 215

Alger, Olive Augusta (Mrs. Amos Cheney), 9, 11, 19, 35, 40, 86, 121, 123, 154, 211, 215, 219, 221, 223, 232, 246-248, 252, 255, 257

Alger, Olive Augusta Fenno, 9, 85, 121, 205

Alger, Thomas, 7

Allen, Joseph, 100

American Idea of Success, The, 254

American Unitarian Assoc., 5

Anderson, John R., 207, 210, 248

Andrews, Annie, 232

Antiquarian Bookman, 255

Babbitt, Walter, 250, 253-254

Ballou's Dollar Monthly, 27, 33, 97, 105, 245

Bangs, Elisha, 3, 5

Barnum, P.T., 145-146

Ben the Luggage Boy, 101-104, 256

Ben's Nugget, 207

260

Bertha's Christmas Vision, 27, 29-30, 246

Blacke, Irving, 220-226, 228-230, 232, 237, 245, 252-253

Boston *Daily Advertiser,* 24, 29, 253

Boston Transcript, 29, 37

Bound to Rise: Up the Ladder, 121-125, 127-128, 257

Boy's Home Library, 215

Brace, Charles Loring, 84, 86-88, 116, 140, 255

Brandeis University, 234

Brave and Bold, 129-139, 161, 257

Brewster, Mass., 1-3, 5-6, 60, 62-63, 73, 82, 99, 234, 241, 250-251, 254

Brown, Bazin and Co., 27, 29

Burt, A.L., Publishing Co., 215, 248

Cardozo, Benjamin, 214

Carleton, G.W. and Co., 202, 247

Charlie Codman's Cruise, 70-74, 257

Chelsea, Mass., 8-10, 14

Cheney, Amos, 86, 121, 123, 211, 215, 221, 223, 232

Coates, Henry T., and Co., 223, 228, 247

Crocker, Thomas, 3, 5

Dana, Charles A., 19

Dan the Detective, 212-213

Dangerous Classes of Society, The, 140, 255

Deerfield Academy, 28, 34, 253-254

Depew, Chauncey, 209

Dillingham, George, W., 114, 130, 202, 222, 224, 247-248, 256

Disagreeable Woman, The, 247

District Telegraph Boy, The, 201

Donahue, M.A., 248

Doubleday & Co., 235, 249

Down, John, 229, 232

Down, Kate, 219-220

Down, Tommy, 229, 232

Encyclopedia of American History, 255

Enslin, Morton S., 255

Fame and Fortune, 80-84, 90, 97

Family Book of Best Loved Poems, The, 214

Fenno, George, 37

Fenno, John, 9

First Unitarian Parish of Brewster, 1-7, 60, 63, 82

"Five Hundred Dollars," 245

$500: Jacob Marlowe's Secret, 245

Flag of Our Union, The, 25

Frank Hunter's Peril, 230

Frank Leslie's Illustrated Newspaper, 49

Frank's Campaign, 40-48, 50, 52, 60, 131, 207, 246, 254

French, James and Co., 30

"Friar Anselmo," 62-63, 84, 254

From Canal Boy to President, 207-209, 211

From Farm Boy to Senator, 209

From Rags to Riches: Horatio Alger and the American Dream, 20

Gallico, Paul, 238

Gardner, Ralph D., 10, 214, 219, 234, 239, 246, 248, 252-257, 259

Garfield, James A., 207-209, 237

Gates Academy, 14-15, 43

Gleason's, 25, 34, 36, 80, 121, 154, 187, 207, 243, 245-246

Goldberg, Max, 234, 250-253, 259

Golden Argosy, 145, 215, 247-249

Golden Days, 207

Golden Hours, 232

Good News, 245, 248

Gould, S.H., 1, 4, 5

Graham's Illustrated Magazine, 33, 245

Grand'ther Baldwin's Thanksgiving, 154

Gruber, Frank, 252, 255

Hale, Rev. Edward E., 3

Hamilton, Arthur (pseud. for Horatio Alger, Jr.), 98, 246

Harper's Monthly, 39, 49

Harvard College, 2, 8, 15-18, 20-23, 32-33, 39, 99, 214, 250, 252-254

Harvard Divinity School, 2, 8, 23-24, 35, 37

Helen Ford, 67-69, 73-74, 255

Henderson, William, 251

Herbert Carter's Legacy: The Inventor's Son, 154-161, 163-170, 258

Holmes, Oliver Wendell, 8, 40, 50

Holt, Rinehart and Winston, 253

Home Companion, The, 207

Horatio Alger: A Biography Without a Hero, 20, 251, 253

Horatio Alger Society, 234, 251

Horatio Alger: The American Hero Era, 234, 248, 251, 253

Huber, Richard M., 254

Huntington Library, (San Marino, Calif.), 251, 253, 259

In A New World, 216-217

Jack's War, 154
Joe's Luck, 190, 200-203
"John Maynard," 64-66, 213-214, 255
Julius: The Street Boy Out West, 140-152, 257

Ladies Library of Brewster, 3, 250-253
Lazell, Edmund, 7
Leslie, Frank, 222
Leslie's, 224
Little Women, 85
Loring, A.K., 41, 48, 50, 60, 66-67, 70, 73-74, 80, 84-85, 104-105, 109, 114-115, 117, 123, 130, 153-154, 170, 186, 189, 199-200, 202, 207, 225, 245-247
Lowe, Rev. Charles, 5-6
Lowell, Knyvet, 30, 32
Luke Larkin's Luck, 217

Macmillan Publishing Co., 235
Marie Bertrand: The Felon's Daughter, 40-41
Mark Manning's Mission, 217
Mark the Match Boy: Richard Hunter's Ward, 84, 90-97, 245, 255
Marlborough, Mass., 11, 14, 15, 18, 23, 26-27, 33, 250, 254
Marlborough Mirror, 36-37, 39
Marlborough Public Library, 254
Maverick, George Nelson, 115
Mayes, Herbert, 20-21, 25-26, 28, 38, 217, 234, 251-253, 256
Memorial of the Descendants of Thomas Alger, 1665-1875, 253
Milstone Plain, Mass., 8
Morris, Richard, 255
"Mortgage syndrome," 238-239
Munsey, Frank, 215-216, 222, 225, 231, 247-248

Natick, 211, 215, 219-221, 223, 225-226, 228, 233, 250
Nation, the, 223
Newsboy's Lodging House, 84, 87-88, 90, 93, 95, 97, 120, 145, 151, 176, 178, 187, 199, 201, 214, 219, 225, 256-257
New York Book Co., 248
New York *Sun,* 19, 29, 37, 40

New York *Times,* 238
New York *Tribune,* 229-230, 239
New York *Weekly,* 40, 121, 129, 190, 200, 248, 254
North American Review, 39
Nothing to Do, 30-33, 246, 254

O'Connor, Charles, 88, 93, 141-142, 145, 178, 199, 214, 217, 225, 257
Ogilvie, J.S. and Co., 209-210, 248
Oliver Optic, 24, 40, 50, 61, 70, 73, 98, 226, 243, 245, 246
Our Young Folks, 64

Paddle Your Own Canoe: The Fortunes of Walter Conrad, 105-108
Padrone system, 115-116, 245, 256
Patterson, Mr. and Mrs. William, 251
Paul the Peddler, 111-114, 116, 256
Paul Prescott's Charge, 3, 4, 50-60, 93, 246, 254
Penn Publishing, 248
Phil the Fiddler, 115-116, 245
Pictorial National Library, 18, 23
Pleasant Hours, 224
Popular Library, 235, 249
Porter and Coates, 207, 247
Potowome Boarding School, 24, 26-28
Preston, Caroline F. (pseud. Horatio Alger, Jr.), 246-247
Proper, David R., 253
Pseudonyms, 98, 215, 246-247
Publisher's Weekly, 251
Putnam, Arthur Lee (pseud. Horatio Alger, Jr.,), 215, 247

Ragged Dick, 74-81, 83-84, 87, 97-98, 100-101, 104, 108, 111, 114, 128, 176, 235, 249, 252, 255
"Rags to riches," 155, 232, 235
Railway Anecdote Book, 49
Ralphy Raymond's Heir, 98, 246
Ray Radford's Reward, 217
Revere (Mass.) Library, 251, 253
Risen From the Ranks, 129
Rough and Ready: Life Among the New York Newsboys, 84, 90, 97, 100
Rufus and Rose, 100, 104

Sams Chance: And How He Improved It, 183, 186
Saracen Dwarf, The, 27-28, 237, 245

Seeking His Fortune, 154

Seelye, John, 189

Seligman, George, 99-100, 105, 107-109, 214

Seligman, Isaac, 99-100, 105, 107-109, 214

Seligman, Isabella, 109, 116, 119, 214

Seligman, Joseph, 99, 105, 214

Series, Atlantic, 215
   Campaign, 215, 246
   Good fortune, 228
   Luck and Pluck, 215, 246
   Pacific, 199, 201, 205, 207
   Ragged Dick, 215, 246
   Way to Success, 215

Shifting for Himself: Gilbert Greyson's Fortune, 184-186, 258

Silas Snobden's Office Boy, 249

Sink or Swim, 161-162, 256

Slavery, 21, 27

Slow and Sure: from the Sidewalk to the Shop, 116, 140, 245

South Natick, 2-3, 35, 37, 39, 41, 85-86, 99, 120, 205

Starr, Julian (pseud. Horatio Alger, Jr.), 247

Stratemeyer, Edward, 225, 231-233, 248-249

Street and Smith, 40, 200, 202, 207, 209, 215, 225, 248

Strive and Succeed: The Progress of Walter Conrad, 108-109, 116-120, 245, 256

Student and Schoolmate, 40, 49-50, 60-61, 73-74, 80-81, 86, 90, 97-98, 100, 104-105, 111, 114, 116, 121, 123, 154, 243, 246, 254-255

Tattered Tom, 109-111, 123, 256

Tebbel, John, 20

Tilden, Rev. W.P., 3

Timothy Crump's Ward, 67, 69, 73-74, 154, 235, 255

Tony the Hero, 201-202

Tracy, C.C., 87, 187

Train Boy, The, 212

Trott, Oren, 219-220

True Flag, 29, 254

Try and Trust: Abner Holden's Bound Boy, 121

Unitarian Church, South Natick, 2, 35

United States Book Co., 245

Vanderbilt, Cornelius, 160-161, 168, 237, 258

Vinal, Charles, 37

Voices of the Past, 18

Wait and Hope: Ben Bradford's Motto, 187, 258

Walter Sherwood's Probation, 228

Webster, Daniel, 209, 211, 220, 237

Western Boy, The, 200

Westgard, Gilbert, II, 214

Whitehead, Charles, 116

Wiley, Mrs. Marion, 251

Winfield, Arthur M. (pseud. Edward Stratemeyer), 232

Yarmouth Public Library, 251, 253

Yarmouth *Register,* 3, 253-254

Young Acrobat, The, 145

Young Adventurer: Tom's Trip Across the Plains, The, 190-198, 200

Young Bank Messenger, The, 231

Young Captain Jack, 232

Young Explorer, The, 202-206

Young Israel, 105, 121, 123, 129, 153-154, 184, 186-187, 190, 207, 245-247

Young Miner, The, 201, 203

Young Outlaw: Adrift in the Streets, The, 170-183, 186, 258